the ordeal of stephen dedalus

the conflict of the generations in

JAMES JOYCE'S *a portrait of the artist as a young man*

Edmund L. Epstein

Southern Illinois University Press *Carbondale and Edwardsville*

Feffer & Simons, Inc. *London and Amsterdam*

to my father

Library of Congress Cataloging in Publication Data

Epstein, Edmund L
  The ordeal of Stephen Dedalus.
  (Arcturus books, AB 114)
  Bibliography: p.
  1. Joyce, James, 1882–1941. A portrait of the
artist as a young man. I. Title.
[PR6019.09P6442 1973]   823'.9'12   73–7714
ISBN 0–8093–0485–6
ISBN 0–8093–0649–2 (pbk.)

ARCT
URUS
BOOKS ®

Copyright © 1971 by Southern Illinois University Press
All rights reserved
Arcturus Books Edition September 1973
This edition printed by offset lithography
  in the United States of America

contents

list of texts used and abbreviation

SH	*Stephen Hero*	All quotations are from the New Directions edition, 1963.
P	*A Portrait*	All quotations from *A Portrait of the Artist* are from the revised text, ed. Chester Anderson, 1964, of the *Portrait*.
U	*Ulysses*	All quotations are from the Modern Library Edition, newly reset 1961. (A few obvious errors have been silently corrected.)
FW	*Finnegans Wake*	All quotations are from the corrected Viking Press edition.

introduction

> *James Joyce always said that
> there was only room for one novel in a
> man's heart (he hadn't even begun
> Ulysses then) and that when one writes
> more than one, it is always the same
> book under different disguises*
>
> —Italo Svevo; quoted in P. N. Fur-
> bank, ITALO SVEVO: THE MAN AND
> THE WRITER (University of California
> Press, 1966, P. 121)

JOYCE TACITLY ACKNOWLEDGED this was true by his preparations for writing *Finnegans Wake*. In his notebooks he headed various pages with the titles of his published works and under these heads wrote commentaries on himself, which he included in the *Wake*. Joyce, therefore, saw all of his lifework as a piece, and we can find a pattern in his creative career only by doing the same.

The pattern that emerges from such an examination is not really difficult to describe. It is a family pattern, the children growing up and maturing, frequently against the strong opposition of their elders, to the point where youth becomes mature, and maturity becomes age. It is my intention to follow the workings of this process through *A Portrait* to its climax in *Ulysses,* always referring to *Finnegans Wake* for corroboration and perspective.

This topic, the growth to maturity of youth, is of peculiar interest to our time, in which youth has so loudly declared its intention to take over its own destiny. This is not the first time in history that youth has knocked at the door; Joyce's work would suggest that every youth welcomes life and goes to encounter, for the millionth time, in his new secondhand clothes, the reality of experience. In the writings of Joyce we see worked out, in detail, patterns and developments which are familiar to us, both in history books and on TV news broadcasts. Even the smallest details are there—the impatience and violence of youth, the young assassins, the "davys" throwing "bombshoobs" at the flaunting big white "harses" of the father-enemy, the boys and girls sending an unmistakable message of defiance to "the old folkers," either in the form of a "Nightletter" signed by "the babes that mean too" or by obscene words chalked on walls and shouted on stages. However, the other half of the message also is applicable to the modern age— the triumphant youthful assassin of the authoritarian Russian General turns into a father figure, as revealed by the careful examination of the brains trusters, as the dawn

prepares to rise; youthful anarchists grow corners and become squares just like their parents. And so the world
wags on.

Special acknowledgment is made for permission to quote
from the following works. From *Ulysses* by James Joyce.
Copyright 1914, 1918 and renewed 1942, 1946 by Nora
Joseph Joyce. Reprinted by permission of Random House,
Inc. Grateful appreciation is also extended to The Bodley
Head, Ltd.

From *Stephen Hero* by James Joyce. Copyright 1943,
1963 by New Directions Publishing Corporation, New
York. Acknowledgment is also made to Jonathan Cape
Ltd., as publishers, and to The Society of Authors.

From *Finnegans Wake* by James Joyce. Copyright
1939 by James Joyce, copyright © renewed 1967 by George
Joyce and Lucia Joyce. Reprinted by permission of The
Viking Press, Inc. Appreciation is also extended to The
Society of Authors as the literary representative of the
Estate of James Joyce.

From *A Portrait of the Artist as a Young Man* by James
Joyce. Copyright 1916 by B. W. Huebsch, Inc., renewed
1944 by Nora Joyce. Reprinted by permission of The Viking Press, Inc. Special acknowledgment is also made to
Jonathan Cape Ltd., as publishers, and to the Executors
of the James Joyce Estate.

I gratefully acknowledge the care, the kindness, the
patience and the many sorts of assistance I received from
Professor William York Tindall during the writing of this
work. I also acknowledge the assistance of Professor F. W.
Dupee and Dean Kevin Sullivan, both of whom kept me
on the track in different ways, and of Professor Chester
Anderson, who contributed many stimulating criticisms.

I also acknowledge the assistance of my colleagues at
Southern Illinois University, especially Alan M. Cohn,

who has participated actively in the creation of this work, Charles Parish, Ted Boyle, Harry T. Moore, Clark Rodewald, John Gardner, and John Howell. Like all Joyceans, I owe a debt of gratitude to all previous workers in the field. I especially wish to acknowledge my appreciation to Father William T. Noon, S.J., for many helpful discussions in the past. Any errors, however, are mine.

I wish to acknowledge the assistance of my father, Alfred Epstein, and my mother, who were always sure that I would finish this work. Finally, I wish to acknowledge this debt, among many other debts, to my wife, Tegwen, without whom it is literally true that this book would never have been written.

E. L. Epstein

Carbondale, Illinois
March 1, 1971

the ordeal of stephen dedalus

1

the conflict
of the generations

We have to had them whether we'll like it or not. They'll have to have us now then we're here on theirspot. Scant hope theirs or ours to escape life's high carnage of semperidentity by subsisting peasemeal upon variables

— FINNEGANS WAKE (P. 582, *ll.* 13–16)

TREATMENT of the conflict of the generations, a universal theme, is also one of the characteristic themes of modern literature. Huxley, Virginia Woolf, Lawrence, Hardy, Dostoyevsky, Turgenev, Dickens, Thackeray, Jane Austen, Henry James,[1] Meredith, Conrad, George Douglas Brown, Synge, Yeats—all of those and many more wrestle with the problem of the conflict of the generations, in realistic or symbolic form. Joyce, however, is unique among the masters of modern literature in his treatment of the father-son conflict. As I hope to show, he is both milder in actual detail and more extreme in principle than any other modern writer.

Two modern authors known to Joyce attack the problem systematically. In Ibsen, young Joyce's favorite author, the conflict of the generations finds careful treatment and analysis. Children have a difficult time in a number of Ibsen plays. Poor little Eyolf is first crippled and then drowned as a direct result of the emotional immaturity and selfishness of his parents. Oswald Alving inherits syphilis from his father in *Ghosts*. In *The Wild Duck*, Gregers Werle's hatred of his powerful father incites him to confuse the weak Hialmar Ekdal into rejecting his little daughter Hedvig, who then kills herself. In *Pillars of Society* Bernick's dishonesty almost ends in the drowning of his son Olaf. However, sometimes children have their revenge; fathers are struck down or otherwise destroyed by young people in *The Master-Builder* and *John Gabriel Borkman*. In *The League of Youth*, the antagonism of youth for age is used by the unscrupulous demagogue Stensgård to further his own career.

Samuel Butler's theories of paternity are carefully worked out in his biopsychological works and underlie

The Way of All Flesh, which was written to exemplify these theories, by showing the irreconcilable antagonism between fathers and sons. *The Way of All Flesh,* which Joyce almost certainly read at some point, portrays a desperate father-son struggle, and shows a father with many weapons in his armory—cruelty, pomposity, hypocrisy, Philistine insensitivity. Butler seems obsessed with the character of the father, Theobald Pontifex, and never tires of citing examples of his attempts to reduce his son Ernest to a cipher, a helpless, characterless slave.

Butler's theorizing on the conflict of the generations, the only really systematic attempt at analysis of the problem before Joyce's in English literature, affected Joyce's theories of paternity by the time of the writing of the final version of *A Portrait,*[2] and in the library scene in *Ulysses,* Stephen seems to echo Butlerian theorizing on paternity and on the father-son conflict: "the son unborn mars beauty: born, he brings pain, divides affection, increases care" (*U* 207). The father therefore finds him first an encumbrance, then an enemy, then a reminder of his own defeat: "He [the son] is a male: his growth is his father's decline, his youth his father's envy" (*U* 207–8). This resembles Butler's declaration, through the mouth of Ernest Pontifex, his hero, that

a man first quarrels with his father about three-quarters of a year before he is born. It is then he insists on setting up a separate establishment; when this has been once agreed to, the more complete the separation forever after the better for both. (*The Way of All Flesh,* Everyman ed. [London, 1933], p. 307)

A reference to *The Way of All Flesh* elucidates a cryptic sentence in the library scene: "[Shakespeare's grandson] never was born for nature . . . abhors perfection" (*U* 208). In chapter 5 of *The Way of All Flesh* Butler announces his principle of the remote inheritance of desirable qualities. (This principle that is also treated in *Life and Habit,* a theoretical work on heredity.)

The more brilliant the success in any one generation, the greater as a general rule the subsequent exhaustion until time has been allowed for recovery. Hence it often happens that the grandson of a successful man will be more successful than the son—the spirit that actuated the grandfather having lain fallow in the son and being refreshed by repose so as to be ready for fresh exertions in the grandson. (*The Way of All Flesh,* p. 17)

However, although Joyce was influenced by Butler's novel and by its theoretical underpinning in his creation of the character of Stephen Dedalus, it is important to note that in Joyce it is symbolic fathers by whom the artist is threatened, not real ones. Poor Simon Dedalus never even comes near to possessing the physical and psychological brutality of Theobald Pontifex. The very worst thing that Simon ever does to Stephen, both in *A Portrait* and in *Ulysses,* is to call him a "lazy bitch" (*P* 175). Of Theobald's bullying nature, his canings, threatenings, and moral blackmailings of his son, there is not a trace in Simon.

This mirrors Joyce's actual relations with his father, whom he once described in a letter of January 17, 1932, written just after his father's death, as "the silliest man I ever knew and yet cruelly shrewd. He thought and talked of me up to his last breath. I was very fond of him always." [3] Although this letter may possibly reflect some degree of guilt on Joyce's part for having been away from his father for so long,[4] the sentiment seems entirely sincere and fits what we know of Joyce's relationship with his father, which was, for the most part, warm and friendly. His brother Stanislaus believed that James liked his father, and suggested that the reason that James's early impression of his father had not embittered James (as they had embittered him) was because young James had been in school most of the time and only saw his father in a holiday mood.[5] They quarreled seriously only once—his father thought that James's hasty elopement with Nora had wrecked his chances in life—but his father apologized handsomely a few years later for his attitude.

Joyce cannot, therefore, claim that he was ever subjected to the sort of abuse that Samuel Butler declared was his lot, and to which he subjects Ernest Pontifex. The only people who physically maltreat Stephen Dedalus are his contemporaries (Wells, Heron and his cronies), or the violent Father Dolan, or, in *Ulysses,* Private Carr. Cranly attempts to bully him, and Aunt Dante and Father Arnall try to frighten him; but Simon Dedalus does not lift his hand or his voice to him.[6] If a father-son conflict is to be discerned in the works of Joyce, the father, unlike Theobald Pontifex, must be a symbolic father.

Joyce puts a theory of symbolic fatherhood into Stephen's mouth in the library scene in *Ulysses.*[7] The words "father" and "son," and their derivatives, are thicker on *U* 206–8 than anywhere else in the book. It is on these pages that Stephen attempts to unite his theories of the sustention and projection of the artist's image and his theories of paternity.

—A father . . . is a necessary evil. [John Shakespeare] rests, disarmed of fatherhood, having devised that mystical estate upon his son. . . . Fatherhood, in the sense of conscious begetting, is unknown to man. It is a mystical estate, an apostolic succession, from only begetter to only begotten. On that mystery . . . the church is founded and founded irremovably because founded, like the world, macro- and microcosm, upon the void. Upon incertitude, upon unlikelihood. . . . What links them [father and son] in nature? An instant of blind rut. . . . When Rutlandbaconsouthamptonshakespeare or another poet of the same name . . . wrote *Hamlet* he was not the father of his own son merely but, being no more a son, he was and felt himself the father of all his race, the father of his own grandfather, the father of his unborn grandson.

In what way was Shakespeare, after writing *Hamlet,* "no more a son"? In the first performance of *Hamlet,*

Shakespeare, playing the ghost, calls to Burbage, playing the prince

by a name:
Hamlet, I am thy father's spirit
bidding him list. To a son he speaks, the son of his soul, the prince, young Hamlet and to the son of his body, Hamnet Shakespeare, who has died in Stratford that his namesake may live for ever . . . [Player Shakespeare spoke] his own words to his own son's name. (*U* 188–89)

Shakespeare has, of course, no father — John Shakespeare was dead by the time of the writing of *Hamlet*. However, this is apparently not enough to make Shakespeare "no more a son." Stephen here suggests that Shakespeare, by acknowledging his son, Hamnet, and his creation, Hamlet, both in the same speech in *Hamlet*, is asserting a double right to the mystical estate of fatherhood. The child in both cases is the projected "image" of the father-artist, that image which is, Stephen declares, "the standard of all experience" (*U* 195) to a man of genius. For this identity of "image" and "child" Joyce leans upon a line from Shakespeare's third sonnet, addressed to his friend who does not wish to marry and have children.

> Look in thy glass, and tell the face thou viewest
> Now is the time that face should form another . . .
> But if thou live, remember'd not to be,
> Die single, and thine image dies with thee.[8]

Moreover, by becoming a "father" Shakespeare has finally overthrown his father, John Shakespeare, who, "disarmed of fatherhood," rots in the grave, a nonentity. It seems that there is room for only one father and one son at a time in a "race," an "only begetter" and an "only begotten," and the father must, therefore, always fear the maturing of his son into fatherhood which will thrust him from his place.

Joyce provides more material for this theory in the Oxen of the Sun chapter. Stephen's friends toast "to his fathership"; they suspect that he has "besmirched the lily virtue of a confiding female." Conforming to the theme of sterility appropriate to the chapter, Stephen declares that, on the contrary, he is "the eternal son and ever virgin" (*U* 392). This is the other half of the theory—a son is characteristically "ever virgin." If this assertion is combined with Stephen's theorizing in the library scene we begin to see the outline of a theory of real and symbolic paternity —a son does not become a father until he becomes capable of projecting his image in the real world in the form of a child, and, in the realm of art, by producing a true work of art.

That this fatherhood refers to symbolic artistic fatherhood as well as paternity of the flesh is well understood by Stephen's friends. "Sonmulligan," as befits his role of "Everyman His own Wife" (*U* 216), strives to bring his obscene play to birth: "Himself his own father . . . I am big with child. I have an unborn child in my brain" (*U* 208), and eventually he projects his image—"Ballocky Mulligan." In the Oxen of the Sun chapter Lynch taunts Stephen for his failure to become a father of works of art.

[Stephen declared that he could call up the phantoms of the past, the images of his Clongowes schoolfellows, since he was "lord and giver of their life."] That answer . . . [declares Lynch] will adorn you more fitly when something more, and greatly more, than a capful of light odes can call your genius father. (*U* 415)

Stephen's theory of physical, moral, and creative "fatherhood" is not just phrases on the lips of fictional characters—Joyce himself believed it. Ellmann notes that Joyce said to his sister Eva, some years after the birth of Giorgio, that "the most important thing that can happen to a man is the birth of a child." [9] This declaration is elucidated by a quotation from Aristotle in Joyce's Paris Notebook of 1903,

The most natural act for living beings which are complete is to produce other beings like themselves and thereby to participate as far as they may in the eternal and divine.[10]

This is an abbreviation by Joyce of a passage from Aristotle's *De Anima:*

The acts in which it [the vegetative soul] manifests itself are reproduction and the use of food—reproduction, I say, because for any living thing that has reached its normal development [*teleia*] and which is unmutilated, and whose mode of generation is not spontaneous, the most natural act is the production of another like itself, an animal producing an animal, a plant a plant, in order that, as far as its nature allows, it may partake in the eternal and divine.[11]

The phrase which is here translated as "any living thing that has reached its normal development and which is unmutilated" appears in Joyce's quotation simply as "living beings which are complete." The word used by Aristotle is *teleia*, which bears the implication of development toward an end, *telos*, which is the characteristic keynote of Aristotelian biology.[12] Indeed, Aristotle makes this clear in the *Metaphysics* where he comments on *teleion*, the word from which *teleia* is immediately derived: "Things which have attained their end, if the end is good, are called 'perfect' [*teleion*]; for they are perfect in virtue of having attained that end." [13] Joyce's "complete," therefore, would contain a suggestion of a completed process of development rather than that of a physical integrity, if his interpretation of Aristotle is that of the majority of translators and commentators on this passage.[14]

Fatherhood, then, would indeed be "the most important thing that can happen to a man"; it is both a sign that he has attained the climax of his development as a man, and, as Aristotle suggests in a subsequent passage in *De Anima* (415^b 3–7) , an attempt to win personal immortality. In Joyce's terms, until the point of fatherhood is reached a man is *faute de mieux* a son, "ever virgin" and immature; after the act of fatherhood is performed, the father starts on the way down from the climax of his life. (This pattern is Aristotelian; see *De Anima*, 2. 9. 432^b 19–25). Stephen suggests this in the Oxen of the Sun chapter.

And as the ends and ultimates of all things accord in some mean and measure with their inceptions and originals, that same multiplicit concordance which leads forth growth from birth accomplishing by a retrogressive metamorphosis that minishing and ablation toward the final which is agreeable unto nature so is it with our subsolar being. The aged sisters draw us into life: we wail, batten, sport, clip, clasp, sunder, dwindle, die. (*U* 394)

The eight stages of life, as outlined by Stephen, have as their center the act of sexual congress; after the clasping and sundering we "dwindle, die." Since the entire Oxen of the Sun chapter contains long hymns of praise to fatherhood and attacks on sterility (see *U* 383, 389, 420–21, 423–24), sexual congress is here the essential act of fatherhood rather than the climax of sterile lovemaking.

Stephen fears that he may never achieve this act of paternity; although "ever virgin" he has slept with whores, but that sort of sexual congress is not enough to qualify him for fatherhood. In an earlier chapter, Stephen asks himself, "Am I father? If I were? Shrunken uncertain hand" (*U* 208). The reference in this last phrase might be to his father Simon's hand which on an earlier page (*U* 207) Stephen remembers touching: "Hurrying to her [his mother's] squalid deathlair from gay Paris on the quayside I touched his hand. . . . The eyes that wish me well. But do not know me." More likely, however, it refers to the "weak wasting hand" (*U* 44) of the exiled Kevin Egan, an unsatisfactory father who can only pass on meaningless fragments of his past to his son Patrice. Stephen fears that that is the sort of father he would be if the prostitute he slept with had conceived a son; a father must, it seems, be more than a fleshly father if he is not to be an ineffectual Kevin Egan or a Simon Dedalus, both of whom have, in Stephen's opinion, abdicated their responsibilities as fathers. It is this refusal of a father to "recognize" his children, to act as a father, that Stephen resents. Simon Dedalus grudges support to his family (see *U* 237–39). Stephen fears that as a son of Simon, as an inhabitant of his "house of decay" (*U* 39), he also may never become capable of being a "true" father, either in the flesh (in which case he would be like Kevin Egan or his own father) or in the spirit, in which case he will never be a creator. In Aristotelian terms he will never attain his *telos,* and will therefore never be a completed organism—his heredity, his environment, is paralyzing the natural processes of growth.

Stephen's (and Joyce's) theory of paternity can be summarized as follows:

1] As reproduction marks the climax of the development of an organism, so fatherhood is the natural climax of the life of man.

2] The production of a child is the climax of natural fatherhood; the production of a work of art is the climax of artistic fatherhood.

3] The father in the flesh and the father in the spirit project their images—the fleshly father produces a child; the artistic father produces a work of art embodying his past, his surroundings. (This is why "Ireland must be important because it belongs to me [Stephen]" [*U* 645].)

4] Physical fatherhood is not enough; it is "an instant of blind rut" if it is only an act of the body and not an assertion of the "mystical estate" of paternity. A man can be a father in the flesh and not in the spirit—Simon Dedalus, Kevin Egan, and Little Chandler in "A Little Cloud," for example.

5] The father in the flesh resents the presence of the son,[15] especially if the son seems to be maturing into fatherhood himself, since the father sinks into meaninglessness when his son becomes a father; there is room for only one father at a time in a "race," (whatever "race" may mean).[16]

To the above summary of what seem to be the main points of Joyce's theory of paternity, it is necessary to add a sixth point, one which is never developed explicitly by Joyce and which, therefore, must be deduced from a study of his major works:

6] Once a father has become a father, either in the flesh, or in the spirit, or perhaps just in the name (Father Arnall, Father Dolan, Father Conmee, and every other "ghostly father" [P 190] in *A Portrait*), he is symbolically the father of every "son." If he encounters a young man exhibiting signs of maturity and creativity he reacts like a fleshly father, that is, he attempts to halt the process of maturity by freezing or paralyzing the son in some way. The son, in his turn, resists the attack of the father, and, in a sense counterattacks by developing, since the son cannot truly create until he is fully matured, that is, until he is ripe for assumption of the mystical estate of fatherhood.[17]

It is easier to support this last assertion by reference to *Finnegans Wake* than to any of Joyce's other books, since all of the major characters in *Finnegans Wake* are symbolic and contain multitudes. (The following section contains only a brief résumé of the main points of paternity as acted out in *Finnegans Wake*. I take up many of these same points in detail in my second chapter.) The hero of *Finnegans Wake*, HCE ("more mob than man" he is called, on *FW* 261.21–22), is most certainly a universal father; one of his names is Haveth Childers Everywhere (*FW* 535.34–35). This aspect of HCE is that of the general fatherhood of a true father—his children, his "all-falling fruits of my boom" (*FW* 535.33–34), are everywhere.[18]

The Haveth Childers Everywhere section comes at the end of a long chapter during which Yawn, the somnolent remnant of Shaun, is being probed for his essential personality. After much surface material is sluiced away, the core of Yawn's nature is reached, and it speaks with HCE's voice. HCE's characteristic obsessive fears are all brought up again—nervous, stuttering denials that he ever thought of incest with his daughter alternate with fearful praise of his wife, and his abject pleas for special consideration as an outcast and criminal modulate gradually into a gigantic hymn of praise to himself as the creator of the city, which he made as a gift for his wife. The inhabitants of the city are his children; in one tremendous sentence which incorporates most of the original charter of Henry II to the city of Dublin, and includes two pages of condensed detail of modern city life from a Victorian sociological treatise, he declares his paternity over the inhabitants in him:

This missy, my taughters, and these man, my son, [all persons within the old boundaries of the city of Dublin] in hommage all and felony, all who have received tickets [the "all" are detailed—each family situation is more sordid and hopeless and "respectable" than the one before it], though their orable amission were the herrors I could have expected, all, let them all come, they are my villeins, with chartularies I have talledged them. (*FW* 543.15–545.14)

And he sets his hand and seal to the charter: "Hereto my vouchers, knive and snuffbuchs. Fee for farm. Enwreak us wrecks" (*FW* 545.22–23). That is, his symbols of control over his civic children are the knife wielded by knaves, and the suffocating-box, to snuff out their lives. He ends with the characteristic phrase of a bloodthirsty giant, "Fee fo fum," [19] and signs the charter with the name "Henricus Rex," which is also the declaration of the effect of the father-city—he "wreaks" (creates) the inhabitants, enwraps them, and wrecks them. No wonder that one of the phrases that his son Shaun employs in an earlier section to describe the father-city is, "We go into him sleepy children; we come out of him strucklers for life" (*FW* 132.8–9). The father has indeed an "eatupus complex" (*FW* 128.36), as

Shaun says; like Cronos, the father attempts to devour all of his children, to destroy any possibility that they can ever function independently of him.

Yet one phrase in the Haveth Childers Everywhere section provides a hint that the father is conscious of forces working for his overthrow: "the loy for a lynch." (*FW* 545.32) "Lynch" was the mayor of Galway who hanged his son with his own hands for a murder, and is thus an excellent symbol of a destroying father. A "loy" was the implement with which Christy Mahon struck down his father in Synge's *The Playboy of the Western World*.[20] The children are often not willing to be absorbed into the body of the father; their teleological drive can be as strong as his, and they may not be willing to be "ordurd"[21] by him. Consequently a fierce battle rages constantly between the generations, full of murderous intent on both sides, and uncompromisingly and cunningly waged.

Through *Finnegans Wake*, HCE is haunted by a vision of three soldiers and two girls who are doing something in a wood. They seem to be his children under light disguise—his two sons Shem and Shaun (plus a third who is an amalgamation of the two), and his daughter Issy (and her mirror image). He is sure that the children are plotting to overthrow him, and he keeps trying to destroy them or, at least, to render them impotent. In the Museyroom section (*FW* 8–10), the father figure, the "Willingdone," orders the three soldiers to be fired upon ("Tonnerre!"), and the soldiers flee in terror: "This is camelry, this is floodens, this is the solphereens in action, this is their mobbily, this is panickburns" (*FW* 9.24–25). The mother figure (Anna Livia Plurabelle, or ALP) knows of the murderous intentions of the Willingdone towards his children, and she tries to shield them behind her crinoline hoopskirt: "This is the crimealine of the alps hooping to shelter-shock the three lipoleums" (*FW* 8.29–30). Eventually the two girls (the "jinnies") run in front of the Willingdone and attract his attention by immodest displays, while the boys (the "lipoleums") behind him prepare to "kill" him.

This is the Willingdone branlish his same marmorial tallow-scoop . . . for his royal divorsion on the rinnaway jinnies . . . This is the dooforhim seeboy blow the whole of the half of the hat of lipoleums off the top of the tail on the back of his big wide harse. (*FW* 9.33–35, 10.19–21)

This fable recurs in many forms throughout *Finnegans Wake*. One of the later recurrences provides further evidence of the father's desire to assure himself that his sons are harmless, that they are not capable of maturing to the point of fatherhood. In the Butt and Taff episode (*FW* 337–55) the Willingdone situation is presented in the form of a horserace.

Pamjab! . . . Lucklucklucklucklucklucluck! It is the Thousand to One Guinea-Gooseberry's Lipperfull Slipver Cup . . . Bumchub! [22] *Emancipator, the Creman hunter (Major Hermyn C. Entwhistle) with dramatic effect reproducing the form of famous sires on the scene of the formers triumphs, is showing the eagle's way to Mr Whaytehayte's three buy geldings Homo Made Ink, Bailey Beacon and Ratatuohy while Furstin II and The Other Girl (Mrs 'Boss' Waters, Leavybrink) . . . are showing a clean pairofhids to Immensipater . . .* The Irish Race and World. (*FW* 342.14–16, 19–26, 32)

The physical order is the same here as in the Museyroom scene: the father, "Immensipater," runs before the three sons, while the two daughters are capering immodestly before him ("showing a clean pairofhids") . "*E*mancipator, the *C*reman *h*unter" (later called "Immensipater") , and "Major *H*ermyn *C*. *E*ntwhistle" are all HCE in various presentations. "Mr Whaytehayte" is the same personage as the "Old Whitehead" who is identified with "Haveth Childers Everywhere" on *FW* 535, so that he also is HCE, a "famous sire." The "three buy geldings" of "Mr Whaytehayte," the "white-hot" HCE, are Shem the Penman, Shaun the Post ("Bailey Beacon" refers to his beltlamp), and the murderous *tertium quid*, the "dooforhim seeboy" of the Willingdone episode, whose name "Ratatuohy" suggests, among other things, a rattle of machine-gun fire. The two temptresses are easily identifiable as Issy and her mirror image. Here the three soldiers are "geldings," that is, they are rendered helpless by the presence of Immensipater who has cornered all the sexuality in the situation: as in *Ulysses*, sons are "ever virgin" until they are ready to become fathers. Here again is suggested the fear of the father that the sexual maturing of his sons will constitute a deadly threat to his monopoly of creation, and his hope that he can keep them helpless puppets, creatures of his will.

The children, for their part, fear the intentions of the father, which are all too clear to them. In book 2, chapter 2, Issy, the daughter of the archetypal family, complains of the attempts of the old man to rape her,[23] and reports her fears that the old man is going to kill all of them.[24] The other children fear him as well: Shaun declares that "the man I go in fear of . . . could be all your and my das" (*FW* 481.32–33). The mob that hangs HCE in his bar says fearfully of him: "He'll be the deaf of us" (*FW* 379.20). The father wishes his children out of the way, so that his power need never be challenged, but the children unite, and send an ominous "youlldied greeding" to "Pep and Memmy and the old folkers below and beyant," signing it "jake, jack and little sousoucie (the babes that mean too) " (*FW* 308.17–19, 24–25).

It soon becomes clear what they mean to do: they mean to counterattack symbolically, by developing to the point of sexual maturity, at which point the father becomes no father, and a new father is created, with all the fears of the old one haunting him. With the old father out of the way, the new holy marriage between brother and sis-

ter can take place (in the archetypal family all sexual relationships are perforce incestuous) .

After the execution of HCE in his bar,[25] all that is left
of the erstwhile father roams around his ruined domain in
the guise of Roderick O'Conor, the last high king of Ireland, (who was left a shadow king when the Normans in-
vaded Ireland) . The "poor old" king, deposed HCE,
drinks up the dregs of his customers' drinks and "slumps
to throne." Then "the stout ship *Nansy Hans*" sails away
with him on board, a dead or meaningless entity. The
name of the ship bears out this interpretation of *FW*
382.27–30: "*Nansy Hans*" contains the name of Nancy
Hanks, the mother of Abraham Lincoln. Lincoln is one of
the masks of HCE; as "Emancipator" or "Immensipater"
he is the father-horse in the reenactment of the Museyroom scene on *FW* 342. Lincoln is in *Finnegans Wake*, it
seems, only because he was a powerful figure who was assassinated, a type of the Russian general, whose killing by
Buckley is one of the main structural elements in the
book.[26] Therefore, the "stout ship *Nansy Hans*" is, in one
sense, the eternal mother bearing the dead father away. It
is, as we see in the next chapter, the site of the merging of
Tristan and Isolde. Around the ship fly the four old men,
the impotent historians, in the guise of gulls, singing a rau-
cous song of praise to Tristan, and mocking poor old King
Mark, the eternal *senex amans* and cuckold, whose fate it
is to represent a "disarmed" fatherhood, an older generation giving way most reluctantly to a new.[27]

This brief analysis of selected passages from *Finnegans
Wake* seems to reveal a complete generalizing of the paternal relationship along the lines suggested above: the father
is the father of every child; the children wish to depose
him; their weapons are time and maturity—if they develop
to the point of sexual and moral maturity, defined by Aristotle, they are, from the father's point of view, dangerously
close to reducing him to a nonentity or, at best, an impo-

tent old praiser of his own past, a lascivious looker-on at the lovemaking of the young, like the four old men in *Finnegans Wake*. The father, for his part, attempts to halt the process of maturity by various means and, in the archetypal situation, always fails—Buckley shoots the Russian general, Tristan steals Isolde from King Mark, the furious "seeboy" in the Wellington Museyroom section attacks the father figure and ends the battle, and the brother and sister consummate their marriage like "boyrun to sibster" (*FW* 465.17) , Byron and his sister.

It is comparatively simple to establish a case for general fatherhood in *Finnegans Wake,* since all of the characters in the *Wake* are multiple in nature. However, can such a case be made for *Ulysses* and *A Portrait*? In those two books the characterization is more naturalistic than in the *Wake*. Of course, in *Ulysses* the "metempsychotic" undertones in the characterization of Stephen and Bloom provide a certain "multiple" depth for them, but the case for a generalized father-son relationship in *Ulysses* and *A Portrait* remains to be established.

In the case of *A Portrait* and *Ulysses,* the three essential questions are:

Has Stephen any other "father" besides Simon Dedalus?

In what way could Bloom be Stephen's "father"?

In what way could Stephen be Bloom's "son"?

These three questions could be merged into one: is there any reason to think that Joyce considered that the father-son relationship could exist between males unconnected by blood?

An approach to the answer to this question may be made by considering Joyce's theory of personality, which, like all of Joyce's general theories, must be gleaned from passages in his works and his notebooks. The earliest statement on personality occurs in the original sketch for *A Portrait of the Artist* which he wrote on January 7, 1904.[28]

The features of infancy are not commonly reproduced in the adolescent portrait for, so capricious are we, that we cannot or will not conceive the past in other than its iron, memorial aspect. Yet the past assuredly implies a fluid succession of presents, the development of an entity of which our actual present is a phase only. Our world, again recognises its acquaintance chiefly by the characters of beard and inches and is, for the most part, estranged from those of its members who seek through some art, by some process of the mind as yet untabulated, to liberate from the personalised lumps of matter that which is their individuating rhythm, the first or formal relation of their parts. But for such as these a portrait is not an identificative paper but rather the curve of an emotion.

Joyce interpreted "individuating rhythm" quite literally by the time of the final version of *A Portrait*—in the course of the book Stephen acquires a characteristic rhythm of speech and thought which never deserts him. In *Ulysses* the rhythm of Bloom's interior monologue is different from that of Stephen, and Molly's is different from either. Other interior monologues are recorded in the book —Father Conmee's, Patsy Dignam's, Mr. Kernan's, Miss Dunne the typist's (all in the Wandering Rocks chapter [*U* 219–55]) —and each is different, each displays a characteristic rhythm. Joyce also intended that his characters in *Finnegans Wake* should display characteristic rhythms in their speech; in one of his drafts for book 1, chapter 6 of the *Wake*,[29] he notes that Issy's speech rhythm is to be trochaic, Shaun's spondaic, and Shem's pyrrhic. The other characters in the *Wake* have their characteristic rhythms also. Joyce sums up his practice of individualizing his characters by speech or thought rhythms in the statement on *FW* 215.17 that "each hue had a differing cry," each "appearance" has an individuating rhythm.

However, the "individuating rhythm, the first or formal relation of their parts" which it is the artist's task to "liberate from the personalised lumps of matter" can be interpreted in a more general way. The phrase "the first or formal relation of the parts" of "personalised lumps of matter" suggests Aristotle's definition of the soul, "The soul is the first grade of actuality of a natural organized body" [30] (*De Anima*, 2. 1. 412^b5–6) which Joyce renders in his Paris notebook as "The soul is the first entelechy of a naturally organic body." [31] As Aristotle makes clear in a subsequent passage (*De Anima*, 2. 1. 415^a9–28), the soul is only the *first* entelechy, or grade of actuality, of a naturally organic body, because in isolation the organism is only potentially a living organism; the *second* entelechy of the organism is the organism in action fully realizing its potential among the society of its fellows.

The first grade of actuality of a body, says Aristotle, is to the second grade as the possession of a quality or faculty is to the exercise of it.

Matter is potentiality, form actuality [*entelecheia*]; of the latter there are two grades related to one another as e.g. knowledge to the exercise of knowledge. . . . It is obvious that the soul is actuality in the first sense, viz. that of knowledge [for example] as possessed, for both sleeping and waking presuppose the existence of soul, and of these waking corresponds to actual knowing, sleeping to knowledge possessed but not employed, and, in the history of the individual, knowledge comes before its employment or exercise. . . . That is why the soul is the first grade of actuality of a natural body having life potentially in it. (*De Anima*, 2. 1. 412^a9–11, 23–28) [32]

This division of soul into potential and actual provides a possible interpretation for Joyce's word "liberate." If the artist were merely to note and observe the potential souls locked up in lumps of matter and record his observations, his work would amount to no more than, at best, a string of Theophrastian character-studies. However, if the artist both apprehends the souls of men and things and then shows these organisms in action, he is allowing the creatures of his mind the same freedom that is enjoyed by natural creations—he is playing the God of Creation, in short. In *Stephen Hero* the process is defined.

The artist [Stephen] imagined [33] standing in the position of mediator between the world of his experience and the world of his dreams—a mediator, consequently, gifted with twin faculties, a selective faculty and a reproductive faculty. To equate these faculties was the secret of artistic success: the artist who could disentangle the subtle soul of the image from its mesh of defining circumstances most exactly and re-embody it in artistic circumstances chosen as the most exact for it in its new office, he was the supreme artist. . . . society is itself . . . the complex body in which certain laws are involved and overwrapped and he therefore proclaimed as the realm of the poet the realm of these unalterable laws. (*SH* 77–78)

The "selective faculty" apprehends the first entelechy of things by "epiphany." In several passages in his early work, Joyce defines the three stages of the apprehension of the soul of an object, an individual, or of a culture.[34] By the third stage, that of *claritas*, "its soul, its whatness, leaps to us from the vestment of its appearance" (*SH* 213). It "leaps" to us because the soul is a "simple" substance incapable of being further subdivided or analyzed into its parts; therefore it must be apprehended by a simple, single act of intuition, by a simple act of the soul.[35]

What is this whatness that is instantly grasped? Aristotle divides thinking into two classes: *1*] intuitive apprehension, and *2*] analytical judgment. The grasp of the whatness of things belongs to the first category. Within this category Aristotle distinguishes three types: *1*] apprehension of what is *actually* undivided in quantity, though potentially divisible by analytical judgment; until we so divide these concepts they are apprehended by a single act of the soul; *2*] what is indivisible in kind by its nature; and *3*] what is indivisible in magnitude, that is, a concept like "white" which is graspable only by contrast with everything that is "not-it." [36] The whatness of an object or of a personality is graspable only by the second of these types of apprehension. What is apprehended is the *infima species,* as it was later called, of the object, that is, the penultimate grade of definition of a thing, that which immediately precedes the individual object or person himself, which is only apprehensible by the third type of apprehension; the last grade of individuality is perceivable only by "privation," by contrast with whatever is "not-it."

Joyce is not concerned with the last stage of individuality. As a good Aristotelian (and Aquinian) he is content to apprehend the whatness of things and not their thisness (their Scotist *haecceitas* which so interested Gerard Manley Hopkins). Critical opinion is divided on this issue: Maurice Beebe, in "Joyce and Aquinas: the Theory of Aesthetics," *Philological Quarterly,* 36 (January 1957), 31, crediting W. K. Wimsatt, declares that Joyce confused *quidditas* with *haecceitas.* Father Noon, who is also influenced by Professor Wimsatt's views, reiterates this point in *Joyce and Aquinas* (New Haven, 1957), pp. 49–51, and expands on it.

The identity which Stephen establishes between claritas and the Scholastic *quidditas* . . . is also questionable if Stephen claims Aquinas as his authority. . . . [The "substantial form" of a thing, its whatness] is not a principle of individuation; it is sometimes called the "specific" form, or *forma specifica,* but the specification is to species, or class. . . . What Stephen seems to mean by claritas may have been expressed by the *haecceitas* of Duns Scotus than by the quidditas of Aquinas [and Aristotle].[37]

According to Father Noon, the specific form, the *quidditas,* is considered by Thomists to be the "inner heart" of an object. S. L. Goldberg finds in Joyce's esthetic theory, as outlined in *Stephen Hero,* "a confusion of aesthetic apprehension . . . and ordinary apprehension" and declares that "consequently a philosophically precise exposition of Stephen's (or Joyce's) meaning is impossible."[38]

The source of these accusations of inconsistency is not easy to find. Perhaps it lies in the unwillingness of men raised in a tradition of Western individualism to believe that a modern writer could deliberately turn his back on the unconquerable citadel of the unknowable individual and conquer the more accessible city of the general type. Joyce proceeds exactly as he says he will—he attempts to grasp and present general types in his works, not idiosyncratic grotesques, or unrepeatable character studies. His books are not called *David Copperfield, Esther Waters, Tom Jones, The Vicar of Wakefield.* They are all named after the general type to which his main characters in their action conform: *A Portrait of the Artist as a Young Man* could not be called *Stephen Dedalus; Ulysses* could not be called *Stephen and Leopold; Finnegans Wake* would be baldly misrepresented if it were called *H. C. Earwicker: His Family and Friends.* It is to general types that Joyce's portraits approximate, and this generalizing process is active in all of his major works.

The above analysis can be summed up as follows: fatherhood and sonhood are "mystical estates," general attitudes into which individuals are born or develop. Once a man has attained the estate of fatherhood he "is and feels himself" the father of all his "race"; a son is also the only son of the only father in his "race," which, in *Finnegans Wake,* tends to be the human race. If Leopold Bloom is a father and Stephen Dedalus a son, they occupy the positions of father and son to each other even if they are not related by blood. The family relationship, then, can be generalized by means of Joyce's Aristotelian definition of personality into the relationship of all men to all other men.

What other general types are there in Joyce's work? By the time he came to write *Finnegans Wake,* Joyce seems to have arrived at an understanding of just how many basic human types there are; all the characters in *Finnegans Wake* seem to be related to the basic types described by

Shaun in answer to the twelve questions set by Shem, in book 1, chapter 6: HCE; ALP; the Four Old Men; Maurice (or Sackerson, or Pore Ole Joe), the manservant; Kate (the maid); the Twelve (jurors or public opinion personified); the twenty-eight Maggies (or little girls); Issy, the daughter-temptress-sister; Shaun and Shem, the two sons, one of whom is also an artist.[39] However, in an earlier chapter, Joyce reduces the number of possibilities to four (or really five).

Four things . . . ne'er sall fail til heathersmoke and cloud-weed Eire's ile sall pall. . . . A bulbenboss surmounted upon an alderman [HCE in his roles as a mountain like Ben Bulben, or Howth, and as an "older man" holding a political office whose name, like his, is Germanic-Scandinavian in origin—*ealdorman / alderman*]. . . . A shoe on a puir old wobban [ALP in her role as the Shan Van Vocht]. . . . An auburn mayde, o'brine a'bride, to be desarted [Issy, the temptress, perhaps attracting to herself the polar opposites of Alpha and Omega, *o*'brine *a*'bride, Shaun and Shem, who strive to win her several times in the book]. . . . A penn no weightier nor a polepost [Shem the Penman and Shaun the Post, the polar opposites, and the eternal sons]. (*FW* 13.20–28)

The "perfection" of human personality reduces itself to five possibilities: father, mother, daughter, sons (and perhaps artist). However, the daughter merges into the wife and mother, when the sons merge into the husband and father, so there are only two great archetypes finally: Man and Woman.[40] Therefore, when young Joyce in *Stephen Hero* had Stephen "[toy] with a theory of dualism which would symbolise the twin eternities of spirit and nature in the twin eternities of male and female" (*SH* 210), he was in reality writing a prospectus for all his future work.

The archetypal method of analysis seems applicable to *Ulysses* as well as to *Finnegans Wake;* it is not difficult to see the father in Bloom and the son and artist in Stephen; even though they are not related by blood they embody the mystical estates of fatherhood and sonhood, and their complex relationship mirrors the archetypal attitudes of father and son. Is this sort of analysis applicable to *A Portrait of the Artist?* The title would suggest that the artist-type is being described, but are the other human types present performing their characteristic tasks, achieving the "second entelechy" of created perfect beings, the activity in society which most completely defines their being?

In the chapter that follows I intend to examine *A Portrait of the Artist* closely, chapter by chapter, to discover the workings of real and symbolic father-son relationships, constantly checking my conclusions with material from *Finnegans Wake,* where the processes of development presented more or less naturalistically in *A Portrait* and *Ulysses* are recapitulated in "fable" form. I will also describe the growth and development of the artist type. After I have outlined the archetypal story underlying the action of *A Portrait* I will examine what I now consider to be a crucial episode in *Ulysses,* the dance of Stephen in the Nighttown scene, and show how this scene, properly unfolded, provides a natural climax to the double development of the artist and the son to fatherhood.

2

a portrait

of the artist

the end he had been born to serve
—A PORTRAIT (PP. 165, 169)

a.   chapter **one,** section one (*P* 7–8)

THE first section of *A Portrait* acts as an introduction to the whole work, like the first chapter of *Finnegans Wake*. The first page of *Finnegans Wake* introduces the characters of the archetypal family; so does the first section of *A Portrait*.

The first paragraph of *A Portrait* introduces the father in a number of different roles. He first appears to the baby Stephen as a storyteller with a "glass" and a "hairy face." As a storyteller, he is a creator, and the hairy face of the creative father is the first thing young Stephen remembers. The hairy face of the creator, this time the famous wall-builder Balbus, is referred to later on, *P* 43:

And behind the door of one of the closets [in the Clongowes lavatory] there was a drawing in red pencil of a bearded man in a Roman dress with a brick in each hand and underneath was the name of the drawing:

Balbus was building a wall.

Some fellow had drawn it there for a cod. It had a funny face but it was very like a man with a beard.

The repetition of the fact that the figure had a beard seems to suggest that Joyce wished to connect this caricature of the classical Balbus, mentioned in Cicero's letters and immortalized in traditional Latin grammars, with the storytelling father. There is no reason to believe that the original Balbus was bearded; indeed, if he followed the practice of patrician Romans, he would almost certainly not have been.[1]

This hairy face turns up again in Joyce's work, in *Finnegans Wake*, at the beginning of the Lessons episode.

With his broad
and hairy face,
to Ireland a
disgrace. *(FW* 260, *l.*1)

This marginal note refers to the sentence in the text "Am shot, says the bigguard." This note is further elucidated by Issy's first footnote, in which she complains about the unwelcome attentions of "old Herod with the Cormwell's eczema," who is, among others, HCE plus Oliver Cromwell plus King Mark of Cornwall, that is, he is the father figure in *Finnegans Wake,* who is as the text suggests, a big blackguard of uncontrollable sexual-creative propensities. Issy declares that she would "do nine months" for him if he attacks her, that is, she would counterassault and spend nine months in jail gladly, or that she would bear his child. The feared and despised being who is after Issy is held, by Campbell and Robinson, to be the Kabbalistic *Makroposopos,* the Great Visage from whom all creation flows, and in whose long white beard the entire universe of men and angels is to be found.[2] If this is so, then hairiness and creation are associated, in Joyce's later work, on the highest possible level.

However, it is not necessary to reach so far for an explanation of the hairy face of the father in *A Portrait;* to a child the hairiness of an adult male would seem the sign of his maturity. In many societies, ancient and modern, the growth of facial hair was held to be the mark of physical and moral maturity. The father with the hairy face at the beginning of *A Portrait* is, at the very least, a mature male, whose appearance contains a covert reference to Joyce's theory of the development of personality; it is a mature, "perfected" organism that has produced its "image," to which it is telling stories.[3]

As we have seen, a son cannot create; he is "ever virgin" by nature. Stephen, in *Ulysses,* attempts to create on several occasions and fails miserably each time: his Parable of the Plums is misunderstood, or at best, only partly understood by Professor MacHugh, and ignored by the rest of his audience; his poem composed on the beach is an unconscious plagiarism from Douglas Hyde; his spontaneous epigram (on *U* 142) turns out to be lifted from Augustine, "From the Fathers," as the paragraph heading states; "Drummond of Hawthornden" helps him during his Shakespeare lecture (*U* 194); his telegram to Mulligan is taken from Meredith (*U* 199, 425). Only a "father" can create.

The subject of the story that the father is telling in the first section of *A Portrait* reveals another aspect of fatherhood. "Baby tuckoo" suggests to some critics a recognition by the father of a "cuckoo" in the nest, an unwanted foreign presence.[4] While in *A Portrait* Stephen's father does not overtly resent his presence, in *Ulysses* it is suggested that a father often sees in the person of his son the presage of his downfall.

The son unborn mars beauty: born, he brings pain, divides affection, increases care. . . . He is a male: his growth is his father's decline, his youth his father's envy. (*U* 207–8)

Bloom obscurely senses that fathers unconsciously resent children: "Frightening them [children] with masks too. Throwing them up in the air to catch them. I'll murder you. Is it only half fun?" (*U* 379).

Later on in *Ulysses* Bloom, seeing Stephen as his lost son, tries gently, firmly, insistently to keep Stephen from becoming an independent creator, and Stephen politely, firmly, unbudgingly refuses to be prevented from developing. In *Finnegans Wake*, as I have suggested in my first chapter, a violent struggle between children and father is one of the basic facts of life. According to the above hypothesis, every child would seem a "baby tuckoo" in his apprehensive father.

After the introduction of the father, with his hairy maturity and creativity and his mixed attitude toward his creation, we are introduced to some aspects of the son-artist which will acquire great symbolic importance later on—"his song," his dance ("the sailor's hornpipe"), and the opposition of warmth and cold that (in combination with darkness and whiteness) is so important in the symbolic structure of *A Portrait* and *Ulysses*. The song and the dance are the symbols of the artist as creator-king, as I will attempt to show in my analysis of the King David figure in the works of Joyce (see below, section on chap. 5). However, it should here be noted that dances occur at important places in Joyce's work. Stephen's "tripudium" in the Nighttown chapter of *Ulysses* (*U* 574–79), for example, immediately brings on the crisis he has been dodging ail day. In *Finnegans Wake* dancing is the sign of Shem the artist; sometimes he is the Gracehoper, who is always "jigging" or "striking up funny funereels" or engaging in a "dance McCaper" like "fantastic disossed and jenny aprils" (*FW* 414–15), that is, dancing like Valentin le Desossé and Jeanne Avril in Toulouse-Lautrec's famous posters. Sometimes he is Dave the Dancekerl (*FW* 462–68), and sometimes Glugg, the "pigtail tarr" who dances up the Maggies to try to win their favor (*FW* 232–33).[5] The clearest association of the artist with dancing occurs on *FW* 513.

—And Jambs, of Delphin's Bourne or (as olders lay) of Tophat? [the investigator asks of Yawn.]

—Dawncing the kniejinksky choreopiscopally like an eastern sun round the colander, the vice! Taranta boontoday! You should pree him prance the polcat, you whould sniff him wops around, you should hear his piedigrotts schraying as his skimpies skirp a . . .

—Crashedafar Corumbas! A Czardanser indeed! Dervilish glad too. Ortovito semi ricordo. The pantaglionic affection through his blood like a bad influenza in a leap at bounding point? (*FW* 513.9–19)

Shem here is the leggy "Jambs" who dances like Fred As-
taire in *Top Hat* (1935), or like the sun at Easter (an old
belief), or like Nijinsky or Taglioni. An imperial dancer,
a "Czardanser," his dances include the tarantella, the
polka, the waltz ("wops"), the rumba, the czardas, and
various dervishlike boundings. "You Should See Me Dance
the Polka" is one of the dance melodies in this passage, and
"Tarara Boom-De-Ay" is another.[6] Apparently "Jambs"
acquired the habit from his father, "the palsied old pri-
amite," who was "trippudiating round the aria, with his
fifty two heirs of age! They may reel at his likes but it's
Noeh Bonum's shin do" (*FW* 513.20, 22–24). (The reel
and the *tripudium* are here the old father's dances.) The
little boy's hornpipe in the first chapter of *A Portrait* is,
therefore, going to play an important symbolic role in the
fortunes of the developing artist.

We are next introduced to young Stephen's mother,
who is juxtaposed in the baby's consciousness with the alternation of warm and cold, and thus with the abstract concept of opposites or alternation.

When you wet the bed first it is warm then it gets cold.
His mother put on the oilsheet. That had the queer smell.
His mother had a nicer smell than his father.

In *Finnegans Wake* woman is associated with opposition,
with polarities, with the breaking up of a single consciousness of unfallen Adam into the "hue and cry" of the senses.
It is also in *Finnegans Wake* that the white radiance of eternity is broken up into seven Rainbow Girls. There is a description of both ALP and the Rainbow Girls in these
terms on *FW* 101–3.

Do tell us all about. As we want to hear allabout. So tellus
tellus allabouter. The why or whether she looked allotty like
ussies and whether he had his wimdop like themses shut? Notes
and queries, tipbids and answers, the laugh and the shout, the
ards and downs. [Here woman is associated with polar opposi-

tions—ups and downs, questions and answers, joy and pain.]
. . . first warming creature of his [HCE-Adam's] early morn
[note the association with *P* 7; 11.13–14] . . . she who shut-
tered him after his fall and waked him widowt sparing and
gave him keen and made him able and held adazillahs to each
arche of his noes, she who will not rast her from her running
to seek him till, with the help of the okeamic, some such time
that she shall have been after hiding the crumbends of his
enormousness in the areyou lookingfor Pearlfar sea (ur, uri,
uria!) stood forth [again the association of woman with urine,
wetting the bed—ALP's initials in "areyou lookingfor Pearlfar" indicate whose sea it is].

Wery weeny wight, plead for Morandmor! *Notre Dame de
la Ville,* mercy of thy balmheartzyheat! . . . But there's a
little lady waiting and her name is A.L.P. And you'll agree.
She must be she. For her holden heirheaps hanging down her
back. He [HCE] spenth his strenth amok haremscarems.
Poppy, Narancy, Giallia, Chlora, Marinka, Anileeen, Parme.
And ilk a those dames had her rainbow huemoures yet for
whilko her whims but he coined a cure. Tifftiff today, kissy-
kissy tonay and agelong pine tomauranna. Then who but
Crippled-with-Children would speak up for Dropping-with-
Sweat?

> *Sold him her lease of nineninenee,*
> *Tresses undresses so dyedyedaintee,*
> *Goo, the groot gudgeon, gulped it all.*
> *Hoo was the C.O.D.?*
>> Bum!
> *At Island Bridge she met her tide.*
> *Attabom, attabom, attabombomboom!*
> *The Fin had a flux and his Ebba a ride.*
> *Attabom, attabom, attabombomboom!*
> *We're all up to the years in hues and cribies.*
> *That's what she's done for wee!*
>> Woe!

Nomad may roam with Nabuch but let naaman laugh at
Jordan! For we, we have taken our sheet upon her stones
where we have hanged our hearts in her trees; and we list, as

she bibs us, by the waters of babalong. (*FW* 101.2–6, 31–32, 102.1–7, 18–35, 103.1–11)

In this section of *Finnegans Wake* the mother, ALP, is indissolubly connected with the differentiation of reality by the senses; she was responsible for the Fall, and we are now "up to the years in hues and cribies," that is, we are now in time and subjected to the hue and cry, the sights and sounds, of the phenomenal world, and also the hue and cry of crybabies in cribs, and to the hue and cry after the criminal Adam. ALP-Eve trapped "the groot gudgeon" HCE-Adam, but she did not get off lightly; although, like the Hebrews in Ps. 137 (King James version) that is echoed in 103.9–11, we are in exile by the waters of Babylon, she herself is "Crippled-with-Children" and has given up one tooth for each child (*FW* 101.34).

Nevertheless, despite her burdens, the great mother and wife actively assists in her husband's pursuit of the Rainbow Girls; in a later section the washerwomen declare that ALP was always "calling the bakvandets sals from all around . . . to go in till him, her erring cheef, and tickle the pontiff aisy-oisy" (*FW* 198.10–12).

[She would] go and trot doon and stand in her douro . . . and every shirvant siligirl or wensum farmerette walking the pilend roads, Sawy, Fundally, Daery or Maery, Milucre, Awny or Graw, usedn't she make a simp or sign to slip inside by the sullyport. . . . throwing all the neiss little whores in the world at him! (*FW* 200.17–21, 29–30)

Since ALP symbolizes, among other things, the flow of time and experience ("if I go all goes" *FW* 627.14), her proxenetical activity would be more than sexual. This activity could be interpreted as the presentation by experience of the facts of the phenomenal world to the senses. Like the hairy face of the father, and the dancing of the son-artist, this association of women with the physical facts of life is first found on the first page of *A Portrait*.

Once the abstract idea of alternation and opposition is introduced, it quickly develops into the idea of conflict and development. Almost immediately the generalized oppositions of warmth and coldness modulate into the localized historical alternates (not yet oppositions) of maroon and green on the backs of Aunt Dante's brushes. Alternates plus history equals conflict: it is after warmth and cold move into the historical plane that young Stephen experiences his first conflict, the concrete social embodiment of opposition.

> The Vances lived in number seven. They had a different [7] father and mother. They were Eileen's father and mother. When they were grown up he was going to marry Eileen. He hid under the table. His mother said:
> —O, Stephen will apologise.
> Dante said:
> —O, if not, the eagles will come and pull out his eyes. (*P* 8)

The phrasing of these sentences is odd. "The Vances lived in number seven. They had a different father and mother." The "they" of the second sentence suggests that Stephen seems to think of "the Vances" almost as the name of a tribe, with "father" and "mother" as the names of the chiefs. At any rate, it shows that he does not yet know the meaning of "husband and wife" or the sexual framework of the family; "father" and "mother" are merely authority-names to him. His declaration that he was going to "marry" Eileen when they both grew up would seem to be a statement with little actual meaning for him.

However, whether or not Stephen means anything by the statement, it provokes a violent reaction from someone. Immediately after Stephen declares that he is going to marry the Protestant Eileen we find him hiding under a table, with his mother and Aunt Dante protecting him from someone or something. Aunt Dante's words provide a clue to the source of the disturbance: "—O, if not, the eagles will come and pull out his eyes." These words, really too frightening to be spoken to a child even in jest, are derived from a passage of the Bible, Prov. 30:17.

The eye that mocketh at his father and that despiseth the labor of his mother in bearing him, let the raven of the brooks pick it out, and the young eagles eat it. [Douay version] [8]

Aunt Dante quotes scripture, or misapplies it, twice during the Christmas Day dinner scene (*P* 32, 38); [9] Joyce strongly establishes this trait as part of her personality. If, then, Aunt Dante is paraphrasing Prov. 30:17, it is a parent that Stephen has insulted. Since it is not his mother, who defends him, it is a father.

This interpretation can be supported by reference to the epiphany upon which this section is based:

[Bray: in the parlour of the house in Martello Terrace]
Mr Vance— (*comes in with a stick*) . . . O, you know, he'll have to apologise, Mrs Joyce.
Mrs Joyce—O, yes . . . Do you hear that, Jim?
Mr Vance—Or else—if he doesn't the eagles'll come and pull out his eyes.
Mrs Joyce—O, but I'm sure he will apologise.
Joyce— (*under the table, to himself*)
—Pull out his eyes,
Apologise,
Apologise,
Pull out his eyes.

Apologise,
Pull out his eyes,
Pull out his eyes,
Apologise.[10]

It is, then, an angry father by whom Stephen is frightened. The biblical verse-paraphrase in the text, shifted from Mr. Vance to Aunt Dante, relates the punishment of a son who scorns and defies his parents. Both of these references tend to support my contention that young Stephen has been threatened by a father for asserting, ignorantly and innocently, his right of growth to maturity, to sexuality, to marriage "when they were grown up."

The father appears in this section in two guises—as the creative, mature father, and as the threatened, threatening father. His appearance in the latter role is so frightening to the son that all explicit mention of who is doing the threatening is burned out of his memory, and can be deduced only from allusions in the text. The removal of Mr. Vance from the final text of *A Portrait* leaves only a generalized paternal threat hanging in the air—Stephen is too frightened to remember whose father threatened him. He remembers it later, however; when he has been pandied by Father Dolan, he has an impulse to hide because "when you were small and young you could often escape that way" (*P* 55).[11]

This double image of the father, along with the song and the dance which are the signs of the artist, and the ideas of alternation and opposition associated with his mother, are the main symbolic contributions of this section to *A Portrait*. As we will see, these symbols here presented in basic terms will be of supreme importance in *A Portrait* itself, and will be the source of important symbolic structures in *Ulysses* and *Finnegans Wake*.

b.   chapter **one,** sections two, three, and four (*P* 8–59)

THE next three sections of chapter 1 of *A Portrait* form a chronological unit. The second section (*P* 8–27) takes place at Clongowes seventy-seven and seventy-six days before the Christmas vacation in the year Parnell died (*P* 10), which would make it about October ninth or tenth, 1891; Parnell died on October 6, 1891. The events of the end of this section would be occurring at the same time as the feverish Stephen imagines them: Parnell's body was brought back to Ireland on October 11, 1891. The third section (*P* 27–39), then, takes place during the Christmas Day dinner of 1891, and the fourth section (*P* 40–59) takes place during Lent, 1892, in the term after the Christmas recess: "He could not eat the blackish fish fritters they got on Wednesdays in Lent" (*P* 53).

Joyce distorts both fictional and real chronology to effect a coincidence of little Stephen's rebellion and the death of Parnell. In *Ulysses* Stephen, remembering Father Dolan, recalls that he was pandied "sixteen years ago" (*U* 561, 563), i.e., in 1888. This would place the time of the pandying three years before the death of Parnell (1891). This lack of congruence might be the result of Stephen's drunken eagerness to see numerical patterns in his disordered life, were it not that this date, 1888, corresponds fairly closely with the facts of Joyce's own life: Joyce entered Clongowes in September 1888 and stayed until just before Christmas 1891. Stephen's memory of his Clongowes days in *Ulysses* corresponds, within one year, to the facts of Joyce's own life. The date of the pandying in *A Portrait* does not; it is deliberately advanced to coincide with the death of Parnell. If the pandying in *A Portrait* follows the death of Parnell it would have taken place during Lent 1892, when Joyce was no longer at Clongowes,[12] and four years after the date Stephen sets for the pandying in *Ulysses*. When Joyce shifts the events surrounding the death of Parnell to Stephen's first year at Clongowes, he is deliberately emphasizing Stephen's heroism in combating those forces responsible for the downfall of Parnell.

The three last sections of chapter 1 form a dramatic unit, therefore, with the death of Parnell as a motivating force. The emotions of the Christmas Day dinner scene, occurring as it does less than three months after the death of Parnell, are exacerbated by the raw emotions surrounding his death; the sudden harshness of the discipline at Clongowes might be due to the fear of rebellion felt by the guilty clerical party after the recriminations that flew back and forth in the months after Parnell's death. It might be said that little Stephen was pandied as a result of a national historical event. The Clongowes Jesuits, responding to the rage of the Parnellites with guilt and fear, suddenly introduce a spirit of terrorism into their dealings with the (potentially) insurrectionary populace under their control; the boys are all conscious of a new stiffening of the school's discipline and tentatively plan a rebellion (*P* 44); Father Dolan's powers are increased, and he is tacitly allowed to execute summary justice on all offenders. Nor can Father Arnall intercede effectively for Stephen; the spirit of suppression has affected him also, so that he is unable to prevent injustice inflicted in the name of order. The sudden rigidity of authoritarian rule in times of stress is no new thing; captive populations soon discover ways of avoiding trouble, as have the boys of Clongowes—all except Stephen. His protest, undertaken out of a sense of personal injustice, is really a protest against a general historical atmosphere, and is therefore a much more serious matter than it would appear to be at first glance. As a serious matter, it is accompanied by signs and omens, which will be analyzed in the following paragraphs.

The decision to appeal to the rector is never consciously made by Stephen. On one page we see him telling himself that

he could not go. The rector would side with the prefect of studies and think it was a schoolboy trick and then the prefect of studies would come in every day the same only it would be worse because he would be dreadfully waxy at any fellow going up to the rector about him. . . . No, it was best to forget all about it and perhaps the prefect of studies had only said he would come in. No, it was best to hide out of the way because when you were small and young you could often escape that way. (*P* 54–55)

Then, almost immediately afterward we see him walking along the matting leading to the refectory door, telling himself that it was impossible, but going on, moved by some unconscious force, which is forcing him to confront his crisis against his childish sense of prudence.

By this act he seems to be striking against the frightening father who terrified him into hiding under the table years before, in the first section: it is that situation he remembers when he reasons that "it was best to hide out of the way because when you were small and young you could often escape that way." However, he does not hide in the fourth section, as he did in the first; he confronts his oppressors and defeats them. It is his first victory as an insurgent son battling against the fathers of his world.

His act of rebellion is accompanied by symbols of rebellion. The last thoughts that pass through his mind outside the rector's door are of Hamilton Rowan, the noble rebel, and of the "ghost in the white cloak of a marshal" (*P* 56). Hamilton Rowan may occur and recur to Stephen because Stephen is also in some sense a rebel, but the reason for the appearance of the marshal is more complex. Although the ghost of the marshal is a local spectre historically associated with Congowes Castle,[13] it is also a symbolic figure of the first importance. The cloak of the apparition is white, and its face is "pale and strange" (*P* 19). Whiteness or paleness in this section of *A Portrait* and after is associated with coldness and dampness, and with the fathers and with repressive authority in general. The evening air of Clongowes is "pale and chilly" (*P* 8) ; the sky is "pale and cold" when Stephen wonders from what window Hamilton Rowan had thrown his hat on the haha (*P* 10) ; the air in the Clongowes corridor chills Stephen: "It was queer and wettish" (*P* 11). Paleness and coldness have already been linked; here they are both tied to dampness. In the classroom Stephen, wearing the white rose, thinks that "his face must be white because it felt so cool" (*P* 12). The bread and the tablecloth in the refectory are damp, and the scullion wears a white apron. Stephen then makes the association between whiteness (or paleness) and coldness and dampness: "He wondered whether the scullion's apron was damp too or whether all white things were cold and damp" (*P* 13). Immediately afterward the white-pale-damp-cold associative group acquires another element:

Nasty Roche and Saurin drank cocoa that their people sent them in tins. They said they could not drink the tea; that it was hogwash. Their fathers were magistrates, the fellows said. (*P* 13)

This conjunction of white-pale-damp-cold with the power of magistrates and fathers is not fortuitous; fathers, in their roles as authority figures, repressors of growth, are generally associated with whiteness, paleness, and coldness, and their minions, their unrebellious tools, are marked by paleness and coldness also. The prefect's hand is cold and damp; "that was the way a rat felt, slimy and damp and cold" (*P* 22). When Stephen wonders what the pain of a caning is like "it made him shivery to think of it and cold" (*P* 45). Mr. Gleeson, the flogger, has "clean white wrists and fattish white hands," and Stephen trembles "with cold and fright to think of the cruel long nails and of the high whistling sound of the cane and of the chill you felt at the end of your shirt when you undressed yourself yet he felt a feeling of queer quiet pleasure inside him to think of the white fattish hands, clean and strong and gentle." Stephen still trusts the cold, white fathers:

And he thought of what Cecil Thunder had said; that Mr Gleeson would not flog Corrigan hard. And Fleming had said he would not because it was best of his play not to. But that was not why. (*P* 45)

Stephen underestimates the sadism of Mr. Gleeson and the repressive fathers; this observation of his occurs only a few pages before his encounter with Father Dolan's old whiteness, his "whitegrey not young" face, his "nocoloured" eyes and his "firm soft fingers" (*P* 50, 52), which, Stephen feels, have betrayed him.

At first [Stephen] had thought [Father Dolan] was going to shake hands with him because the fingers were soft and firm . . . that was to hit it better and louder. (*P* 52)

When Stephen confronts the rector in his office, Father Conmee's hand is cool and moist (*P* 58).[14] Therefore, the whiteness of the cloak of the ghostly marshal identifies him as a father.

Another clue to the symbolic meaning of the ghostly marshal is provided by Joyce during Stephen's vision of home in the dark Clongowes dormitory: "All the people. Welcome home, Stephen! Noises of welcome. . . . His father was a marshal now: higher than a magistrate" (*P* 20). The "magistrate" reference ties up the city marshal that Simon Dedalus was with the associative complex of whiteness, coldness, and dampness that precedes the reference to Nasty Roche's and Saurin's fathers who were magistrates. Therefore, the symbol of the ghost who appeared to the servants in the castle wearing the white cloak of a marshal and holding its hand pressed to its side includes within itself the notions of the whiteness of the flogging repressive fathers and the office of Stephen's real father.

Why should this symbol recur to Stephen's mind just outside the rector's door, just as he is about to attempt to alter a historical mood with his defiant assertion of his "difference," the importance of his name and his personality? I suggest that the wound of the marshal provides the clue. The ghost had received its death wound, and is therefore symbolically a repressive, frightening, flogging father wounded to death. This is what Stephen, an unrepressed and rebellious son, is doing quite unconsciously to the whole world of fathers—wounding it to death by his assertion of his individual worth, of the intention of his growing soul to grow to the point of fatherhood.

This appearance of the white, cold father is not the last in Joyce's work. The father's attributes—his bullying, his haughty and paralyzing power, his intention to engulf and digest his sons so that they may constitute no threat to him, appears all through *A Portrait*, in *Ulysses*, where Stephen's smashing at the lamp repeats this early attack on the white fathers, and in *Finnegans Wake*, where the mortally wounded marshal becomes a Russian general, and where the white, cold father becomes Anna Livia's "cold mad feary father," the sea (*FW* 628.2).

The other side of the opposition, the dark, warm side of life and odors, is developed in this section also. In contrast to the pale, cold, damp atmosphere of the repressive fathers, Stephen feels the presence of a dark warmth which is the filial symbol as the white-cold complex is the paternal, and which eventually, when he overcomes his distrust of it, triumphs over the white coldness of the fathers.[15]

How cold and slimy the water [in the square ditch] had been! . . . [Mother's] slippers were so hot and they had such a lovely warm smell! (*P* 10)

. . . . . .

The air in the corridor chilled him too. It was queer and wet-tish. But soon the gas would be lit and in burning it made a light noise like a little song. (*P* 11)

. . . . . .

It would be lovely in bed after the sheets got a bit hot. First they were so cold to get into. He shivered to think how cold they were first. But then they got hot and then he could sleep. . . . He felt a warm glow creeping up from the cold shivering sheets, warmer and warmer till he felt warm all over; ever so warm; ever so warm and yet he shivered a little. (*P* 17)

. . . . . .

There was a cold night smell in the chapel. But it was a holy smell. It was not like the smell of the old peasants who knelt at the back of the chapel at Sunday mass. That was a smell of air and rain and turf and corduroy. . . . It would be lovely to sleep for one night in [a peasant's] cottage before the fire of smoking turf, in the dark lit by the fire, in the warm dark, breathing the smell of the peasants, air and rain and turf and corduroy. (*P* 18)

. . . . . .

As he passed the door [of the bath] he remembered with a vague fear the warm turfcoloured bogwater, the warm moist air . . . [Stephen does not yet believe that darkness and warmth are his allies; he is still afraid of the dark]. (*P* 22)

. . . . . .

How pale the light was at the window! But that was nice. The fire rose and fell on the wall. . . . He saw the sea of waves, long dark waves rising and falling, dark under the moonless night. . . . [This is the first time that Stephen's interior monologue acquires the mature rhythm it is to keep all through *A Portrait* and *Ulysses*. He loses this rhythm only once; when the fathers succeed in frightening him back to childhood after the sermon on hell.] (*P* 26–27)

. . . . . .

[Stephen's hands and body "burn" and "scald" when Father Dolan pandies him. This is, besides a normal physiological reaction, a sign of the triumph of the warm principle against the fathers' cold, white "not young" principle.] (*P* 50–51)

. . . . . .

The air was soft and grey and mild and evening was coming. There was the smell of evening in the air, the smell of the fields in the country where they digged up turnips to peel them and eat them. . . . The smell there was in the little wood beyond the pavilion where the gallnuts were. (*P* 59)

In this last quotation, Stephen's sense of victory is associated with the coming of darkness and the smells of nature. As we are to see later on, the smells of nature, the feeling of warmth, and darkness are to be much more congenial to the son than is the light, the whiteness, the coldness of the fathers. He hesitates before accepting them wholeheartedly; once, indeed, he rejects them—after the sermon on hell, with its emphasis on the horrors of hellish warmth, darkness, and stink—but he soon recovers from his fright. Warmth, darkness, and odors become his allies; in *Ulysses,* Stephen finds "in my mind's darkness a sloth of the underworld, reluctant, shy of brightness, shifting her dragon scaly folds" (*U* 26). Stephen realizes the bent of his mind; he discovers a resemblance between his mind and those of Averroes and Moses Maimonides,

dark men in mien and movement, flashing in their mocking mirrors the obscure soul of the world, a darkness shining in brightness which brightness could not comprehend. (*U* 28)

At the climax of the book, he smashes the light in the brothel in the name of darkness and sexual development and succeeds in releasing his own paternal light (see chap. 3, below).

Another important aspect of the artist that is developed in this chapter is his sense of "difference" from his fellows. This sense of difference forbids him to mingle with his fellows, or to let his name or his personality be disregarded or insulted. The first questions he is asked insult this sense of difference: "What is your name?" When Nasty Roche hears that his name is Stephen Dedalus he asks contemptuously, "What kind of a name is that?"

(*P* 9). Much later on in the book his schoolfellows will
know his name and will elevate it into a noble and mystical
appellation.

> —Hello, Stephanos!
> —Here comes The Dedalus! . . .
> —Bous Stephanoumenos! Bous Stephaneforos! (*P* 167–
68)

He then accepts their banter as a disguised form of homage, and their cries hailing him as the crown-bearer or
wreath-bearer set off one of the ecstatic moments in that
section of *A Portrait*. In the first chapter of the book, however, he has not established himself yet among his fellows,
and his name and individuality are scorned.

Like all the other abstract elements of the artist's
personality, the idea of difference is first presented in general terms. Young Stephen ponders the general idea of
difference:

> All the boys seemed to him very strange. They had all
> fathers and mothers and different clothes and voices. (*P* 13)
> . . . . . .
> He opened the geography to study the lesson; but he
> could not learn the names of places in America. Still they
> were all different places that had those different names. They
> were all in different countries and the countries were in conti-
> nents and the continents were in the world and the world was
> in the universe. (*P* 15)

Immediately after this association of "difference" with the
definitions of geography, Stephen defines his geographical
position and (by implication) his indivisible personality
and the importance of his name.

> He turned to the flyleaf of the geography and read what
> he had written there: himself, his name and where he was.
>
> *Stephen Dedalus*
> *Class of Elements*
> *Clongowes Wood College*
> *Sallins*

> *County Kildare*
> *Ireland*
> *Europe*
> *The World*
> *The Universe*

That was in his writing: and Fleming one night for a cod had written on the opposite page:

> *Stephen Dedalus is my name,*
> *Ireland is my nation.*
> *Clongowes is my dwellingplace*
> *And heaven my expectation.*

. . . Then he read the flyleaf from the bottom to the top till he came to his own name. That was he . . .[16] God was God's name just as his name was Stephen. (*P* 15–16)

The word "different" is stressed repeatedly thirty-two pages later, just before the entrance of Father Dolan.

It was hard to think what [the teachers at Clongowes would have become] because you would have to think of them in a different way with different coloured coats and trousers and with beards and moustaches and different kinds of hats. (*P* 48)

Two points of injustice affect Stephen deeply after Father Dolan has pandied him: Father Dolan holds his name in so little respect that he had to ask twice what it was, and Father Arnall ignores the difference between him and Fleming. He had not previously felt this "difference" consciously; he had only felt that it was right to defend his name. Now he responds to the "fathers'" attack by a proud and conscious assertion of his difference:

It was cruel and unfair to make him kneel in the middle of the class then: and Father Arnall had told them both that they might return to their places without making any difference between them. . . . he heard the voice of the prefect of studies asking him twice what his name was. Why could he not remember the name when he was told the first time? Was he not listening the first time or was it to make fun out of the name? The great men in the history had names like that and nobody

made fun of them. It was his own name that he should have
made fun of if he wanted to make fun. Dolan: it was like the
name of a woman that washed clothes. (*P* 52, 55)

These last two sentences represent the son-artist's first attempt at counterattack; they also represent the first appearance of the artist's satirical weapon.

Later on in *A Portrait* Stephen's sense of difference
from his fellows, his strong sense of pride in his individuality, and his pride in his name are all going to stand
him in good stead in his struggle with the father and with
the father's obedient sons. In *Ulysses* Stephen develops a
theory of the psychology of the artist based upon the artist's
strong grasp of his own "image," his feeling of pride in his
difference, and upon the artist's pride in his name.

—As we . . . weave and unweave our bodies . . . from day
to day, so does the artist weave and unweave his image. . . .
His own image to a man with that queer thing genius is the
standard of all experience, material and moral. [Shakespeare
felt that his image was damaged, first by Anne Hathaway's
sexual aggression and then by her infidelity, and he piles up
creation to hide this fact from himself.] . . . Belief in himself
has been untimely killed. . . . But, because loss is his gain, he
passes on towards eternity in undiminished personality. . . .
He has hidden his own name . . . in the plays . . . He has
revealed it in the sonnets where there is Will in overplus. Like
John O'Gaunt his name is dear to him, as dear as the coat of
arms he toadied for . . . dearer than his glory of greatest
shakescene in the country. What's in a name? That is what we
ask ourselves in childhood when we write the name that we
are told is ours. A star . . . rose at his birth . . . by night it
shone over delta in Cassiopeia, the recumbent constellation
which is the signature of his initial among the stars. (*U* 194,
195, 196, 197, 209, 210)

And then Stephen, whose own image of himself has been
shaken by a "fall" after his father's telegram and his
mother's death, thinks bitterly:

Read the skies. *Autontimerumenos. Bous Stephanoumenos.*
Where's your configuration? Stephen, Stephen, cut the bread
even. . . . *Stephanos,* my crown. . . . Fabulous artificer, the
hawklike man. You flew. Whereto? Newhaven-Dieppe, steerage passenger. Paris and back. Lapwing. Icarus. *Pater, ait.* Seabedabbled, fallen, weltering. (*U* 210)

Earlier he had recalled a meeting with Synge, who had met
a "faunman" in Clamart woods "brandishing a wine-
bottle." "His image, wandering, he met. I mine. I met a
fool i' the forest" (*U* 200). Stephen sees himself as melancholy Jaques, whose line from *As You Like It* he quotes, no
longer even as Hamlet but as a burlesque of him. This feeling that he has blurred his image of himself contributes
directly to his hysterical desperation in the Nighttown
scene, but eventually he recovers his morale: "Ireland must
be important because it belongs to me" (*U* 645).

In *Finnegans Wake,* the artist's "difference," his conscious fostering of his image of himself and his name, irritates Shaun, the jealous brother of Shem the artist. Shaun
never lets an opportunity slip to deny his brother's origi-
nality or uniqueness, or to attempt to imitate his creations
or his powers of "flight."

Neither of those clean little cherubum, Nero or Nobookisones-
ter himself, ever nursed such a spoiled opinion of his monstrous marvellosity as did this mental and moral defective.
(*FW* 177.13–16)

.   .   .   .   .   .

[Shem's] growing megalomane of a loose past. . . . explains
the litany of septuncial lettertrumpets honorific, highpitched,
erudite, neoclassical, which he so loved as patricianly to manu-
scribe after his name. [The "septuncial" letters of his neoclassical appellation could spell out STEPHEN, DEDALUS,
ULYSSES, or even PATRICK; LEOPOLD is seven letters
also, but it is not "neoclassical."] (*FW* 179.21–24)

.   .   .   .   .   .

You, let me tell you, with the utmost politeness, were very
ordinarily designed. (*FW* 190.10–11)

. . . . . .

I am . . . letter potent to play the sem backwards. (*FW* 419.23–24)

. . . . . .

Obnoximost posthumust! With his unique hornbook and his prince of the apauper's pride. (*FW* 422.14–15)

. . . . . .

And him . . . making his pillgrimace of Childe Horrid, engrossing to his ganderpan what the idioglossary he invented under hicks hyssop! Hock! Ickick gav him that toock, imitator! . . . As often as I think of that unbloody housewarmer, Shem Skrivenitch, always cutting my prhose to please his phrase, bogorror, I declare I get the jawache! (*FW* 423.5, 8–10, 14–17)

. . . . . .

Every dimmed letter in it is a copy and not a few of the silbils and whollywords I can show you in my Kingdom of Heaven. . . . The last word in stolentelling! And what's more rightdown lowbrown schisthematic robblemint! Yes. As he was rising my lather. Like you. And as I was plucking his goosybone. Like yea. He store the tale of me shur. Like yup. How's that for Shemese? (*FW* 424.32–34, 35–36; 425.1–3)

. . . . . .

I can soroquise the Siamanish better than most. (*FW* 425.15–16)

The sense of difference first evoked by the violence of Father Dolan thus becomes one of the distinguishing characteristics of the artist.

This first chapter of *A Portrait* ends with the confrontation of Stephen and the rector and the triumph of Stephen. The confrontation is no mere token battle. Young Stephen, frightened as he is, pushes the rector into a corner and elicits from Father Conmee a complete capitulation.

—O well then, said the rector, Father Dolan did not understand. You can say that I excuse you from your lessons for a few days.

Stephen said quickly for fear his trembling would prevent him:

—Yes, sir, but Father Dolan said he will come in tomorrow to pandy me again for it.

—Very well, the rector said, it is a mistake and I shall speak to Father Dolan myself. Will that do now? (*P* 57)

Perhaps it is not too fanciful to imagine a touch of irritation under the suave amusement in "Will that do now?" Stephen, impelled by the double insult to his "difference" and to his name, goes up against the "fathers" of Clongowes and reverses an injustice that they were ready to countenance in the name of order. No other boy in the school would do more than talk about a "rebellion"; Stephen actually rebels. Moreover, his rebellion is accompanied by the apparitions of the wounded marshal, a symbol of tottering paternity, and of Hamilton Rowan, a noble rebel. Both of these symbols add dignity and measure to Stephen's act.

The cinder path upon which Stephen has been thrown by a schoolboy bicycle racer (*P* 41, 57) and the playgrounds seem to be symbols of history as conflict.

The wide playgrounds were swarming with boys. All were shouting and the prefects urged them on with strong cries. . . . [Stephen remembers his parents shouting goodbye to him as they leave him at school, and then] He was caught in the whirl of a scrimmage and, fearful of the flashing eyes and muddy boots, bent down to look through the legs. The fellows were struggling and groaning and their legs were rubbing and kicking and stamping. (*P* 8, 9–10)

The schoolboy football games and bicycle racing of Clongowes resemble those of the Dalkey school at which Stephen teaches in *Ulysses*, and both suggest the processes and conflicts of history that Stephen comes to dread.

Shouts rang shrill from the boys' playfield and a whirring whistle.

Again: a goal. I am among them, among their battling bodies in a medley, the joust of life. You mean that knock-kneed mother's darling who seems to be slightly crawsick?

Jousts. Time shocked rebounds, shock by shock. Jousts, slush and uproar of battles, the frozen deathspew of the slain, a shout of spear spikes baited with men's bloodied guts. (*U* 32)

. . . . . .

—History, Stephen said, is a nightmare from which I am trying to awake.

From the playfield the boys raised a shout. A whirring whistle: goal. What if that nightmare gave you a back kick? (*U* 34)

Stephen's triumph is a schoolboy triumph, but it contains significant elements: "He could hear the cries of the fellows on the playgrounds. He broke into a run and, running quicker and quicker, ran across the cinderpath." (*P* 58) They had tried to use him as a cat's-paw, but he had not confronted the rector for them; he had followed the dictates of his own nature. Like Parnell, or like Yeats's Irish Airman, he did not love those for whom he fought; again like Yeats's Airman (but unlike Parnell) he did not hate those he fought. Even as a young boy the artist has risen above the conflicts of factions.[17]

In all of his activity young Stephen has been moved by his inner nature toward "the end he had been born to serve yet did not see" (*P* 165). Joyce's concept of personality, based upon Aristotle, is teleological; the soul of man informing the body grows into a *teleion,* a perfected being, by actualizing its potential in society. This is the "end it was born to serve." The Greek for "end" is *telos,* and it is strongly tempting to think that, when the boys shout "Tell us! Tell us! . . . Tell us! Tell us!" at Stephen (*P* 58) they are announcing that he has attained part of his *telos.* (Joyce did not hesitate to insert phrases in Greek, a language he knew only in bits and pieces,[18] at important places in his narrative. Another important ceremony of development in *A Portrait* is introduced by shouts of "Bous Stephanoumenous! Bous Stephaneforos!" and "Stephanos Dedalos!" [*P* 168].) However, whether Joyce

intended a pun on *telos* or not, Stephen certainly has attained his end; he has triumphed over the cold, white
fathers' authoritarian rule, over his cowed contemporaries'
baseness and fear, and over his own youth and ignorance.
Father Dolan's attack was the second attempt at violence of
the fathers against the growing son; the first was the attack,
buried in Stephen's memory, of the angry father in the
overture. He evaded the first attack and countered the
second. From this section on, the fathers will know him for
a danger, and will mount powerful offensives to render
him harmless.

c. chapter two (*P* 60–101)

THIS chapter of *A Portrait* shows the passing of time and
the initiation of Stephen to sex. In this chapter, people
grow old and die – Uncle Charles, Mike Flynn, Aunt Ellen.
In this chapter Uncle Charles is reduced to a nonentity by
the next generation, his nephew Simon, a foreshadowing of
the fate Simon unconsciously fears will be his at the hands
of Stephen's generation. Simon Dedalus struggles with his
fate in vain, and attempts to disguise the fact from himself
that youth and virility are passing from him to his son.
Stephen feels the urges of adolescence, and is enmeshed in
one of the nets which he later declares he will "fly by." The
fathers, the forces of the past, mount a subtle offensive
against the developing son. As a result, Stephen's vocation
is almost lost, and he begins to feel a strong repulsion toward the two most characteristic elements of his personality, his feeling of difference, and his attraction to
darkness and warmth. At the end of this chapter, however,
his unconscious drives preserve him from the fate reserved
for him by his environment, and he pursues sexual experience to a conclusion.

Stephen's "difference," his detachment from his fellows and his family, appears in many guises in this chapter. *The Count of Monte Cristo* appeals to him (*P* 62–63) because of the isolation of the main figure and his discipline in seeking his revenge. As Atherton suggests,[19] the Count's refusal to eat muscatel grapes is only that he will not be hampered in his revenge by having eaten or drunk in the house of an enemy; the food is offered by his former true love who is now the wife of his chief betrayer. Stephen's "sadly proud gesture of refusal" is an attempt to assert his freedom. However, it is not true that he does not eat muscatel grapes; on *P* 61 Uncle Charles thrusts at him "a handful of grapes" (of some sort) , and he presumably does not refuse them. This contradiction of fact is too clear to be accidental. Perhaps Joyce is symbolizing the desire of the older generation, here represented by Uncle Charles, to bind the free boy with its gifts. Stephen's "sadly proud gesture" of refusal is an attempt to show that he realizes the symbolism of the gift and knows that he is in the house of an enemy.[20] This interpretation is supported by the color symbolism of this section as well; the Count is a "dark" avenger, and the house in which Stephen confronts his enemies, in his imaginary sequel to the novel, is "whitewashed" (*P* 63) .

Associated with the figure of his beloved, and the "strange unrest" and "fever" that creeps into his blood when he thinks of her, is the notion, here more clearly enunciated than before, that "he was different from others" (*P* 65) . He also knows that in "darkness and silence" he and his beloved would meet for their "tryst." His "difference," then, is closely tied to his sexual development; the fathers must reduce his difference and halt his development to make him their slave. The important word "image" is also present on *P* 65 – "the unsubstantial image which his soul so constantly beheld." All the elements of the artist's soul are here – his darkness, his image, his difference.

The depressing circumstances of his life, and the decaying fortunes of his family (symbolized by the "dull" fire that would not stay lit on *P* 66) , the fact that his father tries to bind him to the past by attempting to "enlist" him for the battle of the recovery of his fortunes, all these factors tend to embitter him; his sense of isolation and difference acquires a tinge of coldness and weariness. Like the son of Ibsen's John Gabriel Borkman, Stephen in his heart refuses to attempt to redeem the past if it would mean making himself a slave to it. Yet he does not let his anger and his "mood of embittered silence" (*P* 67) affect the clarity of his vision: "He chronicled with patience what he saw, detaching himself from it and testing its mortifying flavour in secret." Even at the children's party at Harold's Cross, Stephen preserves his darkness and his detachment.

His silent watchful manner had grown upon him . . . though he tried to share [the children's] merriment, he felt himself a gloomy figure amid the gay cocked hats and sunbonnets.
But when he had sung his song and withdrawn into a snug corner of the room he began to taste the joy of his loneliness. (*P* 68)

Stephen has been accosted and beaten by his heresy-hunting friends, the first of a series of obedient slaves to their "father," their environment, who will surround the developing son and try to impede his progress. Stephen remembers stumbling down the road sobbing. However, his detachment, his sense of difference, robs the episode of all damaging power.

While the scenes of that malignant episode were still passing sharply and swiftly before his mind he wondered why he bore no malice now to those who had tormented him. He had not forgotten a whit of their cowardice and cruelty but the memory of it called forth no anger from him. All the descriptions of fierce love and hatred which he had met in books had

seemed to him therefore unreal. Even that night as he stum-
bled homewards along Jones's Road he had felt that some
power was divesting him of that suddenwoven anger as easily
as a fruit is divested of its soft ripe peel. (P 82)

Stephen feels that he is in pursuit of "phantoms," perhaps the "phantom" of the "images" he seeks to project
from himself. While pursuing these phantoms he hears the
voices of his environment attempting to divert him from
his path, to enlist him in their service—the voices of "his
father and of his masters" (P 83), of the gymnasium, of
the nationalists, of the practical world urging him to help
his father, of his schoolfriends with their code of comrade-
ship. Yet he tries to detach himself from them all.

It was the din of all these hollowsounding voices that made
him halt irresolutely in the pursuit of phantoms. He gave
them ear only for a time but he was happy only when he was
far from them, beyond their call, alone or in the company of
phantasmal comrades. (P 84)

After the play he feels an overwhelming urge to escape
from the scene of the mummery. Blinded by his half-
understood emotional turmoil he walks for many streets,
until "A power, akin to that which had often made anger
or resentment fall from him, brought his steps to rest"
(P 86).

During the trip to Cork, Stephen feels again that sense
of detachment that is part of his difference, but, influenced
by his environment, he mistrusts it and worries about it;
many adolescents are pursued by a conviction that they are
uniquely deformed or misshapen physically or spiritually,
and Stephen is no exception.

[Stephen] opened his eyes with a nervous impulse. The sun
light breaking suddenly on his sight turned the sky and cloud
into a fantastic world of sombre masses with lake-like space
of dark rosy light. His very brain was sick and powerless. He
could scarcely interpret the letters of the signboards of the

shops. By his monstrous way of life he seemed to have put himself beyond the limits of reality. Nothing moved him or spoke to him from the real world unless he heard in it an echo of the infuriated cries within him. He could respond to no earthly or human appeal, dumb and insensible to the call of summer and gladness and companionship, wearied and dejected by his father's voice. (*P* 92)

It is interesting to see how Stephen's induced mistrust of the signs of his vocation begins to push him into the enemy's camp, how he begins to associate his detachment and difference with the "coldness" characteristic of the fathers:

An abyss of fortune or of temperament sundered [Stephen] from [his father and his Cork cronies]. His mind seemed older than theirs: it shone coldly on their strifes and happiness and regrets like a moon upon a younger earth. No life or youth stirred in him as it had stirred in them. . . . Nothing stirred within his soul but a cold and cruel and loveless lust. (*P* 95–96)

Finally, Stephen's detachment takes the form of isolation from his family. This is an essential step in his progress as as artist and in his development toward maturity; so long as he is and feels himself completely a son he can never develop into a father. His sense of difference cuts him loose from his family.

He had tried to build a breakwater of order and elegance against the sordid tide of life without him and to dam up, by rules of conduct and active interests and new *filial* [my italics] relations, the powerful recurrence of the tides within him. Useless. . . . He saw clearly too his own futile isolation. He had not gone one step nearer the lives he had sought to approach nor bridged the restless shame and rancour that had divided him from mother and brother and sister. He felt that he was hardly of the one blood with them but stood to them rather in the mystical kinship of fosterage, fosterchild and fosterbrother. (*P* 98)

This despair about his detachment is the result of the attack of his environment, his "fathers," upon Stephen. Later he will accept his isolation from his family, especially his mother, as part of the price the artist pays for his difference.

Pascal . . . would not suffer his mother to kiss him . . . Jesus, too, seems to have treated his mother with scant courtesy in public . . . I do not fear to be alone. (*P* 242, 247)

We know that Stephen's depression at his self-exile is only temporary, and is induced by the inimical forces in his environment that would reduce him to a slave; in the diary entries that end the book he reaffirms his isolation and stigmatizes his acquiescent contemporaries as dead, stunted beings with no sense of their own individuality.

[One of the dreams recorded in his diary: a long curving gallery:] Strange figures advance from a cave. They are not as tall as men. One does not seem to stand quite apart from another. Their faces are phosphorescent, with darker streaks. (*P* 249)

This sense of detachment, of difference, although Stephen sometimes worries about it, is the source of the artist's necessary exile, one of the conditions necessary for the projection of his image in the form of art. If he does not isolate himself, or rather, if his developing soul does not forbid him to mingle his life with those around him, he will not be able to preserve his image of himself, that which to a man of genius is "the standard of all experience material and moral" (*U* 195). The greatest works of art are the most original, not because they do not contain elements from the past—frequently they are the climax of a long tradition—but because a self-knowing individual has organized the inheritance of the past—conventions of art, of politics, or of philosophy—and projected his carefully preserved image in them and with them—Dante, Chaucer, Milton, Shakespeare, Beethoven, Michelangelo. All experience is important to these men because it has happened to them. This is not vanity but a necessity of their art. If the growing artist is a true artist (a born artist as Joyce would suggest), he finds that the center of his art, his own personality, isolates itself from the elements of its own past, of its present, to be able to judge them and to be able to project them forth again in terms of art.

Stephen, an adolescent, feels this necessity, but also, being an adolescent, he worries about it. All the voices of his environment shout, "Join me in my endeavors"; his soul says, "You must isolate yourself." Stephen, caught between inner and outer drives, suffers and worries but keeps his difference safe. The artist's detachment annoys his contemporaries; in *Finnegans Wake* Shaun climaxes one of his furious tirades against his brother with a cruel picture of the isolated artist.

If one has the stomach to add the breakages, upheavals, distortions, inversions of all this chambermade music [that is, all the arrangements and rearrangements of the heterogenous material in Shem's inkbottle house, or mind] one stands . . . a fair chance of actually seeing the whirling dervish, Tumult, son of Thunder, self exiled in upon his ego . . . writing the mystery of himsel in furniture. (*FW* 184.3-7, 9-10)

Stephen's filial taste for darkness and warmth is similarly affected by his environment. There had always been an admixture of fear with his longing for darkness; in the Clongowes dormitory the darkness had been peopled with phantoms, the black dog with eyes like carriage lamps and the wounded marshal (*P* 19). In this chapter Stephen's fear of the dark is reinforced by the doubts in his vocation that are being fostered by his environment. Eventually, however, his soul's need for darkness triumphs, and in the last section his surrender to the prostitute is accompanied by images of darkness.

The "dark avenger," the Count of Monte Cristo,

marks the first appearance of darkness in this chapter. The darkness of the Count is found again in Stephen's soul: "The ambition which he felt astir at times in the darkness of his soul sought no outlet" (P 64). This is linked with his feverish unrest: "He returned to Mercedes and, as he brooded upon her image, a strange unrest crept into his blood. Sometimes a fever gathered within him" (P 64). This combination of warmth and darkness is on P 64–65 linked to his sense of difference, and all three lead him to the image of his beloved: "They would be alone, surrounded by darkness and silence" (P 65).

His affinity for darkness stands between him and the activities of the "white" fathers and their pale slaves:

All day [before the play] the stream of gloomy tenderness within him had started forth and returned upon itself in dark courses and eddies, wearying him in the end until the pleasantry of the prefect and the painted little boy had drawn from him a movement of impatience. (P 77)

Darkness and warmth are again associated with sexual development as Stephen attempts to remember the features of his beloved.

He tried to recall her appearance but could not. He could remember only that she had worn a shawl about her head like a cowl and that her dark eyes had invited and unnerved him. He wondered had he been in her thoughts as she had been in his. Then in the dark and unseen by [his friends] he rested the tips of the fingers of one hand upon the palm of the other hand, scarcely touching it. . . . suddenly the memory of their touch traversed his brain and body like an invisible warm wave. (P 82–83)

What Stephen is trying to remember are the circumstances of the events in the empty tram after the children's party in Harold's Cross (P 69–70) when, in the night, Stephen first felt that he could kiss a girl, obviously an important moment in his sexual development.[21] Now during the mummery imposed on him by the cold white fathers, he tries successfully to recapture one of the moments of his past when his maturity suddenly became evident to him.

The mummery ends by disgusting him; it is all too obviously controlled by the forces of the past which are attempting to reassure themselves that the youth can still be manipulated. He rushes away from his waiting family to find comfort in the odoriferous dark.

> A film still veiled his eyes but they burned no longer. A power, akin to that which had often made anger or resentment fall from him, brought his steps to rest. He stood still and gazed up at the sombre porch of the morgue and from that to the dark cobbled laneway at its side. He saw the word *Lotts* on the wall of the lane and breathed slowly the rank heavy air. (*P* 86)

The name, Lotts, the name of a lane off O'Connell Street [22] the opposite side from Belvedere House, is chosen deliberately by Joyce for this episode. Lotts, in its sense of "lots," chances, is here associated with the darkness and detachment congenial to the artist. There is not room here to discuss the role of chance in the works of Joyce. However, it can be said that Joyce always valued chance correspondence, in language or in life, and enjoyed pointing out coincidences to his friends. In *Finnegans Wake*, chance resemblances in language form the style of the book, and chance combinations of events form the events of the universe, "the sameold gamebold adomic structure of our Finnius the old One, as highly charged with electrons as hophazards can effective it" (*FW* 615.6–8).[23] The fact that Joyce seemed to believe that the myriads of human relations in history resolve themselves into a few basic configurations or archetypal patterns seems to point to an acceptance of chance combination as a fact of life. Given enough time, eternity, for example, an infinity of chance relations would form just a few archetypal patterns; even though the pattern of human or natural relations might seem to a limited viewer a "collideorescape," to an artist the patterns resolve themselves into order.

It is chance that Stephen is accepting; even though all things eventually resolve themselves to a few patterns, there is a real difference between the past and the future. The past is determined; certainty belongs to it. As Stephen says to himself in *Ulysses*: "Time has branded them [the facts of history] and fettered they are lodged in the room of the infinite possibilities they have ousted" (*U* 25). The past contains the facts of history, no longer potential, no longer subject to chance and possibility; chance and possibility belong to the rising generation. In his diary at the end of *A Portrait,* Stephen makes the distinction between old beauty and not yet created beauty:

Michael Robartes remembers forgotten beauty and, when his arms wrap her round, he presses in his arms the loveliness which has long faded from the world. Not this. Not at all. I desire to press in my arms the loveliness which has not yet come into the world. (*P* 251)

He places his trust in the future of chance rather than, like Yeats, in the beauty of the past. It is this field of activity, the realm of physical facts, of warmth, darkness, odors, chance, that the young artist takes as his own.

The trip to Cork deepens Stephen's confused mistrust of himself and of the fertile darkness and detachment that are his province. The night train to Cork moves through the darkness:

He saw the darkening lands slipping past him, the silent tele-graphpoles passing his window swiftly every four seconds, the little glimmering stations, manned by a few silent sentries, flung by the mail behind her and twinkling for a moment in the darkness like fiery grains flung backwards by a runner. (*P* 87)

The anatomy theatre, with its "darkness" and the "dark stained wood" (*P* 89) of its desks depresses Stephen.

The letters cut in the stained wood of the desk stared upon him, mocking his bodily weakness and futile enthusiasms and making him loathe himself for his own mad and filthy orgies. The spittle in his throat grew bitter and foul to swallow and the faint sickness climbed to his brain so that for a moment he closed his eyes and walked on in darkness. (*P* 91)

What his "mad and filthy orgies" could have been is hard to imagine. Since, for all we know to the contrary, he is still a virgin, it is probable that his "orgies" are almost entirely mental. His extreme guilty reaction to the past of his father might be the result of the voices of his past warning him of the dangers of development, of the fertile darkness which is his province. Sure enough, when he opens his eyes he sees the sky as full of "sombre masses with lakelike spaces of dark rosy light." His vocation is trying to get through to him, trying to override the voices of the past, of the fathers who fear his development and make him mistrust it. This internal conflict, under the surface of what really seems to be a pleasant trip, sickens and weakens Stephen to the point where he feels that the boy that he was, the boy who won a victory over the fathers, has "faded out like a film in the sun" (*P* 93). He has not, of course; Stephen's later enumeration of significant moments of his life in *Ulysses* includes a clear memory of "I that sinned and prayed and fasted. A child Conmee saved from pandies" (*U* 189–90). Here, however, the adolescent Stephen is on the point of succumbing to the fathers' mental wiles and threats.

In the next section, the image he had been pursuing, that of "life," as she after appears, comes to him in a hideously deformed state, accompanied by images of darkness.

A figure that had seemed to him by day demure and innocent came towards him by night through the winding darkness of sleep, transfigured by a lecherous cunning, her eyes bright with brutish joy. Only the morning pained him with its dim memory of dark orgiastic riot, its keen and humiliating sense of transgression. (*P* 99)

The darkness, however, wins over the paleness of the fathers; Stephen is initiated into sexual maturity amid much darkness, night and warmth.

> He wandered up and down the dark slimy streets . . . He felt some dark presence moving irresistibly upon him from the darkness . . . The yellow gasflames arose before his troubled vision against the vapoury sky, burning as if before an altar. . . . [The young woman] said gaily:
> —Good night, Willie dear! [24]
> Her room was warm and lightsome. . . . [Stephen felt] the warm calm rise and fall of her breast . . . [He was] conscious of nothing in the world but the dark pressure of her softly parting lips. . . . between them he felt an unknown and timid pressure, darker than the swoon of sin, softer than sound or odour. (*P* 99–101)

At this crucial point, darkness, warmth, will, odor, and sexual maturity merge into a symbolic complex. The son-artist here announces his development to sexual maturity; from this point onward the attack of the fathers grows both fiercer and subtler as they sense the presence of the rising generation.[25]

The fathers' attack in this chapter has more aspects than those suggested above. Besides attempting to halt Stephen's development by making him mistrust himself and his characteristic affinities for darkness and detachment, they also attack in more positive ways. The world he wishes to accept, the love he hastens toward, is presented to him in foul and brutal terms. The filthy cowyard at Stradbrook (*P* 63) furnishes the setting for his dream of Hell in chapter 3; the comparison of his love-inspired heart to "a cork upon a tide" (*P* 69) is not what is seems— a few pages earlier he had noted the corks on the tide of the Liffey bobbing "on the surface of the water in a thick yellow scum" (*P* 66), and his trip to "Cork" revolts him;

the sight of his senile relatives and dingy Dublin is repulsive to him—all these encounters with the reality he seeks seem intended to frighten him out of any desire to continue his search. That he does persevere is the truest indication of the strength of his vocation. Though sickened and discouraged by the world he seeks to embrace, he does in the end push through to encounter his fate, to develop to the point of maturity where he will be able to father-forth works of art.

The coldness and whiteness of the fathers appears many times in this chapter. Heron, a precursor of Cranly as a faithful servant of the past, of the fathers, has "pale" hair (P 76) ; Wallis, another minion, has a "pale dandyish face" (P 75) ; the "cold" light of dawn on the train to Cork, and the "chilly" morning breeze (P 87) are the first things that depress Stephen on the journey to Cork; oldness and coldness are equated in his father's song (P 88) ; Stephen's mind, affected by his environment, is "chilled" by Shelley's poem on the moon (P 96) ; the cold October wind around the corner of the Bank of Ireland seems to underline the futility of Stephen's attempt to organize his family's life (P 97) ; the restaurant Stephen selects for the celebration of his achievement is "Underdone's" (his plans are certainly underdone) . But the father's chief attack, the attempt to make Stephen mistrust the signs of his vocation, is accomplished less in terms of paleness and coldness than in Stephen's own terms of darkness and detachment.

Finally, there are the overt attempts on the part of Simon Dedalus and the other fathers to convince Stephen that he is just a child, and by so doing, to keep him a child, an undeveloped being who will be no challenge to them. Simon Dedalus, who, in this chapter, is completely charming and friendly and, one might say, a good father to Stephen, nevertheless tries time and again to discourage Stephen, to remind him that he is a child, and to keep him in his place. The first thing that Simon does is try to rob

Stephen of his pride in his real victory over the fathers of
Clongowes. Although proud of Stephen's courage, Simon
tries to reduce the whole incident to a joke.

—By the bye, said Mr Dedalus at length, the rector, or
provincial, rather, was telling me that story about you and
Father Dolan. . . .
Mr Dedalus imitated the mincing nasal tone of the provincial.
—Father Dolan and I, when I told them all at dinner
about it, Father Dolan and I had a great laugh over it. *You
better mind yourself, Father Dolan,* said I, *or young Dedalus
will send you up for twice nine.* We had a famous laugh together over it. Ha! Ha! Ha! (*P* 72)

The priests organizing the Whitsuntide play are
openly associated in Stephen's mind with his father.

In the middle of the vestry a young jesuit, who was then on a
visit to the college, stood rocking himself rhythmically from
the tips of his toes to his heels and back again, his hands
thrust well forward into his sidepockets. His small head set
off with glossy red curls and his newly shaven face agreed well
with the spotless decency of his soutane and with his spotless
shoes.
As he watched this swaying form and tried to read for
himself the legend of the priest's mocking smile there came
into Stephen's memory a saying that he had heard from his
father before he had been sent to Clongowes, that you could
always tell a jesuit by the style of his clothes. At the same moment he thought he saw a likeness between his father's mind
and that of this smiling welldressed priest. (*P* 84)

This is the second reference to the identity of purpose of
the priestly fathers and Simon Dedalus; the first was the
apparition of the wounded marshal in Stephen's memory
outside Father Conmee's door. All "fathers" are fathers to
the son, and all fear his maturity.

Stephen feels offended by the mummery of the play
because of the repeated insults to his maturity. The mum-

mery, controlled by the fathers, is intended (unconsciously, no doubt) as a device to remind adolescents that they are still children. Wrinkles are painted onto Stephen's forehead and his jaws are painted black and blue in preparation for his part, which is that of an older man. This mockery of his attempts to grow to maturity offends him: "He felt no stage fright but the thought of the part he had to play humiliated him" (*P* 85). Earlier the episode of "little Bertie Tallon" had offended him.

A pinkdressed figure, wearing a curly golden wig and an old-fashioned straw sunbonnet, with black pencilled eyebrows and cheeks delicately rouged and powdered, was discovered. A low murmur of curiosity ran round the chapel at the discovery of this girlish figure. One of the prefects, smiling and nodding his head, approached the dark corner and, having bowed to the stout old lady, said pleasantly:

—Is this a beautiful young lady or a doll you have here, Mrs Tallon?

Then, bending down to peer at the smiling painted face under the leaf of the bonnet, he exclaimed:

—No! Upon my word I believe it's little Bertie Tallon after all!

Stephen at his post by the window heard the old lady and the priest laugh together and heard the boys' murmurs of admiration behind him as they passed forward to see the little boy who had to dance the sunbonnet dance by himself. A movement of impatience escaped him. (*P* 74)

Stephen has good reason to be disgusted with this latest piece of mummery—Bertie Tallon resembles him symbolically. Bertie has a dance to do, as had young Stephen in the overture (*P* 7); the "stout old lady" named Tallon recalls a stout old lady named Dante who had once threatened him with talons of eagles (*P* 8). The unsexing of little Bertie Tallon, and the obvious pleasure it gives to the fathers and their servants to see it, makes Stephen restless and impatient. His first attempt at sexual maturity, the encounter with the prostitute, echoes certain details of the Bertie Tallon episode, as if Stephen were defiantly casting back the father's threats in his teeth; like little Bertie Tallon, the prostitute is dressed in pink (*P* 100), and the word "doll" that stands out on *P* 74 is echoed by the presence of "a huge doll [that] sat with her legs apart in the copious easychair beside the [prostitute's] bed" (*P* 100).

After the play, Stephen sees his family waiting for him. He evades his father's questions with a lie, and breaks away. As I have said before, it is absolutely necessary for his mission as an artist for Stephen to remain independent of his family. In *A Portrait* he has little difficulty accomplishing this, but in *Ulysses* the plight of his sisters and the death of his mother tear at his heart.

> She [his sister Dilly] is drowning. Agenbite. Save her. Agenbite. All against us. She will drown me with her, eyes and hair. Lank coils of seaweed hair around me, my heart, my soul. Salt green death.
> We. (*U* 243)

It is certainly true of Stephen that, as John Eglinton says in *Ulysses* (paraphrasing Matt. 10:35–37): "We have it on high authority [Christ] that a man's worst enemies shall be those of his own house and family" (*U* 206).

On the trip to Cork Simon tries several times to convince Stephen of his status as a child, and to warn and ward him from sexual development. Although Simon probably does not realize what he is doing, that is what many of his comments add up to. His song (*P* 88) begins with the warning that " 'Tis youth and folly / Makes young men marry." Simon repeats his warning later, uneasily, in an indirect manner:

A brisk old man, whom Mr Dedalus called Johnny Cashman, had covered [Stephen] with confusion by asking him to say which were prettier, the Dublin girls or the Cork girls.

—He's not that way built, said Mr Dedalus. Leave him alone. He's a levelheaded thinking boy who doesn't bother his head about that kind of nonsense.

—Then he's not his father's son, said the little old man.

—I don't know, I'm sure, said Mr Dedalus, smiling complacently.

—Your father, said the little old man to Stephen, was the boldest flirt in the city of Cork in his day. Do you know that? . . .

—Now don't be putting ideas into his head, said Mr Dedalus. Leave him to his Maker. (*P* 94)

This concern of Simon to keep Stephen from flirting and marriage is more than the concern of a moral parent to shield an adolescent son from sin; this worrying about the sexual maturing of the young goes back to the overture, where Stephen crouched in terror from the eruption of a father, whose daughter he was going to marry "when they were grown up" (*P* 8).

Simon's story about his father and how he kept his son in his place contains an implicit warning to Stephen about premature assumption of manhood:

I'll never forget the first day he caught me smoking. I was standing at the end of the South Terrace one day with some maneens like myself and sure we thought we were grand fellows because we had pipes stuck in the corners of our mouths. (*P* 91–92)

Another bit of Simon's past that fights with Stephen's sense of maturity is the word "Fœtus" carved on a desk in the anatomy theatre (*P* 89). Stephen overreacts to this technical word; he regards it almost as an obscenity, comparable to those thronging his "monstrous reveries." Why should he feel that "fœtus" is so offensive? I suggest that he feels that he is being mocked, that in being confronted with the technical term for an unborn child he is being reminded of his own immature state.[26]

The Latin phrase upon whose correctness Stephen is

asked to pass, *Tempora mutantur et nos mutamur in illis* (*P* 94), actually could be the epigraph for this whole chapter. Time is indeed changing everything, much as the established order wishes that it would not. J. S. Atherton has discovered that the phrase was used as the title of a poem against envy and ambition by Robert Greene, which has as its second line: "Proud Icarus did fall he soared so high."[27] The coincidence of the Dedalian symbolism of *A Portrait* and this line suggests a hidden meaning to the incident—another warning about Stephen's presumption to think that he could become a man and oust his father from his place of power. Daedalus's invention compassed the death of his son; Stephen himself is threatened by emotional death if he does not accept servitude and stagnation, if he attempts to "soar" too high.

During the conversation with his cronies in the bar Simon attempts, only half-jocularly, to deny the decay of time; he asserts that he is a better man than his son, and incidentally introduces a phrase which becomes a major structural element in *Finnegans Wake*.

—We're as old as we feel, Johnny, said Mr Dedalus. And just finish what you have there, and we'll have another. Here, Tim or Tom or whatever your name is, give us the same again here. By God, I don't feel more than eighteen myself. There's that son of mine there not half my age and I'm a better man than he is any day of the week.

—Draw it mild now, Dedalus. I think it's time for you to take a back seat, said the gentleman who had spoken before.

—No, by God! asserted Mr Dedalus. I'll sing a tenor song against him or I'll vault a fivebarred gate against him or I'll run with him after the hounds across the country as I did thirty years ago along with the Kerry Boy and the best man for it.

—But he'll beat you here, said the little old man, tapping his forehead and raising his glass to drain it.

—Well, I hope he'll be as good a man as his father. That's all I can say, said Mr Dedalus. (*P* 95)

This artificial renewal of his youth is of the same nature as his fierce poking of the fire (*P* 66) at the beginning of his decline and disgrace; it is a reaction to the inevitability of his retreat before the rising generation. His boast that he can keep up with his son in everything is definitely refuted three pages later.

[Stephen] walked on before [his family] with short nervous steps, smiling. They tried to keep up with him, smiling also at his eagerness.

—Take it easy like a good young fellow, said his father. We're not out for the half mile, are we? (*P* 97)

It is not only the passing of time against which Simon fights; he also feels the passing from him of sexual potency to his son. Simon's "Tim or Tom" who is to "give us the same again here" bears a sexual significance. A poem in the introduction to the "1827" edition of *The Merry Muses*, a collection of bawdy poems attributed to Robert Burns, shows "Tom and Tim" engaged on a campaign of sexual imperialism.

> Tom and Tim on mischief bent,
> Went to the plains of Timbuctoo.
> They saw three Maidens in a tent;
> Tom bucked one, and Tim bucked two.

Joyce was introduced to the rowdier poems of Burns by Gogarty, and if Gogarty had shown him the only edition of *The Merry Muses* available to him, Joyce would have known this poem.[28]

Tom or Tim represent many things in *Finnegans Wake*—sexuality, time, resurrection, renewal of youth, maturity. All of these meanings, and many more, belong to Tom and Tim as symbols in the *Wake;* perhaps they mean the same in *A Portrait.* What Simon is asking for symbolically is a renewal of his youth, of his sexual maturity. Of course, he does not get it; a few pages after he has asked for it, we see him asking his son to slow down. As we may suspect from this incident, which occurs a few pages before Stephen gives unmistakable signs of his intentions of sexual maturity by going to bed with a prostitute, Simon is over the hill and Stephen is pressing onward to play his part as father of his race.

The fathers are not yet defeated, however. In the next chapter they launch a powerful offensive against the maturing son; they use his own weapons against him, and almost succeed in frightening him back to childhood.

d.   chapter three *(P* 102–46)

THIS chapter consists of a ferocious sermon on Hell and an account of Stephen's reaction to it. The sermon on Hell occurs directly after Stephen's first sexual experience because the fathers are nervously aware that the son is now physically capable of fatherhood, and they wish to halt his growth in as decisive a way as possible.

The effect of the sermon on Stephen is powerful, but temporary. Why does the sermon drive him almost into a state of nervous collapse? Once driven, why does he recover from the effect of it so rapidly and definitively?

An examination of the sermon and of Stephen's reaction to it provides something of an answer to the first question. "Hell is a strait and dark and foulsmelling prison" *(P* 119). The artist's affinities for warmth, darkness, odors, detachment are exaggerated by the preacher into the characteristic circumstances of Hell, warmth into the fires of Hell *(P* 120–22), darkness into the neverending storm of darkness, dark flames and dark smoke of "burning brimstone" of Hell *(P* 120) mirroring the "darkness and despair" of the damned sinner's mind *(P* 133), odors into the stench of Hell *(P* 120), detachment into permanent exile from the love of God suffered by sinners, the greatest of the spiritual pains of Hell (P 127–28). Having established these as the chief pains of Hell, the preacher then expatiates on the extensity and intensity and eternity of these pains, really rubbing Stephen's nose in it, or, to change the metaphor, stepping again and again and yet again on Stephen's sore toes.

The effect on Stephen is powerful. His affinity for warmth turns mightily against him.

He could not grip the floor with his feet and sat heavily at his desk, opening one of his books at random and poring over it. Every word for him! It was true. It was true. God was almighty. God could call him now, call him as he sat at his desk, before he had time to be conscious of the summons. God had called him. Yes? What? Yes? His flesh shrank together as it felt the approach of the ravenous tongues of flames, dried up as it felt about it the swirl of stifling air. He had died. Yes. He was judged. A wave of fire swept through his body: the first. Again a wave. His brain began to glow. Another. His brain was simmering and bubbling within the cracking tenement of the skull. Flames burst forth from his skull like a corolla, shrieking like voices:
—Hell! Hell! Hell! Hell! Hell! (P 124–25)

The preacher declares that light, in Hell, will be "loathed intensely" (P 131). Stephen's affinity for darkness, then, is a characteristic of a damned soul or of a devil.[29] The "horrible" darkness of Hell (P 120) causes Stephen to fear the darkness of his own room, which now seems to conceal demons.

He went up to his room after dinner in order to be alone with his soul: and at every step his soul seemed to sigh: at every step his soul mounted with his feet, sighing in the ascent, through a region of viscid gloom.

He halted on the landing before the door . . . [He prayed] that the fiends that inhabit darkness might not be given power over him. He waited still at the threshold as at the entrance to some dark cave. . . .

Murmuring faces waited and watched: murmurous voices

filled the dark shell of the cave. He feared intensely in spirit and in flesh. (*P* 136)

(The darkness of the artist's damned soul is a major characteristic of Shem later on.)

The odors that had calmed Stephen's heart in Lotts street now are one of the major components of his terrible dream of Hell.

Clots and coils of solid excrement . . . marshlight . . . ordure . . . An evil smell, faint and foul as the light, curled upwards sluggishly out of the canisters and from the stale crusted dung. . . . Goatish creatures . . . their long swishing tails besmeared with stale shite . . . that was his hell. God had allowed him to see the hell reserved for his sins: stinking, bestial, malignant, a hell of lecherous goatish fiends. For him! For him!

He sprang from the bed, the reeking odour pouring down his throat, clogging and revolting his entrails. (*P* 137–38)

His detachment, his pride over his difference and his name, now are viewed by him with horror and shame as the sources of his isolation from God and from the company of those souls loved by God.

Human life lay around him, a plain of peace whereon antlike men labored in brotherhood. . . . A wasting breath of humiliation blew bleakly over his soul to think of how he had fallen, to feel that those souls [of the "frowsy girls"] were dearer to God than his. The wind blew over him and passed on to the myriads and myriads of other souls on whom God's favour shone now more and now less, stars now brighter and now dimmer, sustained and failing. And the glimmering souls passed away, sustained and failing, merged in a moving breath. One soul was lost; a tiny soul: his. It flickered once and went out, forgotten, lost. . . . He bowed his head upon his hands, bidding his heart be meek and humble. (*P* 126, 140–41)

The effect of the sermon on Stephen is to force him back into childhood again, to horrify him with maturity, with sexual development, and, as I have tried to show above, with the integral "rhythmic" elements of his soul. The cold white fathers (Father Arnall's face is pale and "his voice is broken with rheum" [*P* 108]) succeed in chilling him and arousing in him a fearful if temporary desire for virginal whiteness, a paleness that would mark him as the slave of the fathers. Over and over again, coldness and whiteness and the innocence of harmless childhood are evoked and emphasized (italics mine).

[Stephen] felt the *deathchill* touch the extremities . . . Mad! Mad! Was it possible he had done these things? A *cold* sweat broke out upon his forehead as the foul memories condensed within his brain. . . . No escape. He had to confess . . . — Father, I . . . The thought slid like a *cold* shining rapier into his tender flesh. . . . His hands were *cold* and *damp* and his limbs ached with *chill*. Bodily unrest and *chill* and weariness beset him, routing his thoughts. Why was he kneeling there like a *child* saying his evening prayers? . . . clasping his *cold* forehead wildly, he vomited profusely in agony. . . . His eyes were dimmed with tears and, looking humbly up to heaven, he wept for the innocence he had lost. . . . [His thought rhythms become those of a child:] It was easy to be good. God's yoke was sweet and light. It was better never to have sinned, to have remained always a *child,* for God loved little *children* and suffered them to come to Him. It was a terrible and a sad thing to sin. But God was merciful to poor sinners who were truly sorry. . . . At last it had come. He knelt in the silent gloom and raised his eyes to the *white* crucifix suspended above him. God could see that he was sorry. He would tell all his sins. . . . God had promised to forgive him if he was sorry. He would tell all his sins. . . . God had promised to forgive him if he was sorry. He was sorry. He clasped his hands and raised them towards the *white* form, praying with his darkened eyes, praying with all his trembling body, swaying his head to and fro like a lost creature, praying with whimpering lips.
  —Sorry! Sorry! O sorry!
[After his confession] his prayers ascended to heaven from his

purified heart like perfume streaming upwards from a heart
of *white* rose. . . . [In the kitchen] On the dresser was a plate
of sausages and *white* pudding and on the shelf there were
eggs. . . . *White* pudding and *eggs* and sausages and cups of
tea. . . . [In the chapel] The altar was heaped with fragrant
masses of *white* flowers: and in the morning light the *pale*
flames of the candles among the *white* flowers were *clear* and
silent as his own soul. (*P*, 112, 116, 126, 136, 138, 139, 143,
145, 146)

The "father," in this case Father Arnall, leaves no
doubt open that his mission is to crush rebellion in his
"sons." He begins with a grim little joke about lawlessness
which goes straight to Stephen's guilty heart.

Saturday and Sunday being free days some boys might be in-
clined to think that Monday is a free day also. Beware of making that mistake. I think you, Lawless, are likely to make that
mistake.
    —I, sir? Why, sir?
    A little wave of quiet mirth broke forth over the class of
boys from the rector's grim smile. Stephen's heart began slowly
to fold and fade with fear like a withering flower. (*P* 107)

Stephen seems to sense that the retreat will contain an attack upon his maturity. As the rector announces the retreat, Stephen, remembering Clongowes, feels that "his
soul . . . became again a child's soul" (*P* 109); the effect
of the first sermon causes him to consider his sexual sins
as those of a child: "Their error [Stephen's and Emma's]
had offended deeply God's majesty though it was the error
of two children" (*P* 116).

In the course of the sermon, the fact that it is a paternal warning against filial rebellion is obliquely alluded to
twice. The first warning merely consists of the casual in-
sertion of the word "fathers," which is, however, somewhat
out of place in its context, and is not, moreover, to be
found in Joyce's sources for the sermon: "—A holy saint

(one of our own fathers I believe it was) was once vouchsafed a vision of hell" (*P* 132).[30] The casual mention of
"fathers" identifies the sermon as another attack by the father on the developing son. A more deliberate attack on
the son in the name of the father occurs during the
preacher's description of the blasphemy of the sinners in
hell and their hatred for the fellow sufferers:

The mouths of the damned are full of blasphemies against
God and of hatred for their fellowsufferers and of curses
against those souls which were their accomplices in sin. In
olden times it was the custom to punish the parricide, the man
who had raised his murderous hand against his father, by casting him into the depths of the sea in a sack in which were
placed a cock, a monkey and a serpent. (*P* 122)

This reference to the classical punishment for parricide is
slightly out of the mainstream of the preacher's logic—but
its symbolic purpose is evident.

After all of these attacks on his vocation, these outraged comments of a father on the sins of his son, Stephen
is temporarily cowed: "He had sinned so deeply against
heaven and before God that he was not worthy to be called
God's child" (*P* 137). It is significant that his confession
is made to a bearded priest; Joyce seems to have chosen to
have Stephen confess to a Capuchin father because the
Capuchins were allowed to keep their beards, as opposed
to the clean-shaven Jesuits. Not only is the Capuchin father bearded; "bearded workmen with pious faces" (*P*
141) are at work in the church. Among these many symbolic reminders of the bearded face of the father from the
first paragraphs of the book, Stephen makes his confession
of sexual exploration, and embraces his role as a penitent
child with panicky eagerness.

However, his submission is not all it seems. If his capitulation had been complete, he could never have broken
loose as he does in the next chapter. His rebellious soul

still shapes his surrender for its own ends, and sees to it that he does not feel love for the father who has frightened him. Before the sermon he feels only a "loveless awe of God" the father (*P* 104). After the sermon, in the next chapter, even in his most fervent attempts at piety he finds it easier to accept the idea that God the Father begot the Son out of the contemplation of His own perfection rather than out of love (*P* 149). Stephen never surrenders this last citadel to the father, the surrender of his love.

He *does* love the Virgin and desires to be "her knight": "His sin which had covered him from the sight of God, had led him nearer to the refuge of sinners." He finds no conflict between his veneration of the Virgin, of whose sodality he is prefect, and his visits to whores.

If ever his soul, reentering her dwelling shyly after the frenzies of the body's lust had spent itself, was turned toward her whose emblem is the morning star, . . . it was when her names were murmured softly by lips whereon there still lingered foul and shameful words, the savour itself of a lewd kiss. (*P* 105)

"That was strange," he realizes. Yet it is quite comprehensible if we see the Virgin as yet another aspect of the goddess of life whom he will adore on the beach in the next chapter. His ideas of the Virgin have always been associated with the ivory fingers of Eileen, his first love. It is his unconscious association of the Virgin with sexuality which provides an escape hatch for his cunning soul in its attempts to evade the freezing approach of the father. After the first day of the retreat Stephen, it seems, repents of his sexual adventures; the "jeweleyed harlots" of his imagination flee before the trumpet of doom. Yet what form does his repentance take? Sorrowfully, penitently, he begs the Virgin to confirm him in his love for Emma! The effect is richly ironic. The father is offended and frightened by the sexual adventures of the son; the son is deeply ashamed of his explorations; and yet the son begs the assistance of heaven in his sexual quest.

She [the Virgin] placed their hands together, hand in hand, and said, speaking to their hearts:

—Take hands, Stephen and Emma. It is a beautiful evening now in heaven. . . . Take hands together, my dear children, and you will be happy together and your hearts will love each other. (*P* 116)

Stephen so fears and hates the father that he finds it difficult to mention his name: "Those above, those in heaven, would see what he would do to make up for the past . . ." (*P* 126). When he does force himself to say "Father, I . . ." he feels that a "cold shining rapier" has slid into his tender flesh (*P* 126). Although his child's conscience is terribly frightened, his developing soul still knows who his enemy is, and who is his friend. (Even though the preacher's face is kind, his fingers form "a frail cage" [*P* 127].)

Another flaw in Stephen's submission is that it is his very pride in himself and in his name that forces him into temporary humility: "Could it be that he, Stephen Dedalus, had done these things?" (*P* 137), and later, "Everybody in the chapel would know then what a sinner he had been" (*P* 143). This pride will survive under the cloak of fear, and return when Stephen recovers his morale.

Even when he is most frightened, the sexual demon whispers in his brain, causing him to speculate on the involuntary nature of his erections: "The eyes see the thing, without having wished first to see. Then in an instant it happens. But does that part of the body understand or what?" (*P* 139). Although he prays to his "angel guardian" to drive away the demon, the demon lingers, since it is too deeply part of his soul to be exorcised. Before his confession the heat and murmuring in his blood warn him of the presence of the paternal enemy (*P* 142). He tries to force himself to "love God Who had made and loved him" (*P* 143), but he only forces himself into childish babbling in the attempt, and succeeds only in fearing Him. This, of course, is useless for the father's purpose;

he already knows that the son fears him— the son has hidden under a table from him while only a baby. When the fear is overcome, the effect of the sermons will fade, and the murmuring in the blood will begin again.

Therefore, another attack of the father, the most elaborate and powerful so far, has failed to stop the progress of the son to maturity. Stephen is temporarily cowed by the vision of what his vocation entails—the embracing of stink, heat, chance, isolation, darkness, constant insecurity. However, his vocation is too deeply rooted in his soul to be uprooted at this point, and in the next chapter, under the forcing pressure of this power in his soul, he will affirm his vocation, this time definitively.

e. chapter **four** $(P$ 147–73$)$

FROM the beginning of chapter 4 to the end of the book, the voice of Stephen's environment, "the father," grows weaker and the voice of his soul, his vocation, grows stronger. The attacks of the father do not cease; though not as violent, they are almost as subtle and persistent as before. The soul of the artist, however, is almost mature at this point, and it fights the father with all the symbolic and psychological weapons in its armory.

In the first of the three parts of chapter 4, Stephen seems partly paralyzed from the effects of the sermon. He has constructed a tight artificial schedule for himself, based upon mechanical regularity of observance and mortification of his senses. It is, of course, too rigid a regime for him to follow for long. But it seems to him to be what the father requires of his good children, and so Stephen perseveres in it. He tries very hard to humble himself to the rule of the father.

His day began with an heroic offering of its every moment of thought and action for the intentions of the supreme pontiff. . . . Every part of his day, divided by what he regarded now as the duties of his station in life, circled about its own centre of spiritual energy. (*P* 147, 148)

After the sermon he had sought white meals and pale flowers. He now seeks after paleness and coldness, the signs of the father.

His day begun . . . with an early mass. The raw morning air whetted his resolute piety. . . . The rosaries . . . transformed themselves into coronals of flowers of such vague unearthly texture that they seemed to him as hueless and odourless as they were nameless . . . [As part of his mortification of the flesh he] kept away from the fire [and] left parts of his neck and face undried so that air might sting them. (*P* 147, 148, 151)

He tries to despise the physical life that he was beginning to embrace before the retreat.

The world for all its solid substance and complexity no longer existed for his soul save as a theorem of divine power and love and universality. So entire and unquestionable was this sense of the divine meaning in all nature granted to his soul that he could scarcely understand why it was in any way necessary that he should continue to live. (*P* 150)

All of Stephen's efforts at humbling his heart and slowing the development of his soul toward what it was born to serve are vitiated by the promptings of his vocation, which gives unintended twists to all of his maneuvers. Stephen's desire for darkness and heat, two of the concomitants of creation, creeps in disguised as admiration of elements of piety: at early mass he would occasionally glance up "for an instant towards the vested figure standing in the gloom between the two candles" (*P* 147); was he imagining the "darkness shining in light" that in *Ulysses* becomes a symbol of the artist? In his meditations on the Trinity he seems attracted mostly by the Third Person, who is associated with the creator's darkness and fire.

> The divine gloom and silence wherein dwelt the unseen Paraclete . . . the eternal, mysterious secret Being to Whom, as God, the priests offered up mass once a year, robed in the scarlet of the tongues of fire. (*P* 148–49)

Stephen tries to force himself to believe that the father loves him, but in vain.

> The imagery through which the nature and kinship of the Three Persons of the Trinity were darkly shadowed forth in the books of devotion which he read—the Father contemplating from all eternity as in a mirror His Divine Perfections and thereby begetting eternally the Eternal Son and the Holy Spirit proceeding out of Father and Son from all eternity— were easier of acceptance by his mind by reason of their august incomprehensibility than was the simple fact that God had loved his soul from all eternity, for ages before he had been born into the world, for ages before the world itself had existed. (*P* 149)

Stephen can believe in the father's vanity, a contemplation of his perfections "as in a mirror," rather like Stephen's father in the hotel at Cork "examining his hair and face and moustache with great care" (*P* 88). Stephen cannot believe that the father can love him. A father who has shown such pressing desire to absorb him, to render him entirely childlike, is difficult for him to accept as a loving father, even on a high philosophical plane.

Love does exist in Stephen's universe, however. Although he cannot believe that the father loves him, Stephen loves the father's bride, the created world, and its symbol, woman. Stephen had prayed to the Virgin in his terror in the previous chapter, thus unconsciously fighting off the influence of the father's attack. Now it is basically the thought of woman (artfully and ironically disguised) that "warms" him during his spell of frigid, pale control.

His soul took up again her burden of pieties, masses and prayers and sacraments and mortifications, and only then for the first time since he had brooded on the great mystery of love did he feel within him a warm movement like that of some newly born life or virtue of the soul itself. . . . An inaudible voice seemed to caress the soul, telling her names and glories, bidding her arise as for espousal and come away, bidding her look forth, a spouse, from Amana and from the mountains of the leopards; and the soul seemed to answer with the same inaudible voice, surrendering herself: *Inter ubera mea commorabitur.*

This idea of surrender had a perilous attraction for his mind now that he felt his soul beset once again by the insistent voices of the flesh.[31] (*P* 150, 152)

In the previous chapter Joyce, one feels, had sympathized with his young hero's terror, and had not mocked him. Now Joyce seems to be regarding him with almost open irony. Stephen thinks he is being pious, but his vocation is driving him to sexual maturity. Therefore, despite his fervor, he deceives himself about his own motives and sensations. "I have amended my life, have I not?" he asks himself at the end of this section; but the only thing he has amended is his diction. The ironic overcorrectness of "Have I not?" allows the reader a glance at Joyce's attitude toward his young man. Stephen remembers that "he had felt a subtle, dark and murmurous presence penetrate his being and fire him with a brief iniquitous lust" (*P* 149); in his piety he calls it iniquitous and believes that it has "slipped beyond his grasp leaving his mind lucid and indifferent." In this he is deceiving himself; the dark, murmurous, fiery presence, in various disguises, is still undermining his attempt to be a selfless servant of the father.

Nor has his pride, his sense of difference, left him. Just as in the previous section, pride disguised as humility comes to his aid. Stephen is proud of his mortifications, proud of his ability to resist "spiritual exaltation," proud of his physical and moral austerities. It is finally his sense of difference which provides the first crack in his facade of humility.

To merge his life in the common tide of other lives was harder for him than any fasting or prayer, and it was his constant failure to do this *to his own satisfaction* [my italics] which caused in his soul at last a sensation of spiritual dryness together with a growth of doubts and scruples. (*P* 151–52)

Therefore, the father's most powerful and elaborate attempt has failed to absorb the son. Stephen, under his fear, has kept the seeds of his vocation alive; within a few pages he is going to embrace his vocation, this time definitively.

The father returns to the attack in the second section of chapter 4. One might almost say that he hopes to consolidate a victory already half-won by the sermon on Hell. Of course, the victory is not even half-won over Stephen's soul, as I have tried to show; Stephen's soul stubbornly fights the attempts of the father to halt its growth, and this attack fails, just as the others had.

On the literal level, all that happens in this section is that Stephen is asked whether he thinks he could become a priest and he decides that he could not. That it is an attack upon Stephen's maturity, however, is clear from the vision of the priestly life that is offered to him, "the white peace of the altar" (*P* 159). "He would hold his secret knowledge and secret power, being as sinless as the innocent" (*P* 159), that is, as pure as a child.[32] The coldness of the priest's vocation is again mentioned:

[Stephen thought of the Clongowes jesuits] as men who washed their bodies briskly with cold water and wore clean cold linen. . . . The chill and order of the life repelled him. He saw himself rising in the cold of the morning. (*P* 156, 161)

When he imagines the characters of the name "The Reverend Stephen Dedalus, S.J.," he imagines the raw

red face that would perhaps be his after years of "suffo-
cated anger" in an inappropriate vocation: "Was it the
raw reddish glow he had so often seen on wintry mornings
on the shaven gills of the priests?" (*P* 161) . He would be
uncontaminated by the sins of the women and girls he
would absolve (*P* 159) ; presumably he would be incapable of being sexually stimulated and thus he would have
to renounce the keystone of his maturity. This cold, white,
collective, sexless life is what is being offered him by the
director.

The director makes two mistakes in his presentation
of the priestly life to Stephen: he recalls women to Stephen's mind and he appeals to Stephen's pride in himself.
Both of these factors work against the director. The pride
that the director feels in the power of the priest reminds
Stephen of his pride in his difference, which now emerges
as a full-fledged realization of his destined isolation and insecurity.

A strong note of pride reinforcing the gravity of the
priest's voice made Stephen's heart quicken in response. . . .
A flame began to flutter again on Stephen's cheek as he heard
in this proud address an echo of his own proud musings. . . .
[But later, reconsidering, he asks himself] What had come of
the pride of his spirit which had always made him conceive
himself as a being apart in every order? . . . The voice of the
director urging upon him the proud claims of the church and
the mystery and power of the priestly office repeated itself idly
in his memory. . . . His destiny was to be elusive of social or
religious orders. . . . He was destined to learn his own wisdom apart from others or to learn the wisdom of others wandering among the snares of the world. (*P* 157, 158, 161, 162)

The director mentions the *jupes* of the Capuchins, as a
ruse of some kind, Stephen suspects; perhaps if the director's jocular reference to an order of the church evoked a
flippant or disrespectful echo in Stephen, the director
would know that he need proceed no further in his ap-

proach to Stephen, who would be unsuitable material for a serious vocation. The director does not know, however, that the mention of women's clothes has an inflammatory effect on Stephen.

[Stephen] gazed calmly before him at the waning sky, glad of the cool of the evening and the faint yellow glow which hid the tiny flame kindling upon his cheek.

The names of articles of dress worn by women or of certain soft and delicate stuffs used in their making brought always to his mind a delicate and sinful perfume. . . .[33] But an unresting doubt flew hither and thither before his mind.[34] (*P* 155, 157)

The evocation of two of the primary elements of his soul, warmth and darkness, are enough to turn aside the blandishments of the father. Stephen, after a short period of temptation, easily shakes off any thought of being a priest. His decision is preceded and accompanied by the signs of his personality—warmth, darkness, flames, odors, murmuring unrest, disorder, and chance confusions.

The troubling odour of the long corridors of Clongowes came back to him and he heard the discreet murmur of the burning gasflames. At once from every part of his being unrest began to irradiate. A feverish quickening of his pulses followed and a din of meaningless words drove his reasoned thoughts hither and thither confusedly. (*P* 160–61)

These flames and murmurs and hitherandthitherings will recur in the next section, during one of the transports of his vocational ceremony.

His latest victory over the father is signalized by the emergence of a symbol of great importance in the later books, a symbol of the artist's mission.

He smiled to think that it was this disorder, the misrule and confusion of his father's house and the stagnation of vegetable life, which was to win the day in his soul. Then a short laugh broke from his lips as he thought of that solitary farmhand in the kitchengardens behind their house whom they had nicknamed the man with the hat. A second laugh, taking rise from the first after a pause, broke from him involuntarily as he thought of how the man with the hat worked, considering in turn the four points of the sky and then regretfully plunging his spade in the earth. (*P* 162)

At this point and at other points in *A Portrait* Joyce's important symbols are introduced by juxtaposition to turning points in the story. His symbols seem arbitrarily chosen —hats, knives, buckets, sticks, and so on—and indeed they have little traditional symbolic value when they are first mentioned. They acquire symbolic significance by their proximity to important events, and build up meaning by their deployment in future significant situations. The man with the hat is one such symbol. On the literal level, the image of the man with the hat occurs to Stephen because of his realization that his activity resembles that of the farmhand—he too had gazed the skies in search of a heavenly sign and he too "regretfully" has decided that his work is to be done on the imperfect, chance-ridden, confused earth. However, the hat has a significance beyond this literal psychological one. It is part of an epiphany, "a memorable phase of the mind itself," which follows a victory over the paternal enemy, and one which emerges from the deepest level of Stephen's memory. A man with a hat had been mentioned during the description of Stephen's preparation for his first victory over the father at Clongowes.

The rector would declare that he had been wrongly punished because the senate and the Roman people always declared that the men who did that had been wrongly punished. Those were the great men whose names were in Richmal Magnall's Questions. History was all about those men and what they did and that was what Peter Parley's Tales about Greece and Rome were all about. Peter Parley himself was on the first page in a picture. There was a road over a heath with grass at the side and little bushes: and Peter Parley had a broad hat like a protestant minister and a big stick and he was walking fast along the road to Greece and Rome. (*P* 53)

Stephen in fighting for his individuality rallies to his side the forces of history; "Peter Parley" [35] with his tales of Greece and Rome and his hat and stick broadens the context of Stephen's early rebellion, and is now associated, by juxtaposition, with his victory over the director; the man with the hat, whose actions resemble Stephen's symbolically, wears an article of dress which is associated with victory and with the triumph of the artist's soul over his enemies. In *Ulysses* the hats of Peter Parley and the man with the hat merge into Stephen's "Latin quarter hat" (*U* 17, 41) which makes him look like a protestant minister to the corner-boys in the Oxen of the Sun and Circe chapters and which he regards, only half-ironically perhaps, as the symbol of his name and his status as king-creator: "*Stephanos,* my crown" (*U* 210). After the vocational ceremony in *A Portrait,* and all through *Ulysses* Stephen is *stephaneforos* and *stephanoumenos,* the crowned artist, and the hat is the symbol of his power. There are other honorific hats in the works of Joyce. Parnell's hat, knocked off in a disturbance, was returned to him "as a matter of strict history" (history again!) by Leopold Bloom (*U* 654–55). Bloom's own "high grade ha[t]" (*U* 56, 71, 279, 286, 455, 493) conceals the temples of a hero. It is Bloom who retrieves Stephen's hat after the Nighttown scuffle (*U* 613). In *Finnegans Wake,* the action of Willingdone that drives the "seeboy" mad as a Madras hatter is his "hanking the half of the hat of lipoleums up the tail on the buckside of his big white harse. . . . that was the last joke of Willingdone" (*FW* 10). "Hat" was "flag" in the first draft of this episode; perhaps the hat has come to stand for national honor as well as the artist's crown. What maddens the "seeboy," the visionary artist, is the usurpation of his crown as "conscience of his race." [36] It is no wonder that an image of a hat should flash into Stephen's mind after he has finally shaken off the effects of the most vicious paternal attack on his sovereignty, and just before he is to experience the definitive ceremony of vocation.

One more point, a psychological one, can be made about the last few pages of this episode (P 161–64). Although images and symbols from deep within Stephen's soul flash into his mind and accompany his decisions, his decisions are now made quite deliberately and consciously. When as a little boy he had to decide whether or not to confront Father Conmee, the decision was more or less made for him; he followed the promptings of his soul fearfully. Now he becomes capable of intense self-examination. As his vocational ceremony approaches, his motives emerge and become part of the foreground of his consciousness and, indeed, part of his equipment as an artist. His self-consciousness and self-knowledge never leave him from this point to the end of *Ulysses*.

This section ends in Stephen's family home amid concrete examples of the "vegetable" chaos he has chosen to be his over the peace of the altar. Tea, sugared bread, and "a ravaged turnover," all vegetable products, are scattered on the table. A knife with a broken ivory handle is stuck in the pith of the "ravaged turnover." This knife, like the hat of the man with the hat, becomes an important symbol of historical processes in *Ulysses* and *Finnegans Wake*. Some of the things it symbolizes can be determined by examination of the contexts of its appearance in the later books, and, on the assumption that Joyce's work forms a symbolic totality, the meaning derived from examination of the later works can be reflected back onto the knife in *A Portrait*.

Of course, Stephen Dedalus is "Kinch the knifeblade" in *Ulysses*. However, there are other knife references.

Leopold Bloom helps Stephen pull himself together after the Circe episode, and they enter the cabman's shelter. Stephen then muses upon a knife:

—Liquids I can eat, Stephen said. But oblige me by taking away that knife. I can't look at the point of it. It reminds me of Roman history.

Mr Bloom promptly did as suggested and removed the incriminated article, a blunt hornhandled ordinary knife with nothing particularly Roman or antique about it to the lay eye, observing that the point was the least conspicuous point about it. (*U* 635)

The knife reminds Stephen of Roman history because earlier in the book, meditating on the ineluctable processes of history, he had asked himself, "Had Pyrrhus not fallen by a beldam's hand in Argos or Julius Caesar not been knifed to death?" (*U* 25). The knife-symbol, then, contains connotations of historical necessity and assassination, the fall of great men envied or feared by lesser men.[37] This interpretation of the symbol is enriched by other knives in the Eumaeus section: the "poignards" of jealous Italians and Spaniards (*U* 636, 637), the sailor's claspknife which, he says, resembles a knife used to kill a man in Trieste (*U* 628), and the knives of the Invincibles who assassinated the deputy Lord-Lieutenant of Ireland and his secretary in Phoenix Park in 1882: "[Bloom felt] a certain kind of admiration for a man who had actually brandished a knife, cold steel, with the courage of his political convictions" (*U* 642). Both of these meanings—knives as symbols of political assassination and as instruments of sexual passion—are present in *Finnegans Wake*.

That knife of knifes [that the] treepartied ambush was laid . . . (*FW* 87.35-36)
. . . . . .
The older sisars (Tyrants, regicide is too good for you!) become unbeurrable from age, . . . having been sort-of-nine-knived and chewly removed . . . the twinfreer types [Burrus

and Caseous] are billed to make their reupprearance as the knew kneck and knife knicknots on the deserted *champ de bouteilles*. [The brothers in their local role as Brutus and Cassius are going to kill the old "sisars" and take his place, each perhaps as one of the blades of the new "sisars."] (*FW* 162.1–11)

. . . . . .

Elpis, thou fountain of the greeces, all shall speer theeward from kongen in his canteenhus to knivers hind the knoll. (*FW* 267.4–6) [Both the assassins and their victim, the king, aspire upwards or, perhaps, urinate upwards. (They also hope— *elpis* is Greek for "hope." However, they are all heading towards decay and death; in March, 1909, Synge died in the Elpis Nursing Home.) Issy's footnote to "speer upwards" is "Mannequins' Pose," suggesting the famous Brussels statue of the Manneken-Pis, a bronze in the form of a little naked boy urinating upwards. "Elpis, thou fountain of the greeces" suggests the same thing. A full interpretation of this passage would include the meaning that all men, kings or "knivers" (knaves?) must urinate. Since urination in *Ulysses* seems to be among other things, a symbol of sexuality, male or female (especially on *U* 702–3), the knives of the "knivers" acquire a sexual tinge.]

. . . . . .

[Butt and Taff, describing the killing of the Russian general, argue; Taff reproaches Butt for having hesitated to kill the general while the general was defecating and declares that "you bet your blowieknife" *he* would not have hesitated to kill the general. "Blowieknife" combines "bloody life" and "Bowie knife," another reference to assassination by knife. (*FW* 345.7)]

. . . . . .

How Alibey Ibrahim wisheths Bella Suora to a holy crypt-mahs while the Arumbian Knives Riders axecutes devilances round the jehumispheure. (*FW* 346.4–7) [The reference here is to Gen. 12; Abram called Sarai his sister (*suora*, "sister" [Ital.]) rather than his wife to protect her or himself (in some obscure way) from Pharaoh. Here a holy brother-sister wedding is celebrated amid the mad shootings of the stars (the "night riders" are driving furiously, like Jehu [2 Kings 9:20], around the starry hemisphere) . Knives, axes, and lances are pressed into service as sexual symbols.]

. . . . . .

in the sighed of lovely eyes while his knives of hearts made havoc. (*FW* 405.28–29) [Shaun, the lady-killer, as the knave of hearts.] [38]

The knife in the pith of the ravaged turnover in *A Portrait*, therefore, has a long and distinguished list of descendants in *Ulysses* and *Finnegans Wake*. The conspicuous presence of the knife, with its double connotation of assassination and sexuality, suggests that Stephen has come to the threshold of maturity and is, as it were, ready to "stab" the father with his developing soul. Stephen had imagined a wounded marshal outside Father Conmee's door, and the "marshal" was associated with his father; now Stephen is about to wound the father with his growth to maturity. The vocational ceremony is only a few pages away.

The third section of chapter 4 is extremely complex, both in its form and in its symbolism. All of the episodes in *A Portrait* are carefully chosen for their symbolic importance in the life of the developing artist, but this section contains the moment when the artist, like Hamlet, feels his fate cry out, when the vocation he has been pursuing both consciously and unconsciously becomes manifest to him, when "the end he had been born to serve yet did not see" (*P* 165) finally blazes before him.

This section is built in five parts, with an introduction and a coda. Each of these five parts, with the exception of the second, contains a moment of exaltation in which one aspect of Stephen's vocation becomes clear to him.

INTRODUCTION

Almost every word in the introduction is significant. "He could wait no longer";[39] it is his father for whom he could wait no longer, and once he strides off toward his vocation he dreads being called back: "He set off abruptly for the Bull, walking rapidly lest his father's shrill whistle might call him back" (*P* 164) . He rounds the curve at the police barracks—another symbol of paternal control—and is "safe" from his father's pursuit, a significant choice of words. (All the unconscious symbolism in the book comes to the surface in this section.)

It is at this point that he experiences another sundering of old ties—he separates his life from his mother's. She had attempted to bind him to the past; with an almost reflex action he throws off the thought of her. His powers of "darkness" help him: "A dim antagonism gathered force within him and darkened his mind as a cloud against her disloyalty" (*P* 164) . So he has cast off both his parents.

FIRST EPISODE

The thought of the university sets off the first episode of exaltation. For the first time the whole trend of his past life is completely clear to him.

The university! So he had passed beyond the challenge of the sentries who had stood as guardians of his boyhood and had sought to keep him among them that he might be subject to them and serve their ends. Pride after satisfaction uplifted him like long slow waves. The end he had been born to serve yet did not see had led him to escape by an unseen path. (*P* 165)

This realization of his escape from the nets of the past, from his actual parents and from all the other fathers of his environment, sets off the flames and darkness of his introduction to sex (*P* 100–101) and of his vocation.

It seemed to him that he heard notes of fitful music leaping upwards a tone and downwards a diminished fourth, upwards a tone and downwards a major third, like triplebranching flames leaping fitfully, flame after flame, out of a midnight wood. It was an elfin prelude, endless and formless; and, as it grew wilder and faster, the flames leaping out of time, he seemed to hear from under the boughs and grasses wild creatures racing, their feet pattering like rain upon the leaves. (P 165)

The "formlessness" of his prelude and the sounds of living, moving nature are reminiscent of other aspects of his vocation—his acceptance of the facts of the "funnaminal world" (FW 244.13), the universe of random chances, the "collideorescape" (FW 143.28) which is his to reproduce and mold.

SECOND EPISODE

The second episode contains no exaltation, merely conscious rejection by Stephen of alternatives to his vocation. Stephen asks himself why he has turned aside from what he had "so often thought to be his destiny . . . He had refused. Why?" (P 165). His question is answered by the appearance of the cloddish Christian Brothers "stained yellow or red or livid by the sea," the "cold mad feary father" (FW 628.2), "Old Father Ocean" (U 50), whose "infrahuman odour" he dreads (P 167). Like Stephen's school friends later on (P 168), the Christian Brothers have surrendered to the father. "Brothers" not fathers, they have been "stained" by the paternal sea; they are the possession of the father now and are incapable of independent action. They move as a unit; like the figures in Stephen's dream recorded in his diary "one does not seem to stand quite apart from another" (P 249). They are selfless and serviceable; Stephen is independent, self-conscious, serving nothing but his own vocation. In a long, surely plotted paragraph Joyce rejects any possibility of rapprochement between Stephen and these "absorbed" sons. Stephen finds it "idle and embittering" to try to go against his birthright of "difference" and to try to love them as himself "with the same kind of love" (P 166);

they are slaves and he is free, and no amount of mental striving on his part can bridge the gap and make him one of them. He can, however, use them for his art; perhaps he can also awaken their consciences, after he has forged his own. They are certainly representative of the unawakened Irish conscience, the conscience of "the most belated race in Europe," as Joyce calls the Irish in "The Day of the Rabblement." [40]

Stephen then questions the source of his love of words. His self-examination is completely appropriate in this context—words are the tools of his vocation. He never answers his own question, whether it is the rhythms of words he enjoys more than the "inner world of individual emotions" which he will convey in "a lucid supple periodic prose." At any rate, it is not the raw matter of the world which is primary in his art but his vision of it, his transmutation of it into art. He is not the servant of the world, but the conscious master of it.

Before Stephen gazes toward Dublin, there is a reminder of the cold father ("the air was chilled . . . his flesh dreaded the cold infrahuman odour of the sea" [P 167]). Stephen as a "hydrophobe" in Ulysses (U 673) is here foreshadowed. The sea's odor is infrahuman because absorption renders its Icarian victims part of what has killed them; they are no longer free agents. This sea change is what the fathers intended for Stephen, but he is still free, whatever his contemporaries and compatriots may have become.

The last part of the second episode prepares the way for the ceremony of vocation. Stephen contemplates Dublin through the haze. The modern city lies before him, but his thoughts pierce through; as we later discover, "the ghost of the ancient kingdom of the Danes had looked forth through the vesture of the hazewrapped city" (P 168–69). It is a moment of "metempsychosis," a state which is to claim more and more of Joyce's attention as he strives to break free of the temporal order; in *Finnegans Wake* manipulation of temporal simultaneity becomes his first principle of creation. Joyce implicitly acknowledges this passage as the genesis of his method in *Finnegans Wake* by "prigging" it for a passage in *Finnegan*.

Like a scene on some vague arras, old as man's weariness, the image of the seventh city of christendom was visible to him across the timeless air, no older nor more weary nor less patient of subjection than in the days of the thingmote. (*P* 167)

It scenes like a landescape from Wildu Picturescu or some seem on some dimb Arras, dumb as Mum's mutyness, this mimage of the seventyseventh kusin of kristiansen is odable to os across the wineless Ere no œdor nor mere eerie nor liss potent of suggestion than in the tales of the tingmount. (Prigged!) (*FW* 53.1–6)

Equally important in this context is that the revelation to Stephen is of the past of his race, the Irish. The past of his race provides the greater part of the material of his major work. More to the immediate point, however, his vision provides Stephen with his goal in *A Portrait*—to recreate the conscience of his race, the past of which begins to be clear to him at this point. It is this concept of "race" which sets off the third episode, the second wave of exaltation that sweeps over him, the real beginning of his ceremony of ordination.

THIRD EPISODE

The beginning of the second wave of exaltation is disheartenment: "Disheartened [by his vision of the Irish race's subjection], he raised his eyes toward the slowdrifting clouds, dappled and seaborne" (*P* 167). The reminder of his tools as an artist, the supple periodic prose that he is to mold to tell the story of his race, lifts his depression and sets off a quiet wave of exaltation, in which ancestral voices seem to announce his coming:

The Europe they [the clouds] had come from lay out there beyond the Irish Sea, Europe of strange tongues and valleyed and woodbegirt and citadelled and of entrenched and marshalled races. He heard a confused music within him as of memories and names which he was almost conscious of but could not capture even for an instant. (*P* 167)

Both Stephen and Joyce really believed in the existences of national races; neither of them was a modern internationalist. Joyce was an old-fashioned nationalist, of the school of Herder and Matthew Arnold and Mazzini. Stephen contemptuously rejects MacCann's internationalism later on in *A Portrait* (*P* 195–99) , and in *Ulysses* he pours scorn on international arbitration arranged by peace-loving monarchs (*U* 589) . If the Irish race did not exist it would be useless to try to "forge in the smithy of [his] soul" its uncreated conscience. In 1907 Joyce made a clear statement on the subject of nationality:

Nationality (if it really is not a convenient fiction like so many others to which the scalpels of present-day scientists have given the coup de grace) must find its reason for being rooted in something that surpasses and transcends and informs changing things like blood and the human word. The mystic theologian who assumed the pseudonym of Dionysius, the pseudo-Areopagite, says somewhere, "God has disposed the limits of nations according to his angels," and this probably is not a purely mystical concept. Do we not see that in Ireland the Danes, the Firbolgs, the Milesians from Spain, the Norman invaders, and the Anglo-Saxon settlers have united to form a new entity, one might say under the influence of a local deity? [41] And, although the present race in Ireland is backward and inferior, it is worth taking into account the fact that it is the only race of the entire Celtic family that has not been willing to sell its birthright for a mess of pottage.[42]

Joyce never departed from his belief in national races and always held that the Irish were a race. In 1920 he wrote to Carlo Linati: "[Ulysses] is an epic of two races (Israelite-Irish) ." [43] This does not mean that Joyce was a nationalist of the Nazi type. His nationalism was the nineteenth-century liberal variety which was prevalent in the Ireland of his time, the kind which offered national salvation through a great national *vates,* who, like Mickiewicz or D'Annunzio, would awaken the conscience of his race. Many Irish writers were consciously vying for this position as savior besides Joyce—Yeats, AE, George Moore.[44] Stephen here is responding to a nineteenth-century nationalist call for a savior, and his soul believes that he is the one.

The mention of "race" with all of its mystical and Mazzinian overtones, sets off the process of ordination. Stephen hears a "voice from beyond the world." The voice is, on the literal level, the voice of his friends, calling to him jocularly as they fall into the water, but in Stephen's state of heightened awareness, they are the voices of his race hailing him *vates,* the crowned poet. *"Stephanos,* my crown" Stephen thinks in *Ulysses* (*U* 210); here "Stephanos!" is shouted by his friends. "The Dedalus" combines the Celtic way of referring to a chief of a clan [45] with Stephen's "strange name"; to Stephen it seems that they are acknowledging "his mild proud sovereignty" (*P* 168). They are all "absorbed" sons. Joyce leaves no room for doubt that they are entirely the property of the cold father; like the livid, yellow and red Christian Brothers they are "corpsewhite," "pallid golden," "rawly tanned," and they are covered with cold sea-water.

The roughhewn stones of the sloping breakwater over which they scrambled in their horseplay . . . gleamed with cold wet lustre. The towels with which they smacked their bodies were heavy with cold seawater: and drenched with cold brine was their matted hair. (*P* 168)

They dive, or fall, back into the cold, infrahuman sea, shouting out, like Icarus, "O, cripes, I'm drownded!" (*P*

169). They are symbolically the "belated" race of the Irish that Stephen will arouse. Meanwhile they are completely in the power of the father.[46] At the mention of his name, the name he had once defended from Father Dolan, that of the "fabulous artificer," "he seemed to hear the noise of dim waves and to see a winged form flying above the waves and slowly climbing the air." He knows himself perfectly at that "timeless" moment:

What did it mean? Was it a quaint device opening a page of some medieval book of prophecies and symbols, a hawklike man flying sunward above the sea, a prophecy of the end he had been born to serve and had been following through the mists of childhood and boyhood, a symbol of the artist forging anew in his workshop out of the sluggish matter of the earth a new soaring impalpable imperishable being? (*P* 169)

Stephen feels as if he is flying: "the body he knew was purified in a breath and delivered of incertitude and made radiant and commingled with the element of the spirit" (*P* 169). At certain moments the "incertitude of the void" (*U* 697),[47] the gap between moment and moment, state and state, man and woman, artist and creation, father and son, can be crossed by the possessor of a vocation. Leopold Bloom crosses the incertitude of the void when, keyless, he returns home after rescuing Stephen from the police. The incertitude of the void is more than the doubtfulness of the future; it is the whole realm of chance that the mature artist or father accepts as his domain, confident that he can cross it to certainty, to creation, whenever he needs to. Stephen believes that he is mature enough to cross it, but by the beginning of *Ulysses* he is lying "seabedabbled" (*U* 210), shot down by his father's telegram and doubting his vocation bitterly.

Fabulous artificer, the hawklike man. You flew. Whereto? Newhaven-Dieppe, steerage passenger. Paris and back. Lapwing. Icarus. *Pater, ait.* Seabedabbled, fallen, weltering. (*U* 210)

Something more is needed before the flight can be sustained. I suggest that that something more is to be found near Stephen's dance in the Nighttown section of *Ulysses* (see chap. 3, below) At this point in *A Portrait,* however, Stephen is launched on his maiden flight.

The third episode ends with another realization by Stephen of the "pale service" he has escaped. He starts up nervously to stride onward, accompanied by the flames and darkness of his vocation, and with creation singing in his throat.

He could no longer quench the flame in his blood. He felt his cheeks aflame and his throat throbbing with song. There was a lust of wandering in his feet that burned to set out for the ends of the earth. On! On! his heart seemed to cry. Evening would deepen above the sea, night fall upon the plains, dawn glimmer before the wanderer and show him strange fields and hills and faces. . . . Already one long oval bank of sand lay warm and dry amid the wavelets. Here and there warm isles of sand gleamed above the shallow tide . . . The water of the rivulet was dark with endless drift and mirrored the high-drifting clouds. . . . the grey warm air was still. (*P* 170)

He looks toward Howth, which is to become the supreme father symbol in *Finnegans Wake,* and picks up a stick (*P* 170), the ancestor of his ashplant, his "augur's rod," in *Ulysses,* the other half of his costume as a *vates,* the companion symbol to his crown, the hat. Thus equipped, he is ready for the next stage of his ordination.

FOURTH EPISODE

The fourth episode contains the highest and most powerful exaltation, that evoked by the birdlike girl on the beach. Now the water of the rivulet is "dark with drift," and he and the girl are "alone." He is "alone" and she is "alone and still" (*P* 171) ; it is at this point that Stephen's prediction, made as a very young boy, comes true.

[Stephen and the "unsubstantial image which his soul constantly beheld"] would be alone, surrounded by darkness and silence: and in that moment of supreme tenderness he would be transfigured. (*P* 65)

In this intensely self-revelatory episode the symbolic meaning of the girl is perfectly clear to Stephen.

A wild angel had appeared to him, the angel of mortal youth and beauty, an envoy from the fair courts of life, to throw open before him in an instant of ecstasy the gates of all the ways of error and glory. . . . He felt . . . the earth beneath him, the earth that had borne him, had taken him to her breast. (*P* 172)

The girl symbolizes the realm of "error," "lots," chances, that he has chosen over the dead certainties of the altar of the "absorbing" father; she is the earth itself, the "vegetable chaos" of earthly life. The girl on the beach is the symbolic descendant of Eileen Vance whom Stephen was going to marry, as a baby, thus arousing the frightened, jealous fury of the father; she is E. C., the girl who lingered on the tram step for Stephen's word of love, which did not come. She is Mercedes and the Virgin to whom he prayed in his fear during the sermons on hell. She is the prostitute who initiated him into sex amid flickering gas-flames. (In the 1904 essay "Portrait" the phrase here applied to the bird-girl—an "angel of mortal youth and beauty, an envoy from the fair courts of life" describes the prostitute.) Later she will be the temptress of his villanelle and Molly Bloom and, perhaps, both Anna Livia and Issy in *Finnegans Wake*. Basically, however, she is the dark, warm Earth.

The exclamation of Stephen's soul, "Heavenly God!" accompanying an "outburst of profane joy," is not inconsistent. The sacred and profane here join. Matter and spirit unite in a mystical marriage which, like the archetypal marriages in *Finnegans Wake,* is incestuous, the son married with Mother Earth or, as in the later chapters of the *Wake,* with his sister, like "boyrun to sibster" *(FW* 465.17).

The fifth episode is the most mysterious of all. After his powerful "flight" in the fourth episode, Stephen sinks down "that the peace and silence of the evening might still the riot of his blood" *(P* 172). He feels the earth beneath him and the heavens above him. "He closed his eyes in the languor of sleep" *(P* 172). He dreams of a vast red rose, "trembling and unfolding, a breaking light, an opening flower" *(P* 172). The juxtaposition of Stephen's mystical understanding of the heavens and the earth and the unfolding, developing red rose of "vegetable life" *(P* 162) suggests to me that the red rose is the symbol for Stephen of the universe developing through time to its fulfillment, its *telos,* just as his soul had developed, past obstacles and traps, to its fulfillment in this chapter of ceremonies; Stephen's white rose of innocence has become the red rose of experience, the "rosa mystica" of the litany, with the mystical ceremony of the marriage of earth and heaven. The image of the red rose of the universe recurs in the next chapter, as Stephen attempts to create his villanelle.

An afterglow deepened within his spirit, whence the white flame had passed, deepening to a rose and ardent light. That rose and ardent light was her [the Temptress'] strange wilful heart . . . lured by that ardent roselike glow the choirs of the seraphim were falling from heaven. . . . The roselike glow sent forth its rays of rhyme . . . [Shrinking from the "dull white light" of dawn that is trying to cover "the roselight in his heart" (*P* 218) Stephen stares] at the great overblown scarlet flowers of the tattered wallpaper. He tried to warm his perishing joy in their scarlet glow, imagining a roseway from where he lay upwards to heaven all strewn with scarlet flowers. (*P* 217, 218, 221–22)

In *Ulysses* the red flowers acquire powerful sexual overtones as they appear among the admirers of Molly Bloom. Blazes Boylan carries a red carnation in his teeth as he goes off to his assignation with Molly (*U* 228, 254), and Molly remembers lying with Bloom (himself a flower) on Howth head "among the rhododendrons" (*U* 782). "Id love to have the whole place swimming in roses," thinks Molly as she comes to the ecstatic end of her soliloquy (*U* 781), and the roses are interspersed among her "yeses" on the last page of *Ulysses*. Stephen's image of the universe as a red flower combines powerful elements of creation and of sexual attack and surrender, and is the symbol of the subject matter of the matured artist which he is going to shape into a new reality.[48]

CODA

The third part of chapter 4 ends with a coda. Stephen wakes from his dream of the ardent flowers and looks about him. The moon had risen, and the tide was coming in. The last words of the chapter are a version of one of the few phrases from the first sketch of *A Portrait* composed on January 7, 1904, "the few last figures islanded in distant pools," that survived to the final version of *A Portrait:* "The tide was flowing in fast to the land with a low whisper of her waves, islanding a few last figures in distant pools" (*P* 173). This survival suggests to me that the section of *A Portrait* containing the "ordination ceremony" is one of the most important in the book, one to which

Joyce was leading for many chapters, and one which had been maturing in his mind for ten years.

Indeed, many important things have been achieved in this chapter. The artist's soul has been laid out before us —his love of words, his affinity for warmth and darkness, his quarrel with the signs of the father, coldness and whiteness, his attitude toward absorption by his environment and toward his compatriots and contemporaries who were so absorbed, his acceptance of the "vegetable" realm of development and error and incertitude, and his conscious acceptance of maturity, sexual and emotional, as an indispensable sign of his vocation. He has also acquired his crown, *stephanos,* the symbol of creative mastery as well as a reminder of his important name. He has acquired his stick, his sword "Nothung," his "augur's rod," his "life-wand," (as it becomes in *Finnegans Wake*) the symbol of his mastery over the past of his "race," over the "dead" whom he is to awaken. Finally, the double symbol of the knife is introduced in a context of (perhaps Pyrrhic) victory over his father; in *Ulysses* and *Finnegans Wake* the knife symbolizes the overthrow of an old order and the maturing, usually sexual, of a new order.

All of these implications are laid out before us in chapter 4. We see the "rhythm" of the artist's soul, the ratio of elements in the germinating seed of his personality, the "first entelechy," as Aristotle defined it, of a naturally created body. The "second entelechy" is the organism interacting with its fellows and with the rest of nature; it is this stage of development which Joyce presents to us in the next chapter of *A Portrait* and in *Ulysses*.

In the original sketch of *A Portrait,* Joyce described the process of describing a life in art as tracing "the curve of an emotion." This "curve" is not a phrase from esthetics, the "curve of beauty"; it is a technical term from algebra, and refers to the process of connecting given points on a graph by a line which will include all of them, so that the general equation which generated that curve can be derived and the future course of the curve predicted by extrapolation. This describes exactly Joyce's technique in *A Portrait*. Each section of *A Portrait* contains significant "timeless" moments in the life of the artist, selected from a lifetime of events. The reader's attention traces the line of the curve from one point to the next until the complete curve is defined. At the end of chapter 4 the trend of the curve becomes obvious to the young artist himself; the "end he had been born to serve yet did not see" shines out before him. Both he and the reader became completely aware of the landscape of his soul and the nature of it. From this point on the artist must begin his work, must labor in his vocation among his fellows.

f.   chapter five (*P* 174–253)

THE concluding chapter of *A Portrait*, by far the longest chapter in the book, is exceedingly complex and dense with meaning and implication. In this chapter we see the young artist moving among representative institutions and personalities of his society, his race, and in these circumstances striving to become a "father," to begin his lifework of creation.

The chapter is divided into four parts:

1] (*P* 174–216) – the artist at home and among his university friends, clarifying his own thoughts on his vocation
2] (*P* 217–24) – creation, his villanelle.
3] (*P* 224–47) – another section of discussion, this time more personal than in *P* 174–216.
4] (*P* 247–53) – another creation, the diary.

The form of this chapter—discussion: creation: discussion: creation—suggests that the creation sections are intended to act as summation and commentary (perhaps ironic) on the chapters of discussion that preceded them. However, the discussion sections are more than prologues to acts of creation; they are tremendously rich in materials for understanding the young artist, and they contain many symbols that assume supreme importance in the later works of Joyce. One such symbol—King David, the creator-king—not only sums up the artist's struggle to become a true creator; he furnishes a symbolic frame for *A Portrait,* and helps to elucidate some of the most complex passages in *Ulysses* and *Finnegans Wake.*

The first section of chapter 5 is the longest of the eighteen episodes that make up *A Portrait.* In it, Joyce paints a moral portrait of Stephen's Dublin. By the end of this section we know what the reality of Dublin means to the young artist, and should grasp the magnitude of the task of artistic transformation that he has undertaken.

The first part of this section takes place in Stephen's home, now more disorganized than ever. The colors of nature, the "dark pool" in the jar of dripping that reminds Stephen of the "dark turfcoloured water of the bath in Clongowes" (*P* 174), the vegetable products (tea and bread), are reminiscent of the home scene on *P* 163, and is just as clearly a picture in little of Stephen's homeland. In addition to this vegetable chaos there is a great confusion about time:

His mother straightened the battered alarmclock that was lying on its side in the middle of the kitchen mantelpiece until its dial showed a quarter to twelve and then laid it once more on its side.

— . . . The right time now is twenty past ten.

. . . . . .

The clock in the dairy told him that it was five minutes to five but, as he turned away, he heard a clock somewhere near

him, but unseen, beating eleven strokes in swift precision.
(P 174, 177)

This confusion about the time may be no more than a
humorous observation about the relativity of Irish chrono-
metry, but it may also contain a hint to the reader that he
should expect a certain metempsychotic timelessness or
simultaneity about the events of this section. Joyce's careful observation of the passage of time in *Ulysses* suggests
that this detail is to have more than a casual meaning, and
in *Finnegans Wake* the matter of the mischiming of the
hour is revived in an important context.

> Hark!
> Tolv two elf kater ten (it can't be) sax.
> Hork!
> Pedwar pemp foify tray (it must be) twelve. (*FW* 403)

"It must be twelve," but it only chimes eleven, a symbol of
the world of "error" that Stephen is to transform.[49]
     Stephen is on bad terms with his father. This is the
first and last hint of open friction between Simon and
Stephen; symbolically this is caused by Stephen's assertion
of maturity in the previous chapter. However, Stephen
does not fear fathers any more; he does not think that they
have the power to harm him. Indeed, the attacks of the
father have fallen flat since Stephen recovered from the
sermon on hell. All that fathers do in chapter 5 is fulmi-
nate vainly against the younger generation. The fifth
chapter belongs to the son and to the symbols of his development toward fatherhood. Simon Dedalus overhead
whistles shrilly to his children below and complains vainly;
the dean of studies tries to impress Stephen and fails; authority, sexual potency, and fatherhood are passing from
them to Stephen. (This is not to say that fathers are hence-
forth powerless; on the contrary, when we see Stephen in
Ulysses he is suffering terribly from an attack by the fa-

thers, one that almost annihilates him by the Nighttown episode.)

The mad nun screaming for Jesus when Stephen leaves the house provides a caricature of the attitude of Stephen's mother, whose complaints about Stephen's loss of faith are still comparatively mild. They will soon acquire a more hysterical note, however, and in *Ulysses* they will provide a powerful source of demoralization for Stephen. Even now, Stephen's home has the power to depress him, but the accustomed sights and sounds and smells of vegetable nature, the light on the dripping trees, the scent of moistened earth, have the power to soothe him, both here and at the end of this section (*P* 216). He draws about him the names of the great creators: Hauptmann, Newman, Cavalcanti, Ibsen, Ben Jonson. They are his true peers; his college friends are all, with one exception, debased and marked by their environment and their time.

One by one his school friends are introduced to us. All except Davin are less than human in some degree, monstrous, decaying, bestial, or inhumanly mechanical. The half-mad believer in Mind, the deist Temple, is a complete menagerie of beasts. He tries to "catch each flying phrase in his open moist mouth" (*P* 196) like a toad. He has a "bleating voice" (*P* 196) like a sheep. His olive face is "equine in expression" (*P* 196); he resembles a horse. His laughter is "cackling" (*P* 199) like some kind of fowl. Finally, Cranly calls him an "ape" (*P* 200) and a "goat" (*P* 242). This bestiality of Temple is not accidental; in *Ulysses* Stephen links Temple to *Foxy* Campbell and *Buck* Mulligan as the "oval equine faces" (*U* 39). A man who does not mature, who is content to be absorbed by his environment or the past and is content never to project his image on the future, is not a man but an animal. (Ireland, also bestial to Stephen, is a bat, and a sow that eats her farrow [*P* 203, 238; *U* 595].) Moynihan the

mocker is also an animal; he has a "snoutish face" (P 191).
Lynch is also described as bestial. His laugh is "like the
whinny of an elephant" (P 201). He ate dung (P 205)
like some species of scavenger. His skull under his flat cap
reminds Stephen of that of a "hooded reptile . . . the
eyes, too, were reptilelike in glint and gaze" (P 205, 206).
His mind too is full of animality; Stephen notes that Lynch
finds Cranly's anecdote about pigs more memorable than
Stephen's rarefied lectures on esthetics (P 207), and he
exclaims "Bull's eye!" during Stephen's discourse (P 212).
A pig in human form comes up to tell Lynch and Stephen
about the results of the exams; Donovan is fat and
"bloated," and his eyes are encircled with fat. He also
bears the color of the father's livery; he is "pallid" (P
210). The prefect of the college sodality bites at a "tiny
bone pencil" like a carnivorous animal, and his statement,
"We must make sure of the newcomers," sounds ominous
in this context (P 199).

Some of Stephen's instructors are also bestial or birdlike: "the little priest with feathery hair who wrote de-
vout verses . . . the tall form of the young professor of
mental science discussing on the landing a case of conscience with his class like a giraffe cropping high leafage
among a herd of antelopes" (P 192). The rest of his instructors [50] seem to be clowns (P 192).

MacCann does not resemble an animal, but seems
rather like a toy soldier, mechanically articulated and
comically rigid. Cranly represents an even more extreme
form of paralysis. He has been decapitated, "decollated,"
not so much because of his symbolic role as John the Bap-
tist, but because he is only part of a man, morally truncated, the willing slave of the father. All the signs of the
father are there: his face is "pale" (P 194, 245), "priestlike
in its pallor" (P 178), and he is possessed by a "cold sadness" (P 247). His rigidity is that of a corpse rather than,
like MacCann's, a puppet's. Cranly is associated with sug-

gestions of death: decay and "heavy lumpish phrases" like falling clods surround him (*P* 195). His head resembles a skull, a "deathmask" (*P* 178, 248), with a "widewinged nose" (*P* 178) for the nosehole of the skull, "shadowings" below his "dark . . . eyes" for the empty eyesockets of the skull, and "long," "bloodless," and "faintly smiling" lips for the characteristic set smile of the skull (*P* 178). Cranly, compared to a priest on *P* 178, acts in that capacity in the penultimate section of chapter 5: he tries to get Stephen to confess to him. Here is the pallor and coldness of the priestly fathers in its ultimate form, that of the "deathbone."[51] Father ~~nmee had a skull on his desk when young Stephen confronted him; Cranly greatly resembles that skull. In his corpselike acquiescence to the will of the father, Cranly conforms to a literal interpretation of Loyola's definition of the attitude of a Jesuit: "Let each one persuade himself that he ought to allow himself to be ruled and governed by his Superiors . . . as if he were a dead body (*cadaver*)."[52] (MacAlister, like Cranly, is a skull; Stephen uses that word twice when referring to him [*P* 193]. When Stephen imagines MacAlister's face it is, of course, "wheypale" [*P* 193]; MacAlister is another absorbed son.)

Only one of Stephen's friends is neither corpselike bestial, or mechanical: Davin. He is treated seriously both by Joyce and by Stephen, although the latter does call him "my little tame goose" (*P* 201), and accuses him of subservience: "You used to address the jesuits as father" (*P* 202). The incident Davin relates (*P* 181–83) has deep symbolic meaning. Surrounded by darkness, a possibly pregnant girl invites him to her bed. To Stephen the girl is "a type of her race and his own, a batlike soul waking to consciousness of itself in darkness and secrecy and loneliness" (*P* 183). This incident sticks in Stephen's memory; in chapter 5, section three, he imagines a scene of noble incest, the joyless, passionless embraces of a brother and sister, and the brother's hand is Davin's. "Why were they not Cranly's hands? Had Davin's simplicity and innocence stung him more secretly?" (*P* 228). He had suspected Cranly of competing with him for the love of the girl (*P* 232) who ultimately symbolizes Ireland and the earth, the girl on the beach who opens the gates of error and glory to him. Stephen's mind, however, correctly identifies his chief rival for the love of the bird-girl as Davin the patriot, not the truncated Cranly.

Stephen and Davin will fight for the love of their "sister" Ireland all through *Ulysses,* where Davin will be represented by Buck Mulligan and Haines, by the little rich boys in Mr. Deasy's school, and finally, by Privates Carr and Compton. Buck is a "usurper" of Stephen's position as the "lord" of Ireland. "She [Ireland, the old woman] bows her old head to a voice that speaks to her loudly, her bonesetter, her medicineman; me she slights" (*U* 14). She is also silent before Haines, another usurper. Stephen envies the sex life of the little rich boys in his school.

They knew: had never learned nor ever been innocent. All. With envy he watched their faces. Edith, Ethel, Gerty, Lily. Their likes: their breaths, too, sweetened with tea and jam, their bracelets tittering in the struggle. (*U* 24–25)

No wonder Stephen calls Kingstown pier "a disappointed bridge"; the failure of his flight to creation has also been his failure to mature sexually. "And my turn? When?" he asks himself on *U* 191. Privates Carr and Compton escort Cissy Caffrey, an Irish girl, whose name, significantly, sounds like "Sister." (See also *FW* 267. l.1–3.) It is ultimately for her that Stephen and Carr battle. In *Finnegans Wake* Davin's role is taken by Chuff, who is adored by the Maggies, while his brother Glugg sulks. He is also represented by Jaun who is worshipped by all women; Jaun, however, must call in Dave the Dancekerl (his brother

Shem) to consummate the incestuous marriage of brother and sister, "like boyrun to sibster," like Byron to his half-sister Augusta.

Stephen eventually will triumph, but his rivals for the love of Ireland and the earth are dangerous till the end. Shem and Shaun are here opposed for the first time, as rivals for the love of their sister. This is why Davin is treated respectfully by Joyce—he is a great polar symbol.[53] The son is trying to become a father, but he has exterior and interior obstacles to overcome. Not only does the father stand in his way—those of his contemporaries who are not gelded by the father are also striving for fatherhood. At this point they are more successful than Stephen; he, still immature, roughly rejects the young flowergirl immediately after recalling Davin's story (*P* 183–84), and he never quite solves the problem of woman within *A Portrait* (see *P* 248, 249, 250, 251, and finally 252—"O, give it up, old chap!").

The interview with the dean of studies has a different meaning. Here we see a representative of the (temporarily) defeated father deploying his remaining weapons almost without hope, kneeling before the rising generation.

The symbolic meaning of the dean is clear, in terms of the symbolism of the rest of the book—he is a representative of the old father, with a few tricks left in him, getting ready to surrender paternity. His eyes are "pale" ·(*P* 185, 186); the coldness of his soul is suggested by the fact that, as Stephen sees it, "in his eyes burned no spark of Ignatius' enthusiasm. Even the legendary craft of [the Jesuits] . . . had not fired his soul with the energy of apostleship" (*P* 186). The fact that the dean suddenly quotes Epictetus apropos of very little (see Appendix) also contributes a detail to his characterization. Epictetus was a lame slave; the dean is lame (*P* 186) and, Joyce suggests by this detail, also a slave. Stephen sneers openly at the dean's choice of Epictetus as a subject of conversation; Stephen's reference to Epictetus as an "old gentleman" conceals a gibe at the dean's age and debility.

Even though the dean is old and fading, he is a danger to youth. Stephen's description of him contains a scenario of age threatening youth and keeping it from maturity.

Similiter atque senis baculus, he was, as the founder would have had him, like a staff in an old man's hand,[54] to be left in a corner, to be leaned on in the road at nightfall or in stress of weather, to lie with a lady's nosegay on a garden seat, to be raised in menace. (*P* 186)

The old man travels, at night or in storm, to talk to a lady on a garden seat, and to menace—whom? Perhaps the young man whose nosegay the lady has placed on the garden seat. The old man is using a selfless instrument to frustrate the maturity of the young, just as the father is trying to use the dean to prevent Stephen's maturity. There is an episode in Wagner's *Siegfried* which resembles this scenario. Wotan stops Siegfried with his spear, the spear of law, and tries to keep him from seeking his destiny with the maiden Brunhilde on the rock surrounded by flames. Wotan volunteers the information that it was he who with this spear shattered his father Siegmund's sword Nothung and caused his death. Siegfried, outraged by this information and by Wotan's obstruction, shatters Wotan's spear with Nothung, newly forged from the fragments of Siegmund's sword. Wotan steps sadly aside and lets the young hero (his grandson) pass by to the end he sought to serve. In his notes to *Exiles* Joyce refers to the relationship of Wotan and Siegfried: "Wotan . . . in willing the birth and growth of Siegfried longs for his own destruction."[55] Perhaps it is this story that directs the course of Stephen's thought on the *senis baculus;* there are other Wagnerian echoes in this chapter. Therefore, the cry of "Nothung!" as Stephen shatters the lamp in *Ulysses* bears the significance of an attack upon the father, the last of many.

Although Wotan tries to stop the development of his heroic offspring, eventually he acquiesces in his own defeat. If Stephen feels the hostility of the father in the appearance of the dean, the dean himself is humble before the son. The fire that he lights symbolizes the acquiescence of the old order in its own supersession. In *Ulysses*, Stephen remembers six fires that have been lit in his presence, as Leopold Bloom prepares to light the kitchen fire (*U* 670). Each of these fires has been lit by a representative of an old order when the emerging order was beginning to be recognized. On *P* 23, 26, Brother Michael rakes and then lights the infirmary fire just before the news of the death of Parnell is announced; as I have tried to show above, Stephen steps in and alters the historical situation of fear and subservience that accompanied the reaction to Parnell's death, and is therefore in some degree Parnell's successor. On *P* 65–66 Simon Dedalus stands before a dying fire, proclaiming a faith in himself which is, we see, unjustified; he is about to step down unwillingly in favor of his son. A fire burns in the house of the dying sister of Stephen's godmother on *P* 67; the atmosphere is heavy with senile decay and the passing old order cannot even recognize the new order. Stephen's mother (presumably) has lit a fire on the eve before Stephen's communion after his terrified confession of his sins following the sermon on hell (*P* 146); by the time of the fire, however, Stephen has basically come out from under the father's influence. The dean of studies' fire is the fifth mentioned on *U* 670. The last is the fire kindled by "his sister Dilly (Delia) in his father's house in Cabra." This is possibly a reference to the squalid home-scene recalled by Stephen on *U* 620. (Dilly was serving Stephen by boiling "some weak Trinidad shell cocoa" for him.) The dean of studies, by his action of lighting the fire, takes his place among those who serve the young artist, who symbolize by that act the passing of their power or their willing submission to his. The dean of studies is not only a lame slave, "a humble server" (*P* 185) of the father, he is in some degree a slave or server of the maturing son. Stephen in his turn is so sure of his victory that he can afford pity to this "half-brother of the clergy . . . one whom he would never call his ghostly father" (*P* 190), and he generously exonerates him and the Jesuits as a whole from Pascal's charge of laxity and casuistry. This detached justice is the final sign of Stephen's freedom.

Other episodes of symbolic importance occur during and after Stephen's refusal to sign MacCann's petition supporting the Tsar's campaign for international arbitration of disputes. Of course the insurgent son rejects the notion of arbitration; he thinks he is going to win. The Tsar and the other monarchs, the great authoritarian father figures who advocate world understanding, would seem, from the son's point of view, to be recommending a freezing of the status quo which the son, hoping to topple the father from his place of power, could not accept. After having avoided this trap, Stephen repels another attack launched by Davin in the name of patriotism. In keeping with Davin's metaphysical dignity as a Shaun-figure, Stephen addresses him as if he were Ireland and rejects orthodox nationalist agitation as his role, although Stephen is in his way as dedicated a nationalist as Davin. It is not that Stephen rejects nationalism for internationalism; we have just seen him rebuff MacCann. Stephen's nationalism is more purely "internal" and Mazzinian than Davin's, and he insists on a Mazzinian awakening of the racial conscience before any struggle for freedom can have any meaning. If unawakened Ireland attempts to keep the souls of its sons from "flight" with its nets of nationality, language, religion, then it is not ready for freedom; it is "the old sow that eats her farrow" (*P* 203) .[56]

In the course of his rejection of Davin's invitation Stephen shows how clear the process of development of his soul toward its *telos* has become to him.

The soul is born . . . first in those moments I told you of. [Stephen apparently had told Davin about some of the significant episodes in his life, some of the points through which the curve of his personality could be traced.] It has a slow and dark birth, more mysterious than the birth of the body. (*P* 203)

Stephen is almost entirely self-conscious now, conscious of the outline of his personality and of his vocation. The darkness of the soul's birth has provided one of the major affinities of his personality; it is in the name of the necessary nourishing darkness of the soul's development that he will strike at the light in *Ulysses*. He is not, however, completely mature; although his vocational ceremony has stamped him an artist, he is not yet a "father" or prepared to be one in any creative or moral sense. The "cold violence" (*P* 203) of his insult to Ireland should mark it as coming from some other source than the "warmth" of the young artist; "coldness" is an attribute of the forces that oppose the artist's growth. (Indeed, Joyce himself in his maturity never wrote about anything but the old sow that ate her farrow; *Dubliners*, *A Portrait*, *Ulysses*, and *Finnegans Wake* are all gigantic portraits of Ireland.)

The longest narrative unit in this section contains Stephen's lecture on esthetics. I do not intend to analyze Stephen's doctrines in detail; that has been done often enough. For my purposes, it is possible to see the lecture in another light than that of a guide to Joyce's own methods of writing. It is not as a hint to the reader about what to expect in the writings of Joyce, but as a setting for an extremely important symbol of the matured creator, King David, that I intend to treat this section.

Joyce himself in two places in this section hints that the lecture is not to be taken *au pied de la lettre*.

They had reached the canal bridge and, turning from their course, went on by the trees. A crude grey light . . . and a smell of wet branches over their heads seemed to war against the course of Stephen's thought. (*P* 207)

In other parts of chapter 5, however, the smells of moist nature encourage Stephen and soothe his heart. At the beginning of the chapter

as he walked down the avenue and felt the grey morning light falling about him through the dripping trees and smelt the strange wild smell of the wet leaves and bark, his soul was loosed of her miseries. (*P* 176)

At the end of this section, wet nature calms his spirit again and mollifies his attitude toward what he believes to be his beloved's disloyalty.

The quick light shower had drawn off, tarrying in clusters of diamonds among the shrubs of the quadrangle where an exhalation was breathed forth by the blackened earth. . . .

And if he had judged her harshly? If her life were a simple rosary of hours, her life simple and strange as a bird's life? (*P* 216)

These two passages occur at the very beginning of chapter 5, section 1, and at the very end, as if Joyce were insisting upon the symbolic meaning and effects of the scents of nature upon Stephen's soul. (Joyce himself was often soothed by Nature's moister aspects; see Ellmann, p. 208.) If, therefore, moist nature is congenial to Stephen's spirit and soothing to his sensibilities, the fact that the smell of wet branches seems to "war against the cause of Stephen's thought" suggests to me that Stephen's soul, his vocation, is fighting his static doctrine of art, that his theory of esthetics is an incomplete collection of other people's insights. The dray loaded with old iron that interrupts the climax of Stephen's lecture on *P* 209 is literally an "ironic" portrait of Stephen's theorizing; both the dray and the lecture contain nothing but sounding fragments of the disjected past.

In Joyce's own terms, the esthetic principles enunciated by Stephen are incomplete. In the Paris notebooks of 1903 which contain the original version of the esthetics lecture, Joyce insists that the highest form of art is *comic* art; "tragedy is the imperfect manner and comedy the perfect manner in art." He was determined to write a comedy after his first book of poems, as he declared to his mother, in a letter of March 20, 1903 (*Letters* 2:38). All theorizing about comedy is deliberately omitted from Stephen's lecture, perhaps to make him more rigidly solemn than Joyce himself was at that age.[57]

Whether or not the lecture on esthetics is to be taken literally as Joyce's guide to the understanding of his work, one thing does stand out from Stephen's definition of the process of artistic apprehension—the supreme role of the artist. The artist is not a mere servant of the muse, a nameless conduit through which pours the unordered universe. It is the artist's timeless moments of apprehension that are considered worthy of being embodied in their perfect rhythmic analogues and sent forth as art; conversely, anything that is "epiphanized" to him is *ipso facto* material for a work of art. This blind trust in the ability of the man of genius to make no errors in his life or his art (see *U* 190) characterizes both Stephen and Joyce; Stephen's vocation, growing within him, has kept him from deviating from his line of growth as a true artist; young Joyce considered his epiphanies worth writing down, and mature Joyce rejected very little that experience handed him, confident that the mind of a born artist could not absorb irrelevancies for his art; hence the relevance of the tons of material gathered without apparent system for *Ulysses* and *Finnegans Wake*.

This lordly definition of the artist finds a perfect symbol within the esthetics-lecture episode. On *P* 210

Lynch, amused by Stephen's earlier claim that he is able to "express, to press out again, from the gross earth or what it brings forth, from sound and shape and colour which are the prison gates of our soul, an image of the beauty we have come to understand" (*P* 207), sings a stanza from Venantius's hymn *Vexilla regis prodeunt*. It is not the first stanza, as one might expect, but the fourth. Lynch's deliberate choice of this stanza makes Stephen appear as King David preaching to the nations the advent of Christ, who is in this case an esthetic Messiah.

> Impleta sunt quae concinit
> David fideli carmine
> Dicendo nationibus
> Regnavit a ligno Deus.

The figure of David, the artist as king and priest, appears many times in many guises in the works of Joyce and sums up Joyce's mature conception of the development, nature, and role of the artist. As an exceedingly full and complex symbol, Joyce's David includes within himself many of the interpretations of David throughout history, from Augustine to the German romantics. Lynch hints at the most exalted possible interpretation of David —the predictor and type of the Messiah. David is also, however, the model of the kingly creator, the creative artist at his most mature, and the goal toward which young Stephen has been striving from his earliest childhood. Joyce was aware of traditional interpretations of David, and his employment of the symbol is based upon these interpretations. In approaching the meaning of the King David symbol in Joyce, I will first outline the development of the historical meaning of David, touching only upon writers Joyce may have read or otherwise encountered, and then point out how and where Joyce uses and expands these interpretations in his books.

To the modern mind, the David of the Bible is perhaps the most clearly characterized personality in the Old Testament. As the initiator of Israel's golden age, he and the history of his reign are covered in close detail in the first and second books of Kings and again in Chronicles. He is many things—shepherd, musician, composer of the psalms, therapist (for Saul), false madman like Hamlet (1 Sam. 21:10–15), guerrilla warrior, dancer, king, adulterer, unhappy father, builder of the Temple of Jerusalem, guardian of the Ark of the Covenant, and finally, descendant of Ruth and ancestor of Christ. Each age has its own interpretation of David; each finds in him a symbol of the deepest concerns of its time.

The middle ages found in David a rich source of symbolism. Primarily, he was a prophet of the coming of Christ and a prefiguring in his own person and life of the life of Christ. The medieval commentators on the psalms declare this unequivocally, and in medieval illustrations of the psalms he is often painted as Christ in majesty, with the dove of the Holy Spirit descending on his head.[58] He was also the ideal king; Byzantine emperors were called *novus David*.[59] His talents for song and dance were similarly exalted by the middle ages. Like that of Orpheus, his playing attracted and subdued the beasts.[60] (Indeed, the illustrations of David harping in ancient Irish art seem to have been influenced by drawings of Orpheus playing to the beasts.)[61] David's music, inspired by the spirit of revelation, was in itself a microcosm of the just order of the universe; Augustine, basing his analysis of David's psalms on the Pythagorean belief that the universe is constructed on harmonic proportions, declares that

David was a man skilled in songs, who dearly loved musical harmony, not with a vulgar delight, but with a believing disposition, and by it served his God, who is the true God, by the mystical representation of a great thing. For the rational and well-ordered concord of diverse sounds in harmonious variety suggests the compact order of the well-ordered city.[62]

As the prophet and symbol of world order, David represents the meeting-point of the great symbolic systems of
the universe; Joachim of Flora considers him the link
between earthly and heavenly order.[63] In some medieval
illustrations he is surrounded by the Four Daughters of
God—Prudence, Fortitude, Temperance, and Justice—
and by representatives of other quadripartite symbolic
entities—the four seasons, four elements, four humours,
the Quadrivium, and so on.[64] Neo-Pythagoreans linked
David's composition of the psalms to the creation of the
universe from the ten numerals.[65]

In addition to his role as prophet, David was considered the model of the *princeps litteratus,* the educated
ruler. This strong tradition lasted through the renaissance
and influenced the theorizing of the minnesingers. The
emperor Henry VI, who was a minnesinger, appears in a
famous illustration as a typical David-figure.[66] As a royal
sage David was also a *vates,* a poetic prophet. Germanic
tradition had always assigned such a role to kings; [67] now
the tradition was fortified by religious symbology.

In the middle ages, therefore, David became the
symbol of inspiration, of ability to read the future and to
control the present by means of his art, his majesty, and
the grace of God. The reference to David in the stanza
from Venantius is in this tradition. David sings to the
nations that God shall reign from wood, in a medieval
version of Ps. 96:10. In modern versions of the psalm the
verse merely declares that God will reign; in some early
Christian texts the words "from wood" appear after
"reign." Augustine, anticipating medieval belief, declares, in his comment on Ps. 96 in *Expositions of the
Book of Psalms,* that this verse contains a clear prophecy
of the coming of Christ.[68]

Dante draws upon the medieval tradition about
David twice in the *Commedia.* In *Purgatorio,* 10. 64–69,
David's dancing before the Ark (2 Sam. 6) is carved in

marble as an example of humility to the proud who are expiating their sin. David had brought the Ark of the Covenant to Jerusalem and was so overcome with joy that he danced before it clad only in a linen "ephod," or short mantle. His wife Michol, seeing him capering before the Ark, despised him in her heart, and later reproached him for making a spectacle of himself before the people. Dante interprets David's dancing as a mark of humility before the Lord: "In that hour he was more and less than King." [69] Although condemnations of dancing were not rare in the middle ages, David's dance was specifically excepted from this condemnation. Ambrose defends David on the grounds that everything is seemly which is done for religion.[70] Manuscripts and scriptures from all over medieval Europe show David dancing, in a great variety of postures.[71] Some drawings show him as a naked, prancing, idiotlike figure; others have him doing a sort of war dance or sword dance, in which he juggles swords, knives, and helmets.[72] David's dancing is as prominent a characteristic of this *princeps litteratus* as his singing. As a symbol of artistic achievement he sums up in himself three art forms —music, dancing, and poetry. In *Finnegans Wake* Joyce resurrects this tripartite talent of David in the figure of Shem in his role as "Dave the Dancekerl" ("Dave the Dancer" in the first drafts of *Finnegan*).

Perhaps a more important aspect of David is shown in *Paradiso,* 20. 31–42. David is shown to Dante in the heaven of Jupiter, the heaven of those rulers who have striven for the public good. David is in the pupil of the eye of the heavenly eagle which addresses Dante.

> Fix firm thy gaze on me, and view that part
>   Which in your earthly eagles," thus it said,
>   "Sees and endures the sun's most fiery smart;
>
> For of the fires wherewith I've architected
>   My figured shape, the chief of rank and mark
>   Are those with whom the eye shine in my head.

> Midmost, as 'twere the pupil, burns that spark
> Which was the minstrel of the Holy Spirit,
> And once from town to town bore forth the ark;
>
> And now he knows how much his own songs merit,
> So far as 'twas his art that shaped the strain,
> For even as he deserved, he doth inherit . . .
> (*Laurence Binyon trans.*)

The revelation of the nature of God vouchsafed to David is here symbolized by David's position in the eagle's pupil; in life, David "saw" the order of the universe, and sang it forth in his creations. This interpretation of David is of great importance to the form of *A Portrait*. In the first section, Aunt Dante refers to eagles and eyes: "O, if not the eagles will come and pull out his eyes" (*P* 8). In the epiphany upon which this episode is based, it is Mr. Vance, Eileen's father, who makes the reference to eagles and eyes. Joyce deliberately shifts the statement to Aunt Dante as an allusion to this passage from *Paradiso* and ties together the first chapter and last of *A Portrait* by the reference to David, the visionary artist-king. (A sheet of notes for the Circe episode, BM Add. Mss. 49975, contains the words "eagle eye" crossed out in red.) David's most important characteristic for Dante is his reality-piercing vision. It is important for Joyce also; in *Finnegans Wake* a "seeboy" named Davy strikes at the Willingdone (*FW* 10.12–22).[73]

Joyce was acquainted with Dante and with at least the names of the medieval commentators on the psalms whose interpretations of David are given above, either directly or from some secondary source. He takes considerable pains to introduce quotations from Augustine and Ambrose in *Ulysses*. Augustine's *Confessions* 7. 12 is quoted on *U* 142 and there is a reference to his doctrines on *U* 391.[74] On *U* 49 a phrase from Ambrose's *Commentary on Romans* floats into Stephen's mind.[75] Joachim of Flora puts in an appearance both in *Stephen Hero* (*SH* 176) and in *Ulysses* (*U* 39).[76]

Joyce conceals the names of many medieval commentators on the psalms in *Finnegans Wake*. Six are mentioned in the Dave the Dancekerl section (*FW* 461–68) : Augustine, Ambrose, Sedulius Scottus (the ninth-century Irish monk who defined the character of David as the *princeps litteratus*) , Basilius, Eucherius of Lyons, and Priscus: Augustine, (*FW* 468.4), Ambrose (*FW* 467.5), Eucherius (*FW* 462.1), Sedulius (*FW* 466.21),[77] Basilius (*FW* 463.22) , and Priscus (*FW* 467.32) . Augustine, moreover, is a major source of phrases in *Finnegans Wake;*[78] in his 1912 lecture on Blake, Joyce showed familiarity with the *City of God*.[79] The names of the medieval commentators on David that appear in the Dave the Dancekerl section, and many others, are scattered throughout the *Wake* in various guises;[80] some, like Gregory the Great, Gregory of Nyssa, Bruno Carthusius, Bruno of Wurzburg, St. Jerome, Hilary of Poitiers, and John Chrysostom (mentioned on the first page of *Ulysses*) , are hidden by the names of major figures in the *Wake*—Matthew Gregory, Giordano Bruno, Jerry, the twin of Kevin,[81] Hilary, the twin of Tristopher, and Shaun. Others put in appearances in one form or another; Ambrose appears at *FW* 85.32, 127.36, and 605.30, as well as in the Dave the Dancekerl section; Barnabas, the author of a second-century note on the relationship of the Old and New Testaments, appears at *FW* 337.36 and 572.34; Basilius appears at *FW* 463.22, and perhaps in many other places; the name of Bede is hidden by the word "bead" which appears in many places; Cassiodorus appears at *FW* 255.21; Eusebius appears at *FW* 409.36 and perhaps at 528.14; Eucherius of Lyons appears at *FW* 110.34 and 304.R3, as well as in the Dave the Dancekerl section; Haymo of Halberstadt appears at *FW* 68.5, 247.14 and perhaps at 499.11; Hrabanus Maurus appears at *FW* 72.13; Ivo of Chartres seems to appear at *FW* 29.4 and 31.32, but his name is partly hidden by "Iveagh," one of the brewing brothers of Iveagh and

Ardilaun, the brewers of Guinness; Priscus appears at *FW* 494.11, as well as in the Dave the Dancekerl section; Rufinus of Aquileia appears at *FW* 366.23.

On the basis of these references, it seems likely that Joyce was acquainted with at least the names of the medieval interpretors of the psalms who made David out to be a clear-sighted visionary into the processes of the universe and a consummate, lordly artist who bodied forth his vision of the universe with his arts of song and dance.

Joyce also knew of renaissance views of David as a mage and a cabalist which enriched his concept of this symbol. Pico della Mirandola, the renaissance prodigy and cabalist, with whom Joyce was acquainted (he mentions him on *U* 40 and in his 1907 lecture, "Ireland, Island of Saints and Sages"),[82] held that the psalms of David were magical compositions

incantations powerful for the works of Cabala, as the hymns of Orpheus are of value for natural magic. . . . Thus a practical Cabalist singing a psalm is performing a rite similar to the natural magician intoning an Orphic hymn—similar, but more powerful, because we are told in another Orphic conclusion . . . that the Orphic hymns have no power unless "the work of Cabala" is added to them.[83]

Pico's interpretation of David as a mage whose works contain magical clues to the nature of the universe obviously owes something to Augustine's view of David's psalms as symbols of the holy city and to the medieval tradition of David as the seer of God. This interpretation of David as mage could not have been uncongenial to Joyce: his Daedalian artist, the hawklike man, derives from this renaissance tradition of the artist as magical seer. Giordano Bruno in his *La cena de le ceneri,* dial. 1, defines the mage's vision in terms of flight.

And now, what shall I say concerning the Nolan? . . . If in days of old Tiphys was to be praised who invented the first

ship and voyaged across the ocean with the Argonauts . . . if
in our times Columbus receives honour . . . what then shall
be said of him who has found a way to mount up to the sky
. . . ? The Nolan . . . has released the human spirit, and set
knowledge at liberty. Man's mind was suffocating in the close
air of a narrow prison house whence only dimly and, as it
were, through chinks could he behold the far distant stars. His
wings were clipped, so that he might not soar upwards through
the cloudy veil to see what really lies beyond it . . . Behold
now, standing before you, the man who has pierced the air and
penetrated the sky, wended his way amongst the stars and over-
passed the margins of the world.[84]

The mage (in this case Bruno the Nolan himself) and the
artist are equated by Joyce and symbolized by him as
Daedalus.[85] Bruno's definition of the mage as seer and
Pico's definition of David the artist as mage both influenced Joyce's definition of the artist as seer, or "seeboy";
Davy the "seeboy" in the Willingdone Museyroom episode
of *Finnegans Wake* (*FW* 10) "sees" through the nature
of the universe and then strikes at the father's power.
    David becomes the patron and practitioner of a
learned and deliberate art among the German *meistersingers* of the fifteenth and sixteenth centuries. The *Posten-
brief,* the shield hung up to announce meetings of the
meistersingers of Iglau in Moravia, showed a garland and
a *Davidgroschen,* prizes for the best singer and composer,
and David enthroned in the background, as well as two
scenes from the psalms and one of David with his harp.[86]
The historical Hanns Sachs of Nürnberg composed five
plays about the life of David. David, among the meistersingers, is the symbol and inspirer of their deliberately
controlled and shaped art—he is an esthetic model rather
than, as above, a magical one. Joyce was familiar with
this interpretation of David through Wagner's *Meistersinger,* which he said was his favorite Wagnerian opera; [87]
in the opera a large portrait of David enthroned and play-

ing on his harp is borne before the Meistersingers in the third act as they parade out to the contest of song.

David acquires additional significance in the eighteenth century. In response to the deistic attack on David as an unworthy vessel of God's election launched by Pierre Bayle in the *Philosophical Dictionary* and followed up in English by Thomas Chubb, Patrick Delany, the friend and biographer of Swift, wrote a three-part defense of David which reveals the state of speculation about David in the eighteenth century.[88] The first part of *An Historical Account of the Life, and Reign of David, King of Israel* . . . was published in 1740, and the second and third parts in 1743. Delany is fertile in inventing doubtful history. Quoting Isaac Newton's *Chronology*, he suggests that David originated the arts of letters, poetry, and music, which were then carried by the Phoenicians to the Greeks and thence to the rest of the world. "David was the first of all, that were, properly and professedly poets." [89] He also suggests that David and Orpheus were the same man, although he admits "it may be thought a wild conjecture." [90]

David was the sweet singer of Israel. If we derive *Orpheus* from the Greek, it is a composition of two words, which signify a *fine* or *sweet* voice ([*horaia phone*]).[91]

Delany also suggests various influences on Homer from the psalms,[92] a suggestion that Joyce, with his eagerness to believe in Semitic influences on Homer, would find congenial.

The deists had also reproached David for his naked dancing before the Ark; Delany fiercely defends him. Dancing is graceful, joyful, healthful, and conducive to the formation of manners, piety, and virtue. Orpheus was a dancer, Delany declares upon the evidence of Lucian, and he made dancing part of worship; David's dancing was also religious in origin, and was therefore not a frivolous amusement but an act of worship and invocation.[93]

It was practiced on solemn occasions in the ancient world; Delany especially singles out for mention the dancing of the Salii, the Roman priesthood, whose practices, he says, were derived from those of the Jewish priesthood performing David's psalms.[94]

Joyce was acquainted with Delany; he mentions him twice in *Finnegans Wake* (*FW* 43.33, 84.8); the name of Delany's famous house in Glasnevin, Delville, appears on *FW* 43.26 and 503.17. Moreover, Joyce used Delany's association of David's dancing with the religious dancing of the Greeks and Romans in his works. In a sheet of notes for the Circe episode of *Ulysses* (BM Add. MSS. 49975) he has written "jig: warlike: relig (jews) esth (Gr)" just above the words "eagle eye" (which refer to David: see above). In the Circe episode in *Ulysses* Stephen distractedly mutters something about the "priests haihooping round David's that is Circe's or what am I saying Ceres' altar" (*U* 504). The dance of the Salian priesthood mentioned by Delany is a war dance as well as a religious dance —it is a *tripudium*. The Salian priesthood, according to Livy, were appointed by Numa, and their worship included a war dance called the *tripudium:* "Salios . . . ancilia . . . ferre ac per urbem ire canentes carmina, cum tripudiis sollenique saltatu jussit." [95] The twelve Salian priests would go through the city with their hourglass-shaped shields singing their sacred songs, and dancing the *tripudium* gravely. That the *tripudium* is a war dance or sword dance is clear from other references in Livy. The Galatian Celts sang as they went into battle, and danced the *tripudium* and clashed their shields to terrify their foes: "cantus ineuntium proelium et ululatus et tripudia." [96] At another place in Livy, book 21 of the *History*, Hannibal returned their weapons to captured Iberian (Celtic?) mountaineers in order to give them a chance for freedom; they snatched them up and burst into their customary war dance: "exsultans cum sui moris tripudiis." [97]

(Joyce certainly knew of this reference; he read book 21 of Livy's *History* for his second-class honors in Latin at the university.) [98] One of the facets of David's personality that Joyce derived from a combination of Livy and Delany, therefore, is an interpretation of David's dance before the Ark as a close relative of the war dance of the Salian priesthood in Rome, a war dance which was also performed by Galatian and Iberian Celts, and by Stephen Dedalus in Bella Cohen's kip.[99] (I will analyze this part of *Ulysses* in a later section.)

Delany's David was considered by him to be the source of the major arts, a characteristic postrenaissance interpretation. A later interpretation of David was offered by the continental romantics, that of the young artist who fights the old-fogy Philistines. In 1835 Robert Schumann, battling musical conservatives in his new musical journal, the *Neue Leipziger Zeitschrift für Musik,* created a brotherhood of kin-spirits called the *Davidsbund.* The Davidsbund was composed of Schumann himself under three pseudonyms, a few of his friends, his wife Clara, Chopin, Brahms, Berlioz, Mendelssohn, and many allies from the past, including Bach and Mozart. This little band, similar in conception and purpose to many fictional, quasi-Masonic organizations of the time such as Carl Maria von Weber's *Harmonic Union* and E. T. A. Hoffman's *Serapionsbrüder,* was designed to organize plots against the stodgy *grossvaters* of the world, to wake them up to the fact that a new generation had come along to destroy the old world with new art. Nor did Schumann rest content with his journalistic creation; in *Carnaval,* his suite for piano written in 1834–35, the pieces are named for members of the *Davidsbund,* and the last piece is a full-scale musical depiction of a battle between the *Davidsbund* and the Philistines. In this *Marche des Davidsbundler contre les Philistins,*[100] a proud, thrusting youthful melody battles a fatuous old folksong, whose text originally praised "the way things were done in grandfather's time" and which represents everything Philistine, limited, and old. Schumann followed up *Carnaval* with the *Davidsbundlertänze* in 1837. In Schumann's circle David came to stand for the power of art to overthrow the forces of dullness, and for the power of rebellious youth to supersede age on the throne of authority. Joyce was almost certainly acquainted with this interpretation of David by the time of the writing of *Finnegans Wake;* one of his closest friends in Paris was Marcel Brion, a contributor to the *Exagmination* in 1929 and an authority on Schumann. Brion's book on Schumann, *Schumann et l'ame romantique,* Paris, 1954, contains a full account of the *Davidsbund.*[101] Joyce's David, like Schumann's, attacks the older generation. In *Ulysses* Davy Stephens, a "king's courier" (*U* 116) who combines in his name King David and Stephen, reveals the secret of the sexual inadequacy of the older generation symbolized by Bloom (*U* 469), and in *Finnegans Wake* the "davy" in the Willingdone Museyroom throws a bomb at the "big wide harse" of the older generation (*FW* 10).

A less militant but equally uncompromising view of David as the romantic artist is to be found in Goethe's *Wilhelm Meisters Lehrjahre,* the archetypal *bildungsroman* and *entwicklungsroman,* the model for the genre to which *A Portrait* belongs.[102]

Wilhelm Meisters Lehrjahre, the first section of *Wilhelm Meister,* is a carefully plotted book.[103] Although on the literal level the novel contains little more than the journeyings of young Wilhelm with a theatrical troupe, it is basically the story of the development of an artistic soul toward "fatherhood," in every sense of the word, and therefore close to *A Portrait* in its underlying theme. *Wilhelm Meisters Lehrjahre* is a symbolic tale of the growth of an artist amid the Philistinism of his time.[104] Young Wilhelm, interested in the theatre from his youth, joins a theatrical company and travels with it throughout Germany. After many adventures he is inducted into a mystical order, the Brotherhood of the Tower, and from the head of the order discovers the great secret of his life—he is a father. It turns out that Wilhelm had fathered a little boy, Felix, upon an actress, but this casual liaison is explained by the head of the order as the most important act of Wilhelm's life (an Aristotelian conclusion).[105] Wilhelm returns home, to discover that the bosom companion of his youth, Werner, has become a melancholy, commercial drudge. The book ends with the contrast of the "fulfilled" creative Wilhelm, an adult and a father, with the sterile, futile Werner.

King David presides over the beginning of the fortunes of Wilhelm. The earliest creative endeavor of Wilhelm is to stage the conflict of David and Goliath on his puppet stage. He later proceeds to stage other episodes from the life of David with his puppets.[106] In the carefully controlled symbolic world of *Wilhelm Meisters Lehrjahre* this positioning of David is of the greatest importance. By staging the life of David, Wilhelm sets out on his development in art, and shows his difference from Philistines like Werner. David's significance in Goethe is very close to that he bears among the Schumann set of the *Davidsbund*—the inspiration of the romantic artist, and his ally against the Philistines.[107]

Joyce was obviously acquainted with the works of Goethe and with *Wilhelm Meister*.[108] It is unlikely that the prominent symbolic role played by David escaped him or failed to affect his image of the romantic artist as a being in conflict with the stodgy Philistine giants of his time.[109]

The personality that emerges when these historical versions of David are added up is extremely rich and dense. David is the prophet and type of the Messiah, a singer of true songs and a dancer of warlike, sacerdotal dances, a king and a poet, whose works proceed from a clear-sighted grasp of the nature of reality and which reflect this knowledge by being in themselves magical microcosms, the practitioner and patron of a learned art, and the progenitor of the historical genres of art who, by his activity, causes the old order to yield place unwillingly to the new.

Joyce's artist contains all of these elements in his personality. Stephen sees himself as kingly; his difference from his fellows is constantly asserted, and on the beach his falling schoolmates remind him of "his mild proud sovereignty" (*P* 168). Stephen's name means "crown," and he is conscious of its significance: *"Stephanos,* my crown" (*U* 210). Stephen thinks of Buck Mulligan as a "usurper" (*U* 23) of his rightful kingdom. In the Oxen of the Sun episode Stephen reasserts his sovereignty over the past that is his to form into art.

You have spoken of the past and its phantoms, Stephen said. Why think of them? If I call them into life across the waters of Lethe will not the poor ghosts troop to my call? Who supposes it? I, Bous Stephanoumenos, bullockbefriending bard, am lord and giver of their life. (*U* 415)

Finally Stephen surprises Bloom by asserting that Ireland belongs to him (*U* 645). Ireland is in the memory of an artist who will make it the subject of immortal art—in this sense Stephen is the king of his country.

David's song and dance are also Stephen's. In the very beginning of *A Portrait,* on the first page, young Stephen has a song and a dance:

> *O, the wild rose blossoms*
> *On the little green place.*

He sang that song. That was his song. . . . [his mother] played on the piano the sailor's hornpipe for him to dance. He danced:

> *Tralala lala*
> *Tralala tralaladdy,*
> *Tralala lala*
> *Tralala lala* (*P* 7)

Stephen feels his throat "throbbing with song" at the height of one of the waves of exaltation of his vocational ceremony (*P* 170), and the inspiration for his first composition in his new role as king-creator, the villanelle of the Temptress, comes to him accompanied by "faint sweet music" (*P* 217). In *Ulysses* (*U* 504) David's 18th psalm is the occasion for much metaphysical theorizing on Stephen's part,[110] and Stephen's dance, his "tripudium," causes the dead to rise and precipitates the final conflict. After Private Carr has delivered his celebrated sock in the jaw and dispelled Stephen's hesitancy, Stephen sings incessantly. In fact, he sings almost more than he speaks, although earlier in the book he did not sing at all; (Almidano Artifoni reproaches him gently for neglecting his singing on *U* 228; see also *U* 394, 518, 519). Even while Stephen is unconscious from the effect of Private Carr's blow, he begins to sing (*U* 608).

STEPHEN
. . . (*he sighs and stretches himself, then murmurs thickly with prolonged vowels.*)
    Who . . . drive . . . Fergus now.
    And pierce . . . wood's woven shade?

(The "prolonged vowels" indicate that Stephen is singing the setting of Yeats's poem that he mentions on *U* 9). Walking home with Bloom, Stephen performs "exquisite variations" on an air *Youth here has End* (a significant title) by Jans Pieter Sweelinck, and sings an old German song about sirens by Johann (not Johannes) Jeep (*U* 663). Once in Bloom's house, Stephen sings the Harry Hughes song (*U* 690–91) and quotes the first line of the Irish song *Shool Aroon* (*U* 688). Finally, as if to nail down the identification of Stephen with David, Stephen leaves Bloom's house intoning *"secreto"* David's 113th psalm, *In exitu Israël de Egypto* (*U* 698), and as Stephen walks away under "the chariot of David" (The Big Dipper) (*U* 700),

the "double vibration of a jew's harp" is heard on Eccles
street (*U* 704). The message that can be deciphered from
these songs is simple: I am no longer a child, to be enticed
into danger and destroyed; I intend to walk safely, out of
the house of bondage. Stephen has found his voice again
and has passed out of the dreadful period of guilt and
sterility induced by his father's telegram and his mother's
death. A *princeps litteratus,* he is finally ready for creation.

David appears in his traditional role as the Messiah,
the Davidic King who is the focus of Jewish hopes for
secular deliverance, in two places in *Ulysses.* One refers to
his political significance; the other treats him as a mystical-sexual saviour.

In Bloom's home, Stephen and Bloom begin to com-
pare the Irish and the Jews. The last point of similarity
between them is the Irish and Jewish hope for autonomy
and national self-determination, "the restoration in
Chanan David of Zion and the possibility of Irish political
autonomy or devolution" (*U* 688–89). Bloom then sings
the first "distich" of *Hatikvah,* which helps to elucidate
the words "Chanan David." On a set of notes for the Ithaca
chapter (BM Add. Mss. 49975/733E) Joyce has written
down and crossed out (in blue) the first two lines of the
first stanza of *Hatikvah* in the form they appear in *Ulysses;*
underneath on the notesheet appears Joyce's version of the
last two lines of the first stanza, which Bloom could not recall due to "defective mnemotechnic":

> Luschuw l'erez abatejnu
> Erbah David chanah.

The first line is not crossed out; the second is crossed out
in blue, indicating its use in the Ithaca chapter. Joyce obviously got these lines from the same source that provided
the first two, probably a Germanic one (Svevo?), as the
transliteration conventions suggest. (Joyce has not got
them completely right, of course; the lines should sound

more like "Lashuv l'eretz avotenu, / Le'ir ba David chanah.") "Chanah," or "Chanan" as Joyce allows it to be misspelled in *Ulysses,* is not a Hebrew version of "Canaan" as Joyce seems to think; it simply means "dwelled" or "camped," and the whole distich means "To the land of our fathers / where David dwelled." *Hatikvah,* "the hope," was the Zionist anthem and is now the Israeli national anthem. The first stanza, now altered to fit the happy ful-fillment of Zionist hope, expresses the longing of the Jews for the Messianic deliverance from exile, so similar to Ulysses's longing for home; the land of Israel is identified with David, the greatest king of Israel, the model for all earthly kings, and the ancestor of the Messiah.[111] David is, therefore, the symbol of political deliverance to the Jews and, in this context, to the Irish also. In *A Portrait* (*P* 253), Stephen expresses his intention to forge the uncre-ated conscience of his people and thus prepare them for their autonomy. In *Ulysses* the identification of Stephen with David reinforces Stephen's pledge to free his people.

David appears as another form of Messiah within the Circe chapter of *Ulysses.* Bloom, ascending the ladder of glory in his mind (he has just been crowned "emperor president and king chairman"), is about to become the Messiah and attain a debased form of martyrdom. A voice asks him, "Bloom, are you the Messiah ben Joseph or ben David?" Somewhat at a loss, Bloom gives Christ's reply be-fore Pilate, "You have said it" (*U* 495). As we later dis-cover, Bloom has a "sewn pamphlet" in his library, *Phi-losophy of the Talmud* (*U* 708), in which this matter is (presumably) treated and from which he draws the neces-sary knowledge about this dark matter. (In fact, however, it is doubtful if the book exists; it is not to be found in the catalogues of the British Museum, or in the Library of Congress, or in the Hebraic collection of the New York Public Library.)[112]

Wherever Joyce acquired his knowledge of Hebrew

Messianism, he must have known that he was getting into
deep waters. The *Zohar*, the main text of Hebrew mysticism, declares that there are four Messiahs to come.[113] The
Talmud's treatment of the Messiah limits his representatives to two: the Messiah ben Joseph, the suffering servant
of Isa. 53, where it is declared that the Messiah will suffer
and die for his people, and the Messiah ben David, the
triumphant prince and redeemer of Israel, as in Isa. 9 and
11. (Jewish tradition does not accept the reconciliation of
these predictions by the resurrection of Christ.) [114] Bloom
cleverly resolves the problem by answering in Christ's
words; Christ was the descendant both of David (see Matt.
1:1–6, and Luke 3:23–28) and of "Joseph the joiner." [115]
However, Bloom's hallucinatory career stops short with
(comfortable) martyrdom; presumably he is not to be the
triumphant Messiah ben David.

The Messiah ben David, according to the *Zohar*, will
play an extremely important mystical-sexual role upon his
appearance: he will reconcile the four letters of the Tetragrammaton, the ineffable name of God, which were torn
apart from each other upon the destruction of the Temple
and the dispersal of the Jews. The *Zohar* holds that the
third and fourth letters of the name of God, *Vau* and *He*,
symbolize the eternal daughter and eternal son respectively, and that the coming of the Messiah ben David will
bring them together again.[116] Stephen, the son in *A Portrait*, seeks maturity throughout the book. However, even
at the end of *A Portrait* he has not arrived at a clear understanding of his relationship with the girl on the beach, his
"subject matter." He breaks off his speculation on his beloved with "O, give it up, old chap! Sleep it off!" (*P* 252).
In *Ulysses* Stephen envies the sexual freedom of his stu-
dents (*U* 24–25) and yearns vainly to be tumbled in a rye-
field by his own Ann Hathaway (*U* 191). A man cannot
become a father by himself; if he cannot find a woman to
bear his child he is condemned to be, in Buck's terms,

"Everyman His own Wife" (*U* 216). After smashing at the light in the brothel Stephen rushes out and accosts Cissy, an Irish girl, perhaps as a sign of his new freedom or as a last hope of maturity, and gets a sock in the face for his reward. Although we may suspect that Stephen has altered after the scene in the brothel, it is not finally certain whether the Messiah ben David has come for Stephen; certainly we do not see him linked to his "sister" in *Ulysses*.

We certainly do see him linked to her in *Finnegans Wake*. The ithyphallic David appears in two major forms —Dave the Dancekerl and the "davy" in the first chapter. Dave the Dancekerl is introduced to Issy, his sister, by Jaun as his "darling proxy" which he is leaving behind for her "consolering" (*FW* 462.17).[117] and he throws Dave and Issy into each other's arms.

Be sure and link him . . . as often as you learn . . . He's . . . as nasal a Romeo as I am . . . Canwyll y Cymry, the marmade's flammel . . .[118] Be introduced to yes! [119] This is me aunt Julia Bride . . . dying to have you languish to scandal in her bosky old delltangle. . . . That's his penals. . . . Come on, spinister, do your stuff! Don't be shoy, husbandmanvir! . . . Up the shamewaugh! She has plenty of woom in the smallclothes for the bothsforus . . . ! Hatch yourselves well! Enjombyourselves thurily! . . . Embrace her bashfully by almeans at my frank incensive and tell her in your semiological agglutinative yez, how Idos be asking after her. . . . To be had for the asking. Have a hug! . . . ["kissing her from me . . . all over" is] good for her bilabials . . . You [Issy] try a little tich to the tissle of his tail. . . . Why, they might be Babau and Momie! . . . Shuck her! Let him! What he's good for. Shuck her more! Let him again! All she wants! . . . Ruffle her! . . . In the beginning was the gest he jousstly says, for the end is with woman, flesh-without-word, while the man to be is in a worse case after than before since she on the supine satisfies the verg to him! . . . And pull up your [Issy's] furbelovs as farabove as you're farthingales. That'll hint him how to click the trigger. Show you shall and won't he will!

. . .[120] So dactylise him up to blankpoint and let him blink for himself where you speak the best ticklish. (*FW* 462.22–23; 463.6–8; 464.6; 465.1–3, 5, 6–7, 8–10, 11–13, 22, 26, 29–30; 466.1, 15–17; 467.6; 468.5–8, 13–15, 16–18)

Dave the Dancekerl and his sister are violently joined in a parody of the holy marriage of brother and sister symbolized by the conjugation of the third and fourth letters of Tetragrammaton at the coming of the Messiah ben David. "Like boyrun to sibster" (*FW* 465.17), like Byron and his half-sister Augusta Leigh, they are joined in an incestuous union, but on an eternal scale. After they join, the sun rises, the lovers separate, the curtain goes up for another performance of the cosmic drama amid thunder and lightning, and the universe is created anew: "Echo, read ending! Sipparioramoci! But from the stress of their sunder enlivening, ay clasp, deciduously, a nikrokosmikon must come to mike." [121] The problems of physical and moral maturity, the *sine qua non* of fatherhood, with which Stephen wrestles unsuccessfully in *A Portrait*, and with no clear success in *Ulysses*, is triumphantly solved on a vast scale in *Finnegans Wake*, by the prowess of an esthetic Messiah gifted with universal powers of conjugation. The true identity of the seducer, King David as artist, is strongly suggested at *FW* 468.36–469.1–2 by an allusion to one of Joyce's earlier works: " 'Bansheeba peeling houri-haared while her Orcotron is hoaring ho. And whinn muinnuit flittsbit twinn her ttittshe cries tallmidy!" And when, at midnight, he (Dave the Dancekerl) flits between Issy's (Bathsheba's) tits, or thighs, she cries: "Christ tall and Almighty!" or "Christ Talmudically!"—the Messiah ben David.[122] It is King David, both as the talmudic Messiah and as the romantic artist, the phallic attacker of the old-fogy Philistines, who is here shown in a sexual role that changes the balance of power in the family; the son is trying to become "a cataleptic mithyphallic" (*FW* 481.4), a father.[123]

King David attacks the old order and overturns it

most explicitly in the Willingdone Museyroom episode of *Finnegans Wake*. As in the Dave the Dancekerl episode, Dave is ithyphallic; his weapon is the organ of mature sexuality. He combines many traditional views of David with Joyce's additions.

After the Willingdone is introduced (*FW* 8.16–21), we encounter the three "lipoleum boyne," three soldiers —an "inimyskilling inglis," a "scotcher grey," and a "davy," a Welch Fusilier. The suggestions of slaughter in the names of the first two soldiers—'killing," "scotching" —are borne out at the end of the episode; the first two soldiers incite the "davy" to throw a bomb at the Willingdone. That the attack is sexual is suggested by a number of elements. The "davy" is first shown as "stooping" below the other two.[124] (*FW* 8.23–24) By the end of the battle he has been incited by the other two soldiers to rise up "between" them; the first soldier "hiena hinnessy" is "laughing alout at the Willingdone," the second soldier "lipsyg dooley" catches the spark from the hinnessy ("krieging the funk," *kriegen,* to seize [Ger.], *funk,* spark [Ger.]), and the "hinndoo Shimar Shin," combining the hinnessy and the dooley, Shem and Shaun, has now risen up "between" the twins where previously he had been "stooping" below them.[125] When the "hinndoo seeboy" sees the Willingdone desecrating the hat of the "lipoleum boyne," he waxes "ranjymad" for a bomb. Within the symbolic structure of *Finnegans Wake* "ranjymad" suggests wild sexual excitement. "Ranjy"—Prince Ranjitsinghi—was a famous Anglo-Indian cricketer at the beginning of the twentieth century who bought a castle in Ireland at the end of his career, and whose feats young Joyce followed avidly.[126] Cricket in *Finnegans Wake* is powerfully associated with sex. At *FW* 583–84, the old man wakes and attempts sexual congress with his wife; this section is filled with dozens of cricketing terms.[127] "Ranjymad," therefore, suggests the sexual madness of a Hindu, which is what the "davy" has become. The aroused hinndoo seeboy Davy, or Shimar Shin, sees his duty and does it—"upjump and pumpim"—and, mad as a hatter and shouting what seems like Hindustani or English sexual insults at the Willingdone, he blows the hat off the "big wide harse" and redeems his mission. Like the David of Schumann and Goethe, the tumescent Davy overthrows the old order; it is this sign of physical maturity that the father fears to discover in his son.[128] In *A Portrait* the hell-fire sermon follows immediately after Stephen's introduction to sex, and seems to be intended to frighten him away from the maturity he seeks. The father knows that if the son becomes capable of becoming a father, then he, the father, will become a nonentity, a chirping, malicious old bystander. The son, on his part, feels the Aristotelian drive for the perfection of his soul, the high point of development when the organism becomes capable of reproducing itself, and rebels against the past to pursue maturity regardless of the cost.

King David in the Willingdone Museyroom symbolizes man's physical maturity, the revolutionary force which keeps the wheel of history turning. He is also a "seeboy," a visionary as defined by Augustine, Dante, Pico, and Bruno. Augustine's David has "seen" through the structure of universal reality, and reflects universal order in his psalms. Dante's David is eagle-eyed for truth, as is the David of the *Zohar* whose intention it was to "see" his heavenly Master close at hand.[129] The Renaissance mage of Pico and Bruno created magical works because of his Daedalian flights through the universe to "see" all of reality. And an epiphany is a "seeing," after all.

As usual, Joyce contributes facets of his own to the concept of King David as visionary. For one of his interpretations he leans upon Aquinas; A. D. Hope, in an article on Joyce's esthetic theory, comments that

beauty in fact is regarded [by Joyce] as a particular class of "good" . . . the good is defined [by Aquinas] simply as that by which an appetite is appeased. . . . But it pertains to the nature of the beautiful that the appetite in question is appeased by the mere *sight* [my italics] or contemplation of its object. . . . Aquinas . . . makes a sharp distinction between the senses of taste and smell, appetites which are appeased by sensual gratification, by actual possession of their objects, and those of sight and hearing which are appeased by the contemplation of them.

Aquinas's "seeboy" would be capable of exercising his vision not only upon the moral attributes of the Father, but upon the beauty, the "radiance," of his creation as well.[130]

Davy the seeboy sees more than Ham saw of his father [131] or Moses saw of the nature of the creator of the universe. Joyce provides a clue to the meaning of the Museyroom episode on *FW* 8.8: "For her passkey supply to the janitrix, the mistress Kathe." In view of the Hindu complexion of the fable [132] I take this to be a reference to the Katha Upanishad.[133] In this upanishad, one of the most important statements of classical Hinduism, a son is sent to visit Death by his irritated father and returns with information about the most secret workings of the universe. Death agrees to grant the youth three wishes. The first wish is that the father pardon the son; the second refers to knowledge about specific religious ceremonies; but the third, a question about death and the survival of human personality, is answered by Death only after initial reluctance. Death's answer, which reconciles the fact of individual death and the moral nature of the universe, underlies most of the philosophical basis of Hindu religion. The youth returns with his knowledge and preaches the truth about the universe to the world. The relevance of the Katha Upanishad to the Willingdone Museyroom episode is that the youth in both works has been threatened with death, real or moral, by the father, and in both cases he has become a "seeboy," a visionary, piercing with his vision the secrets of the universe, and thus performing David's characteristic act, according to Augustine, Dante, the *Zohar,* and Pico. If the Katha Upanishad really supplies a "passkey" to the meaning of the Willingdone Museyroom episode, we find in it a relationship that stresses, first, a father's attack on his son, second, the journey to death (which Shem makes also, to return as Dave the Dancekerl), and third, the return with knowledge that changes the old order completely. He combines creation and destruction in himself, the creation of a new order, and the destruction of an old.

Davy the seeboy is represented in Joyce's worksheets for the Willingdone Museyroom episode by a symbol which combines Shaun's $\wedge$ and Shem's $[\ ;\underline{\bigwedge}$. Joyce's King David is indeed a combination of Shem and Shaun. He is creator and destroyer. He is Shem as the artist, the esthetic and political messiah, the visionary of the Katha Upanishad, the *Zohar,* Dante, and Pico, who discovers the secrets of the universe, Augustine's creator miming God's Heavenly City in the proportions of his work, Delany's originator of the arts, especially those of song and dance ("a Czardanser indeed!" [*FW* 513.16]), the mythmaker, and the *princeps litteratus* of Sedulius. David is also Shaun, as the destructive, murderous Butt or Buckley, the revolutionary destroyer of the Philistine *Grossvaters,* as Goethe and Schumann would have him, Dave the Dancekerl in his ithyphallic aspect, the "davy" rising up to attack the father from behind, and the revolutionary and scurrilous Hosty or Davy Stephens who attacks the father in public. David is lifewand and deathbone, anabolism and katabolism. What he represents in the work of Joyce is the double development of the artist as artist and as man, as Shem and Shaun, to maturity. At one point, both of these aspects of man, having reached the height of their development, fuse and overthrow the father, to become the father in their turn, suffering from guilt at having attacked their father, but creating, as a natural soul must, images of itself—children and works of art—to fulfill its Aristotelian drive to- ward perfection. HCE is called "a cataleptic mithyphallic" by the old men in *Finnegans Wake* (*FW* 481.4), and that is precisely what he is—a cataleptic mixture of mythmaker and ithyphallic man—a fallen man and a father.

With these interpretations of the figure of David in mind, the overall plan of *A Portrait* and *Ulysses* becomes clear. In *A Portrait* the artist as Shem, David as myth- maker, becomes certain of his vocation, receives his hat and stick, and attempts to practice his art. However, David as Shaun is not yet fully developed; in *A Portrait* the artist is still a "young man." Stephen has not yet come to terms with his "anmal matter" (*FW* 294.F5), the material world symbolized by his mother, by the girl on the beach, and by his beloved; he exclaims about women in his diary "O give it up, old chap! Sleep it off!" It is not until he smashes the lamp in the Nighttown brothel that he finally develops as Shaun, that is, it is not until he strikes at the paternal white light that has been attacking and hindering him all through *A Portrait* that he can become a man and con- template Molly side by side with Leopold. Both Davids then merge; Stephen begins to sing and walks out of *Ulysses* accompanied by the sound of his (or David's) harp.

What is introduced, then, in *A Portrait* between paragraphs of Stephen's lecture on esthetics to Lynch is a double-faced symbol of great importance in the works of Joyce, one which sums up in itself more than three thou- sand years of cultural history, and one which, when under- stood, clarifies the general structure of Joyce's novels— King David as the symbolic goal or model of the son-artist trying to become a father.

Stephen's character does not change noticeably in the last three sections of chapter 5. At this point, judged against the ideal of the artist, King David, the creator and destroyer, Stephen seems incomplete, immature. Like the

limbo of Temple's definition, Stephen is "neither my arse
nor my elbow" (*P* 237). He is certain that he is an artist,
but he seems less certain that he is a man. The father still
attacks him, but the main hindrance to his maturity is the
immaturity of his own mind. He is able to fend off the attacks of the father, but his own internal lack of definition
pursues him to the end of the book (and beyond, to *Ulysses*), undercutting his attempts at creation with irony.

The father in his customary form of coldness and
whiteness, or in the person of one of his servants, attempts
to hinder Stephen's creativity. An analysis of the circumstances of the composition of the villanelle suggests that
Stephen is developing his *own* white paternal light: inspiration is accompanied by waves of "pale cool" light (*P*
217); the "instant of inspiration" flashes forth like "a
point of light" and a "white flame" and is specifically identified as "Gabriel the seraph" coming to the virgin's chamber (*P* 217). The white flame deepens to a "rose and ardent light." The roselight, as in Stephen's vocational
ceremony, symbolizes the receptive female reality waiting
to be impregnated by the paternal creator. The white
light, therefore, is the light of paternity, now not the light
of Stephen's elders but his own. The villanelle, feeble as
it is, is an attempt by the son to become a father, to project
his image.

The father, sensing a new attack, immediately throws
up hindrances to Stephen's thought. His white light attempts to smother Stephen's creative act: "The dull white
light spread itself east and west, covering the world, covering the roselight in his heart" (*P* 218). A remembrance
of the coarse humor of Moynihan, an "absorbed" son, a
minion of the father, again interrupts the current of Stephen's inspiration.

The earth was like a swinging smoking swaying censer, a ball
of incense, an ellipsoidal ball. The rhythm died out at once;
the cry of his heart was broken. (*P* 218)

. . . . . .
What price ellipsoidal balls! Chase me, ladies, I'm in the
cavalry! (*P* 192)

The father attacks constantly in the third section of
chapter 5. He warns Stephen, through the mouth of Temple, that "reproduction is the beginning of death" (*P*
231). The father's weapon of brightness distresses Stephen's mind and disturbs his inspiration. Birds associated
with his vocational ceremony fly about "the jutting shoulder of a house in Molesworth Street" (*P* 224). Stephen's
inspiration on the beach was a bird-girl; he himself is a
hawklike man; he holds an augur's rod (*P* 225). In addition, these birds are "dark"; they symbolize all of the most
intimate aspects of his vocation. Joyce repeats "dark" many
times so that there can be no mistake about their symbolic
meaning.

Their dark darting quivering bodies flying clearly against the
sky . . . bird after bird: a dark flash . . . the dark frail
quivering bodies wheeling and fluttering and swerving round
an airy temple of the tenuous sky soothed his eyes. . . . They
came back with shrill cries over the jutting shoulder of the
house, flying darkly against the fading air. (*P* 224, 225)

After an interlude, Stephen stands again on the porch of
the library, and his beloved passes by. She is immediately
fused with the dark birds as a symbol of the darkness which
has been and is still necessary for Stephen's development.

The swallows whose flight he had followed with idle eyes
were sleeping.
    She had passed through the dusk. . . . Darkness was
falling.
            Darkness falls from the air.
    A trembling joy, lambent as a faint light, played like a
fairy host around him. But why? Her passage through the
darkening air or the verse with its black vowels and its opening sound, rich and lutelike? (*P* 232–33)

The "unrest" of his vocational ceremony, and the odors of her body, both elements of his soul's need, reinforce the darkness of her presence. The father, scenting danger, immediately counterattacks within Stephen's mind ("Could his mind then not trust itself?" [P 233]):

Eyes, opening from the darkness of desire, eyes that dimmed the breaking east. (P 233)

The father will not have his light dimmed by the darkness of Stephen's desire:

What was their languid grace but the softness of chambering? And what was their shimmer but the shimmer of the scum that mantled the cesspool of the court of a slobbering Stuart (P 233)

"Chambering" is the first unfriendly word, the first overt attacking weapon of the father, in this offensive, and it is a good one. This unusual word appears in only a few texts in English. Its most prominent appearance is in the King James Bible, at Rom. 13:12–14, most likely Joyce's source:

12 The night is far spent, the day is at hand: let us therefore cast off the works of darkness, and let us put on the armour of light.
13 Let us walk honestly, as in the day; not in rioting and drunkenness, not in chambering and wantonness, not in strife and envying.
14 But put ye on the Lord Jesus Christ, and make no provision for the flesh, to fulfill the lusts thereof.

Under the stress of the father's attack, Stephen immediately drops his joy in darkness, casts off the works of darkness and quickly buckles on the constraining armor of light: the dark birds, flying like his thoughts, and whose voices were specifically described as "unlike the cry of vermin" (P 224), now turn into bright vermin, lice falling from the air, and his thoughts become verminous in his altered opinion, "born of the sweat of sloth."

In the darkness he saw the brittle bright bodies of lice falling
from the air and turning often as they fell. Yes; and it was not
darkness that fell from the air. It was brightness.

> *Brightness falls from the air.*

He had not even remembered rightly Nash's [*sic*] line.
All the images it had awakened were false. His mind bred
vermin. His thoughts were lice born of the sweat of sloth.
(*P* 234)

And he rejects his beloved, as the father would have him
do: "Well then, let her go and be damned to her" (*P* 234).
He may have misremembered Nashe's line, but it was a
significant error, an error in the right direction. The father
corrects his error and turns him into the wrong direction.

Cranly also is an instrument of the father, a cadaver
obeying the father's orders, with the paleness and coldness
of the father upon him as signs of his allegiance. Just before he goes on his walk with Stephen he detects the blasphemy of Glynn and drives away the heretic Temple like
an avenging angel (*P* 237). As he starts off on his walk,
Stephen receives a signal that Cranly is going to try to
poison his mind in the name of the father: "They crossed
the quadrangle together without speaking. The birdcall
from *Siegfried* whistled softly followed them from the steps
of the porch" (*P* 237). Siegfried, in Wagner's *Siegfried*,
suddenly understands the meaning of the bird's song after
he has slain the dragon and tasted its blood. The bird
warns him of the malevolent intentions of Siegfried's
foster-father Mime, who intends to poison him and get the
dragon's horde for himself. Mime does attempt to cajole
Siegfried into drinking a poison cup, but Siegfried sees
through his plans and finally, disgusted by his insistence,
kills him with one blow from Nothung. Stephen is receiv-
ing an allusive warning not to trust Cranly, who represents
the father and who does not mean Stephen well. Cranly
also shares the father's unwillingness that Stephen think

of women or attempt to love them, and his "coldness" rises
to the surface at Stephen's mention of them.

—Have you never loved anyone? Cranly asked.
—Do you mean women?
—I am not speaking of that, Cranly said in a colder tonè
(*P* 240)

Cranly attempts to divert Stephen with the pure, sexless
"woman as she appears in the liturgy of the church": she
is a "whiterobed figure, small and slender as a boy" (*P*
244). Although Cranly does not mention it, the woman he
has picked for Stephen, besides being boyish and white-
clad, is dangerous. Her words, "the first words of a woman
which pierce the gloom and clamour of the first chanting
of the passion," are the words of the woman who recog-
nizes Peter and tries to force him to admit that he too was
with Jesus of Galilee (Matt. 26:69). Cranly says of his
Rosie O'Grady, "There's real love," to which the suspi-
cious Stephen answers, "I want to see Rosie first" (*P* 244,
245).

The livery of the father which Cranly wears so openly,
his pale face and his "elder's affection" (he calls Stephen
gaily "my child" [*P* 247]) which conceals his cold sadness,
finally irritates Stephen to the point where he specifically
rejects his native land which, for the first and last time in
A Portrait, he calls "my fatherland" (*P* 247). The form
of the word suggests that Stephen intends the father to
know that, like Siegfried, he sees through his poisonous intentions and intends to avoid them.

Stephen's revolt against his father extends throughout
his diary entries.

21 March, night. Free. Soulfree and fancyfree. Let the dead
bury the dead. Ay. And let the dead marry the dead. (*P* 248)

"Let the dead bury the dead" is a hostile glance at the
father, as the source, Matt. 8:21–22, indicates:

18 Now . . . Jesus . . . gave commandment to depart unto the other side. . . .
21 And another of his disciples said unto him, Lord, suffer me first to go and bury my father.
22 But Jesus said unto him, Follow me; and let the dead bury their dead.

Stephen feels that he can leave the father behind and fly off on his mission, while the other dead, Cranly and the other "absorbed" sons in this case, marry with their destined mates.

The diary entry for 3 April (*P* 250) shows Stephen's father in the role that Bloom will take in *Ulysses*—the friendly, cunning creator of bonds to keep Stephen in Ireland, helpless, his task unperformed. Just after Stephen declares to Davin that exile is the shortest way to kingship of Ireland, Simon Dedalus appears and, after a little friendly talk with Davin, he tries to get Stephen to join a rowing club and to read law, that is, to reproduce his father's past and redeem his father's present failure, as Stephen seems to interpret it. Stephen exclaims bitterly in his diary "More mud, more crocodiles," a reference to Cranly's riddle in the diary entry for 30 March. Stephen seems to see in the low cunning of the greedy crocodile the cunning of the forces that intend to swallow him down, to reduce him to harmlessness in his fatherland. In the diary entry of 30 March he exclaims:

This mentality, Lepidus would say, is indeed bred out of your mud by the operation of your sun.
     And mine? Is it not too? Then into Nilemud with it!

Stephen's father is playing the role of the crocodile in his life, friendly smile and all. The father is explicitly identified as a crocodile in *Finnegans Wake:* "crocodile" on *FW* 273.22 is glossed by the sentence "Yes, there, Tad, thanks, give, from, tathair, look at that now." Besides "Tad" and "tathair," respectively Welsh and Irish for "father" ("the father" is [*an*] *tAthair* in Irish), there are other fathers concealed in the phrase. "Da," colloquial Irish for "father," is also Russian for "yes," Italian for "from," German for "there," Sanskrit for "give" (really *dā*), and perhaps means "thanks" in some other language. Bloom, for all his warmth and friendliness, plays the same part in *Ulysses* (see *U* 644–45, 658–59, 663–64, 695–96).

The famous last sentence of *A Portrait,* "Old father, old artificer, stand me now and ever in good stead" (*P* 253), conceals ironic allusions to Stephen's immaturity. A source for Joyce's "old father" may be found in Yeats's dedicatory poem to *Responsibilities* (1914), in which Yeats addresses his actual and spiritual ancestors.

> Pardon, old fathers, if you still remain
> Somewhere in ear-shot for the story's end . . .
> Pardon that for a barren passion's sake,
> Although I have come close on forty-nine,
> I have no child, I have nothing but a book,
> Nothing but that to prove your blood and mine.

This poem, dated January 1914,[134] may have supplied Joyce with his "old father"; it is certainly true that Stephen, although not forty-nine, has no child, not even a book, and in his state of immaturity is not likely to achieve either. What Stephen thinks he is doing is quite clear; he is praying to Daedalus to support him in his flight to creation. The irony of this later becomes obvious; in *Ulysses* Stephen realizes how Daedalus has answered his prayer.

> Fabulous artificer, the hawklike man. You flew. Whereto? Newhaven-Dieppe, steerage passenger. Paris and back. Lapwing. Icarus. *Pater, ait.* Seabedabbled, fallen, weltering (*U* 210)

The "old father" of Stephen's prayer has become "Old Father Ocean" (*U* 50). (See also *U* 572 for another hawklike paternal betrayer.) All fathers have failed or betrayed the immature Stephen by the time of this passage in

Ulysses. As he discovers, he will not be ready to be an artist until he is mature as a man, until he wins his weapon Nothung in the Circe chapter by attacking the father. Until then, fathers will attempt to keep him a son to affirm their own fatherhood, while he, obeying the order of his life, will strive vainly for maturity.

Besides these attacks of the father, Stephen has to wrestle with his own internal youthful confusions about women and about his subject matter, the "life" that they represent. In these last sections of the book, his ideas about his beloved vacillate from forced ecstasy to weak suspicion to arrogant dismissal, from a desire to consider her white and pure to an urge to find her dark and sensual. Finally, he breaks off his theorizing about her impatiently and the book ends with Stephen's problem still unsolved.

Before and during his composition of the villanelle his feelings swing wildly from desire to repulsion.

She too stood silently among her companions. She has no priest to flirt with, he thought with conscious bitterness . . . Lynch was right [in his cynical, physical ideas about desire]. . . . And if he had judged her harshly? . . . That rose and ardent light was her strange wilful heart, strange that no man had known or would know, wilful from before the beginning of the world . . . At certain instants her eyes seemed about to trust him but he had waited in vain. She passed now dancing lightly across his memory as she had been that night at the carnival ball, her white dress a little lifted, a white spray nodding in her hair. . . . The white spray nodded to her dancing and when she was in shadow the glow was deeper on her cheek. . . . Bah! he had done well to leave the room in disdain. . . . Rude brutal anger routed the last lingering instant of ecstasy from his soul. . . . [He imagines all of her debased representatives—flower girls, kitchen girls, factory girls.] He had left the classroom in disdain that was not wholly sincere, feeling that perhaps the secret of her race lay behind those dark eyes upon which her long lashes flung a quick shadow. He had told himself bitterly as he walked through the streets that she was a figure of the womanhood of her country, a batlike soul waking to the consciousness of itself in darkness and secrecy and loneliness . . . [He remembers the scene after the children's party at Harold's Cross (*P* 69–70).] She came up to his step many times between their phrases and went down again and once or twice remained beside him for- getting to go down and then went down. Let be! Let be! [Would she show the verses to her family?] No, no: that was folly. Even if he sent her the verses she would not show them to others. No, no: she could not.

He began to feel that he had wronged her. . . . Might it be, in the mysterious ways of spiritual life, that her soul at those same moments had been conscious of his homage? It might be. [Then he yields himself to an image of his beloved as "conscious of his desire," dark, odourous, warm, naked, and radiant.] [135] (*P* 215–16, 217, 219, 220–21, 222, 223)

The passage on the noble incestuous lovers (*P* 228) shows Stephen's lack of confidence in himself as a wooer; it is Davin's hand that caresses the sister, not Stephen's. Later, after his beloved passes through the dusk, she sets off the desire for dark sensuality which is countered by an attack by the father. As a result of the father's attack, his opinion of her veers violently toward rejection and disdain.

Well then, let her go and be damned to her. She could love some clean athlete who washed himself every morning to the waist and had black hair on his chest. Let her. (*P* 234)

Remembering Davin's story, he comes close to realizing that his immaturity is barring him from connection with his beloved, from approaching the soul of his country.

And under the deepened dusk he felt the thoughts and desires of the race to which he belonged flitting like bats, across the dark country lanes . . . A woman had waited in the doorway as Davin had passed by at night and, offering him a cup of milk, had all but wooed him to her bed . . . But him no woman's eyes had wooed. (*P* 238)

Stephen's hostility toward his mother also contributes to his confusion about women. In his discussion with Cranly, every avenue seems to lead to a sarcastic comment about women from Stephen, whether the woman is Rosie O'Grady or the mothers of Pascal, Aloysius Gonzaga, or Jesus. Stephen obviously believes that he has hardened his soul against sentiment, but all that his uncertainty about women has done is cause him to oscillate violently from one pole to the other.

In his diary, his confusion about the proper approach to women is extreme. He tries following a hospital nurse with Lynch, but the obvious animality of the quest disturbs him. He satirizes his beloved as unwell and sees her in his mind's eye being fed solicitously by her mamma. Nevertheless, he worries about her, and about himself. On 24 March, the eve of Lady Day, the feast of the Annunciation, he rambles on in his diary:

Went to library. Tried to read three reviews. Useless. She is not out yet. Am I alarmed? About what? That she will never be out again.
Blake wrote:

> I wonder if William Bond will die
> For assuredly he is very ill.

Alas, poor William!
I was once at a diorama in Rotunda. At the end were pictures of big nobs. Among them William Ewart Gladstone, just then dead. Orchestra played O, Willie, we have missed you. (P 249)

The association of his beloved ("her strange wilful heart") with five different "Wills"—Blake, Shakespeare, William Bond, William Ewart Gladstone, and Willie—is not fortuitous. "Will" in Joyce always has a strong sexual tinge, as it had in Elizabethan and Jacobean times (see note 24). In addition, the William Bond of the Blake poem is suf-

fering from lovesickness; the first two lines of the poem
that Stephen omits are

> I wonder whether the Girls are mad,
> And I wonder whether they mean to kill.

William Bond, like Stephen, is torn by the problem of sex,
whether his beloved should be bright and pure or dark
and human. The moral of the poem declares a victory for
the forces of darkness.

> I thought Love liv'd in the hot sun shine,
> But O, he lives in the Moony light!
> I thought to find Love in the heat of day,
> But sweet Love is the Comforter of Night.

Stephen's confusion remains with him to the end of *A Portrait*. In a frivolous diary entry, he repudiates his desire
for dark sensual girls:

5 April: Wild spring. Scudding clouds. O life! Dark stream of
swirling bogwater on which appletrees have cast down their
delicate flowers. Eyes of girls among the leaves. Girls demure
and romping. All fair or auburn: no dark ones. They blush
better. Houp-la! (*P* 250)

He veers to satire of his beloved in the entry for 6 April
(*P* 250–51), and relapses helplessly in the entry for 11
April.

11 April: Read what I wrote last night. Vague words for a
vague emotion. Would she like it? I think so. Then I should
have to like it also. (*P* 251)

His last mention of his beloved, the story of his meeting with her in the street (*P* 252), begins with a tone of
conscious controlled irony and ends in total confusion; the
reference to Dante merely reinforces the effect of Stephen's
confusion by the contrast with Dante's heroic control in
the *Vita Nuova*.

15 April: . . . She shook hands a moment after and, in going
away, said she hoped I would do what I said.

Now I call that friendly, don't you?

Yes, I liked her today. A little or much? Don't know. I liked her and it seems a new feeling to me. Then, in that case, all the rest, all that I thought I thought and all that I felt I felt, all the rest before now, in fact . . . O, give it up, old chap! Sleep it off! (P 252)

And this is the last we hear of Stephen's desire for maturity as a man until *Ulysses*. We are left with the feeling that the artist certainly is a young man, and that his flight is foredoomed to failure.

In various sections of *A Portrait*, Stephen has received signs that his vocation as an artist is real. The fathers around him realize this and try to halt his growth. One-half of him is ready for creation. However, before he can become King David, a royal creator, a lord of his country and of reality, before he can forge Nothung in the smithy of his soul, before he can transmute the daily bread of life into the sacrament of art, the immaturity that Joyce observes in him with such delighted irony must be burnt out of him. Stephen must smash at the white light in Nighttown to liberate his own light; he must leave Bloom's house singing before his maturity can be complete. Shem and Shaun must unite to form the "davy" who will overthrow the father and become the father of the race in his turn.

3

stephen's dance

THE technique employed by Joyce in the writing of *A Portrait,* the recording of significant moments in the development of a young man, could have produced a fragmented, formless work. To crowd the life of a man from his earliest infancy to his coming of age in a few hundred pages would be a difficult feat to accomplish even if the young man were a much less remarkable fellow than Stephen Dedalus. That Joyce accomplishes his task in *A Portrait* is partly a tribute to his sense of form and partly an evidence of the consistency of the character that he draws. It is the personality of Stephen Dedalus that ties together the dozens of moments separated in time and makes *A Portrait* a tightly organized book.

The elements of Stephen's character are set from the very first section of *A Portrait*—his song and dance, his attempts to find a sexual partner, the struggle with his father, are all parts of his soul, of the "rhythm" of his personality which never alters but only develops. From the beginning of *A Portrait* he grows to be what he was "ineluctably preconditioned to become" despite the opposition of the forces of the past who see in him the future which will supersede them. They oppose him with terror and violence, and with cajolery and blank obstruction; they attempt to halt his growth and to make him a tool of their wishes, a good son content to be no more than a son, and thus perpetually to reaffirm them in their mystical estate of fatherhood.

Stephen, however, moves onward to the end that he sees he must serve, recovers from the fathers' violence, and avoids their traps. By the end of *A Portrait* Stephen is confirmed in his vocation as artist and is reaching for maturity as a man. He is approaching the condition of an esthetic Messiah, a King David combining maturity and creativity. There are flaws in him; he is too confident in his own powers, and he does not realize how confused some of his ideas are, especially those on the subject of women. However, he bravely essays his first flight, fluttering up out of the diary entries that end *A Portrait*.

When we see him again, in *Ulysses*, he is waking up to what is probably the worst day in his life. His flight has ended abruptly; his father's telegram has called him back to his mother's bedside; he has "fallen" heavily and is trying dazedly to collect his morale. What has happened between the end of *A Portrait* and the beginning of *Ulysses* is that the fathers have launched one last attack on the growing artist, one last desperate attempt to keep him harmless. We see Stephen struggling with the effects of this attack all day in *Ulysses*. In other words, *Ulysses* is a gigantically expanded version of an episode, like many of the episodes in *A Portrait*, where the father tries to keep the son down, and the son eventually wins through.

I do not intend to analyze *Ulysses* in detail in this chapter; I will avoid close analysis of the personalities of Bloom and Stephen and confine my attention to an analysis of the attitudes toward fatherhood that Stephen displays in the course of the book and to an examination of Stephen's dance in the Circe chapter, which I believe is a moment when Stephen finally turns the tables on the forces of the past and throws open the door of creation to himself.

The tone of Stephen's relationship with his actual father Simon Dedalus has altered significantly from that displayed in *A Portrait*. In *A Portrait* Stephen, while seeing through his father (and once calling him a crocodile), nevertheless remains on more or less cordial terms with him. In *Ulysses*, Stephen feels a bitter resentment toward his father, both for having stopped his "flight" with a blue French telegram (*U* 42) and for neglecting his family.

Stephen finds it more and more difficult as the day goes on even to call him "father," or to avoid creating bitter synonyms for the word. On *U* 38 he calls him "the man with my voice and my eyes"; immediately afterward the image of Arius breathing his last in a Greek water closet comes to Stephen's mind and he calls Arius "widower of a widowed see." "Widower" is what Stephen savagely calls his father on *U* 207: "the widower." On that page he also describes his father's "eyes that wish me well. But do not know me." On *U* 188 Stephen, fearing that Eglinton will say the word "father," interrupts him, with creeping flesh:

—He will have it that *Hamlet* is a ghoststory, John Eglinton said for Mr Best's behoof. Like the fat boy in Pickwick he wants to make our flesh creep.
List! List! O List!
My flesh hears him: creeping, hears.
If thou didst ever . . .
—What is a ghost? Stephen said with tingling energy. (*U* 187–88)

He does not want to ask himself if he ever loved his dear father. On *U* 195 he prevents Richard Best from finishing the word *"grandpère."* He stops dead in Nighttown when he is about to finish the Prodigal Son's declaration that he will arise and go to his father (*U* 517). In Nighttown Simon Dedalus appears as a useless comic figure, a misleading guide with his maxims of gentlemanly conduct, a buzzard father advising his vulture son.

STEPHEN
No, I flew. My foes beneath me. And ever shall be. World without end. (*He cries.*) *Pater!* Free!
BLOOM
I say, look . . .
STEPHEN
Break my spirit, will he? *O merde alors!* (*He cries, his vulture talons sharpened.*) Hola! Hillyho! (*Simon Dedalus' voice hilloes in answer, somewhat sleepy but ready.*)

SIMON

That's all right. (*He swoops uncertainly through the air, wheeling, uttering cries of heartening, on strong ponderous buzzard wings.*) Ho, boy! Are you going to win? [1] Hoop! Pschatt! Stable with those halfcastes. Wouldn't let them within the bawl of an ass. Head up! Keep our flag flying! An eagle gules volant in a field argent displayed. [2] Ulster king at arms! hai hoop! (*U* 572)

Simon has nothing to offer to help Stephen in his flight but the tired exhortations to gentlemanly conduct and snobbery that he left with him at Clongowes (*P* 9). He is a carrion-bird, a buzzard, because he is guilty of his wife's death; Stephen, as his son, is a "vulture," for the same reason. Earlier in the Circe episode, a clownish cardinal, Simon Stephen Cardinal Dedalus, appears, declaiming tragedy and comedy with high-spirited and sentimental insincerity (*U* 523–25). The Simon Dedalus of *Ulysses,* with his weak sentimentality and equally weak resentment of his paternal responsibilities, is a shadow of the optimistic Simon of *A Portrait.*

Stephen distrusts and fears his father, and, characteristically, he generalizes this attitude toward his father into a mistrust of fatherhood. This mistrust of fathers appears in many places in *Ulysses.* Stephen significantly misremembers Buck's description of his *Hamlet* theory— "Hamlet's grandson is Shakespeare's grandfather and . . . he himself is the ghost of his own father" (*U* 18) – and reproduces it as "Shakespeare's ghost is Hamlet's grandfather" (*U* 28). Stephen so dislikes the idea of being thought "the ghost of his own father," an unsubstantial replica of his father, that he unconsciously changes the relationship of the Ghost and Prince Hamlet from father and son to grandfather and son. [3] According to Samuel Butler, useful talents are transferred only between remote degrees of relationship; the father and the son always are antagonistic and have less in common than the grandfather and the grandson. (That is why Shakespeare's grandson never was born according to Stephen; nature abhors perfection [*U* 208].) In the library scene Stephen, only partially realizing what he is doing, delivers a disquisition on fatherhood that is filled with mistrust, hatred, and fear of the paternal forces which have, as he sees it, hounded him throughout his childhood and young manhood.

—A father, Stephen said, battling against hopelessness, is a necessary evil. . . . Who is the father of any son that any son should love him or he any son?

What the hell are you driving at?

I know. Shut up. Blast you! I have reasons. . . .

Are you condemned to do this?

—They are sundered by a bodily shame so steadfast that the criminal annals of the world, stained with all other incests and bestialities, hardly record its breach. . . . The son unborn mars beauty: born, he brings pain, divides affection, increases care. He is a male: his growth is his father's decline, his youth his father's envy, his friend his father's enemy. . . . What links them in nature? An instant of blind rut. (*U* 207–8)

There are many bad or neglectful fathers in *Ulysses:* Simon Dedalus, who refuses to support his family (*U* 226–27, 237–39); Reuben J. Dodd, "bad shepherd" (*U* 497, 506); Kevin Egan (*U* 43–44); Gerty MacDowell's drunken father (*U* 354); Bridie Kelly's drunken father who will not interfere with her professional activities (*U* 441). The "absentminded beggar" of the song that echoes throughout *Ulysses* is, in the original song by Kipling and Arthur Sullivan, a father who does not know his own son. The ocean that swallows the fallen Icarus and bleaches him "saltwhite" (*U* 21, 50) is a father, "Old Father Ocean" (*U* 50). Even God becomes a devouring father to Stephen. Children die young because the "omnivorous being" that swallows down and digests so many different kinds of people "find[s] gastric relief in an innocent collation of staggering bob" (*U* 420), the meat of a newborn calf; God is the "corpsechewer" to Stephen at the climax of the Nighttown scene (*U* 581). Even Bloom mildly suspects that fathers might want to murder their children (*U* 379).

It is not unreasonable for Stephen to suspect the motives of fathers; he is a son who has been attacked constantly by them. Stephen's attitude toward fatherhood has another side, however. He realizes that he must become a "father" before he can be a true creator. "Father" is the word Stephen uses for Shakespeare as a creator; Shakespeare was not only a father of his actual children but "the father of his race" when he succeeded in attaining personal and artistic maturity.

Fatherhood, in the sense of conscious begetting, is unknown to man. It is a mystical estate, an apostolic succession, from only begetter to only begotten. . . . When [Shakespeare] wrote *Hamlet* he was not the father of his own son merely but, being no more a son, he was and felt himself the father of all his race, the father of his own grandfather, the father of his unborn grandson. (*U* 207–8)

Shakespeare as creator is the father of his race and the author of his plays. Later in *Ulysses,* Lynch taunts Stephen with the "capful of light odes [that] call [his] genius father" (*U* 415), and Stephen feels despairingly that he will never be a father, never fertilize his subject matter with his will, that he is "the eternal son and ever virgin" (*U* 392). Logically, since there can be only one father-creator in a "race" at a time, the son is debarred from creation, either physical or spiritual, by his own immaturity and by the stifling presence of the paternal creator. When, however, the son breaks through his "virginal" lethargy, when he is ready for creation, the father gives way and the new father begins to create.

This point is reached during the Circe episode in *Ulysses,* after Stephen's frenzied *tripudium*. Since this is an extremely complex section of *Ulysses,* I will analyze its elements one by one, and then try to show how Joyce achieves a symbolic synthesis of these elements to illustrate the crucial point of the son's development to fatherhood.

All that happens on the literal level is that, after dancing, Stephen strikes at a light with his ashplant. Let us examine these elements in turn—the *dance,* the *ashplant,* and the *light.*

Dancing is one of the prime symbols of the Davidic artist. Stephen dances on the first page of *A Portrait;* in *Finnegans Wake* dancing is one of the signs of Shem, and one of the elements of the name of Dave the Dancekerl. Stephen's dance in Nighttown is, then, more than mere capering; it is an assertion of his identity as an artist, an assertion bravely advanced amid desolation of spirit.

Stephen's dance is identified as a *tripudium* (*U* 574) , an ancient sword dance mentioned by Livy as having been practiced by primitive Celts to celebrate receipt of their weapons and by the Salian priesthood of Rome. Like an ancient Celt dancing the *tripudium,* Stephen is dancing with a "weapon," his ashplant, which he has many times called his "sword" (*U* 37, 192, 210) , and which he calls "Nothung!" at the climactic point of the scene (*U* 583) . *Tripudium* has other significances as well. It is obviously derived from *trēs* and *pes;* it is a "three-foot" dance.[4] "My Girl's a Yorkshire Girl," the melody to which Stephen is dancing, is a heavy, pounding waltz (*U* 575) ; the triple rhythm of the *tripudium* underlies Joyce's deliberate choice of this melody for his hero to dance to.[5] The "three-foot" nature of the dance conceals another symbolic association, a phallic one. The "Three Legs of Man" are mentioned earlier in the Nighttown chapter (*U* 507) . In addition to being a reference to the coat of arms of the Isle of Man (a "triskelion," with three armored legs joined at the hip) , it also contains a reference to the "middle leg" of man to which the whores refer in the beginning of the section.

How's your middle leg? . . .
Eh, come here till I stiffen it for you. (*U* 450)

The third leg (actually "foot") of the *tripudium* is the phallus in this connection. Sterne, an author Joyce knew well,[6] employs *tripodium* (obviously the same word as *tripudium*) with this meaning in *Tristram Shandy* 1:21, where the *Argumentum Tripodium* is strongly opposed to the *Argumentum ad Rem;* "one is the best answer to the other," says Sterne. Stephen's dance is, then, a weapon dance celebrating the acquisition of Nothung, a sword, which is at the same time a phallic symbol, a symbol of manhood (as it is in Wagner's *Ring* itself). Stephen's ashplant, his "augur's rod," the symbol of his vocation as an artist, is now the third leg of a three-legged dance, and a sword, and a phallus.

It will be recalled that young Siegfried uses Nothung to kill his foster-father Mime who was trying to poison him, and to break his grandfather Wotan's spear of law with which Wotan hoped to bar the young hero's way to his beloved. Wagner's phallic sword of maturity is also Joyce's. In striking at the light Stephen employs the sword that killed one "father" and disarmed another in the *Ring.* This sword is at the same time the symbol of his maturity as an artist and his maturity as a man. It is therefore the weapon of a "David," a double-faced creator and destroyer, an attacker and overthrower of the old order, like the "davy" in the Willingdone Museyroom.

If the ashplant is a symbol of the artist as an insurgent son striving for fatherhood, the lamp at which he strikes represents the old order, the fathers who have hindered and frightened Stephen ever since the first episode of *A Portrait.* The color-symbolism of *A Portrait* and *Ulysses* supports this view. In *A Portrait,* as we have seen, darkness is congenial to the son, and light or whiteness is the symbol of fatherhood. In *Ulysses* the symbolic opposition between light and dark becomes clear and overt. Stephen realizes, sometimes despairingly and sometimes defiantly, that darkness is congenial to his mind in many ways, initially as a negation of paternal brightness, but also as the proper environment of love, and as a companion symbol of "incertitude." Early he identifies his mind's bent for darkness: "in my mind's darkness a sloth of the underworld, reluctant, shy of brightness, shifting her dragon scaly folds" (U 26). He finds a sympathy in himself with the mind of the Moors and Jews who created algebra:

Across the page the symbols moved in grave morrice, in the mummery of their letters, wearing quaint caps of squares and cubes. Give hands, traverse, bow to partner: so: imps of fancy of the Moors. Gone too from the world, Averroes and Moses Maimonides, dark men in mien and movement, flashing in their mocking mirrors the obscure soul of the world, a darkness shining in brightness which the brightness could not comprehend.[7] (U 28)

Mr. Deasy emphasizes the "darkness" of Jews who "sinned against the light" (U 34); Stephen, defending them, defends their darkness and his. On the strand Stephen experiments with darkness and declares that "I am getting on nicely in the dark" (U 37). He opens his eyes and sadly discovers that the world was "there all the time without you: and ever shall be, world without end" (U 37). To create his vampire poem Stephen sits with his back to the sun and finds that "darkness is in our souls, do you not think?" (U 48). He tries to project his "image" in the poem as his shadow is produced by the sun, "manshape ineluctable." (See also U 243: "shadow of my mind.") The part of the Circe episode directly leading to the smashing of the lamp begins on U 560 with Stephen's allusion to the twilight of the gods. A little later (U 573) Stephen sees himself as the unfavored "dark horse" Throwaway fleeing past the winning post riderless, a symbol of the victory of darkness and incertitude over light and certainty, a victory won not by the power of controlled reason but by hysterical self-assertion. Stephen's victory, the smashing of the light, destroys time "and in the following darkness" ruins space (*U* 583). The darkness of the son has destroyed the light of the old father.

The father in *Ulysses* is represented by symbols of whiteness or paleness and light as he is in *A Portrait.* Stephen's enemies, all "fathers" or tools of fathers, bear the signs of the father; Buck's fair hair is the hue of "pale oak," and his teeth are white (*U* 3, 5, 6, 8); Haines's eyes are as cold and pale as the sea (*U* 18, 20, 30); (the sea itself is "Old Father Ocean" [*U* 50] and bleaches the victims of its cold waters [*U* 45] "saltwhite" [*U* 21, 50]); [8] Privates Carr and Compton are both blond (*U* 430), as are Richard Best (*U* 191, 198) and the paternal old fool Garrett Deasy (*U* 29). [9] Edward VII, the father whose "sons" attack Stephen, wears a white jersey and sucks a red jujube white (*U* 590, 591). The sun as well as the sea is enlisted on the side of the father. Buck's name is as "tripping and sunny" as he is (*U* 4); his voice and the sunlight are linked on *U* 10 and 11. Mr. Deasy's blond hair is "bleached" by the sunshine (*U* 29); his eyes are animated by a sunbeam while he shares his "old wisdom" with Stephen about the Jews' sin against "the light" (*U* 33–34). After he tells Stephen his joke about Ireland's exclusion of the forces of darkness, the sun flings spangles, dancing coins, on his shoulder in reward (*U* 36). Mr. Deasy is identified in Stephen's mind as a cold seafather on *U* 38; the waves, the "whitemaned seahorses, champing, bright windbridled," remind Stephen of Deasy and his letter, and in the following paragraph, of his "consubstantial" father Simon Dedalus. Father Conmee is surrounded by sunlight as he moves through the city; see *U* 219 for three references to sunlight. Finally, Edward VII's face begins to shine with pleasure at the impending slaughter on *U* 591. Clearly, when Stephen strikes the brothel lamp, he is trying to destroy the shining symbol of the father's power. Joyce's symbols for paternity have surrounded Stephen from the beginning of *A Portrait;* on *U* 583 Stephen finally strikes out at the fathers who have been trying to slow down his growth to maturity and creation, and ends their reign.

Their reign *is* ended; in the description of the effect of Stephen's blow Joyce makes it clear that this marks the end of an era, a goal toward which Stephen's history had been moving from the beginning of *A Portrait*.

(*He lifts his ashplant high with both hands and smashes the chandelier. Time's livid final flame leaps and, in the following darkness, ruin of all space, shattered glass and toppling masonry.* [*U* 583])

The idea that history moves toward the last judgment, toward the destruction of time and space in eternity, is first found in *Ulysses* in the Nestor episode.

Fabled by the daughters of memory. And yet it was in some way if not as memory fabled it. A phrase, then, of impatience, thud of Blake's wings of excess. I hear the ruin of all space, shattered glass and toppling masonry, and time one livid final flame. What's left us then? (*U* 24)

Joyce, in his early essay on Mangan, considered that it was history that was "fabled by the daughters of Memory." [10] By the time of the writing of *Ulysses* Joyce had modified this concept. The ultimate source of this phrase was found by Ellmann [11] to be Blake's addition to his catalogue of pictures for the year 1810, p. 68.

The Last Judgment is not Fable or Allegory, but Vision. Fable or Allegory are a totally distinct and inferior kind of Poetry. Vision or Imagination is a Representation of what Eternally Exists, Really & Unchangeably. Fable or Allegory is Form'd by the daughters of Memory. Imagination is surrounded by the daughters of Inspiration. [12]

History in Blake's terms is somehow not as Memory fables it because it leads up to the last judgment, an event graspable only by the visionary mind. Stephen imagines the end of the world in terms of the collapse of space and time, the shattering of glass and the toppling of masonry.[13] Stephen's smashing of the lamp is, then, a type of last judgment, an end of the world. Joyce's idea of apocalypse is not really Christian; the references to the *Ring*, to Nothung and to Götterdämmerung in *A Portrait* and *Ulysses* and to Ragnarök in *Finnegans Wake*[14] suggest that his idea of the great goal to which all history moves is not the permanent establishment of the City of God, but a pagan cyclical apocalypse, one occurring at the end of each cycle of history, when the old order yields place most grudgingly to the new. When Stephen smashes at the lamp with his phallic sword he is causing, or signalizing, the *ricorso* of history, the changeover from one set of fathers to another, himself becoming the father-creator.

The nature of the two-headed octopus mentioned by AE on *U* 165, which reappears as The End of the World on *U* 507, provides further support for this apocalyptic interpretation of *U* 583.

—Of the twoheaded octopus, one of whose heads is the head upon which the ends of the world have forgotten to come while the other speaks with a Scotch accent. (*U* 165)

The phrase "the head upon which the ends of the world have forgotten to come" is a parody of Pater's famous description of the Mona Lisa, in his book on the Renaissance: "Hers is the head upon which all 'the ends of the world are come,' and the eyelids are a little weary." However, in Pater's sentence the phrase "the ends of the world are come" is itself a quotation, from 1 Cor. 10:11.

Now all these things [various disasters overtaking the ancient jews under the old Law] happened unto them for ensamples: and they are written for our admonition, upon whom the ends of the world are come.

The meaning of this passage is that Christians of Paul's day should take heed of the flaws in the old Law, of the disasters which overtook even firm believers in the old interpretation of God's covenant, so that they may perfect themselves in the new ways, since it is in them, the new believers, that history is to have its fulfillment.[15] "The ends of the world" is equivalent to "the fulfillment of history" in Paul and in Pater. (Pater's Mona Lisa has lived and died many times and is immeasurably old.) AE's octopus, as he interprets it, is a being or a civilization that has missed its chance for historic fulfillment. The next time we see the octopus, however, it is called "The End of the World" and is part of a comic apocalypse (*U* 507). It whirls down through the murk from the zenith "in the form of the Three Legs of Man." The Three Legs of Man, as we have seen above, refers to the middle leg of man, the phallus. Therefore, if The End of the World represents the historical fulfillment of the world, the great goal toward which all history moves, it is a phallic end of the world. Stephen's ashplant smashes the paternal light and causes the old world to end; Stephen's maturity as a man forces the old father to give way to the new father, the old world to give way to the new; in *Finnegans Wake* (*FW* 10), the "davy's" bomb blows the hat off the whiteness of the father, and ends the fable.

The lamp, however, is a double symbol. The light within the lamp symbolizes the power of the old fathers; the light flashing out of the broken lamp chimney represents the new father, Stephen, the mature creator. In the foreshadowing of the lamp-smashing episode, at the beginning of the Circe episode, the light is liberated from the lamp, shattered "over the world" – "*[Stephen] flourishes his ashplant shivering the lamp image, shattering light over the world*" (*U* 432). In *A Portrait*, Stephen's first creation, the villanelle, feeble as it is, first comes to him surrounded by a white paternal light, his own, and is "opposed" by the dull white light of the older fathers. Released light is the symbolic representation of the primal act of fatherhood in the Oxen of the Sun chapter, as Bloom remembers his first sexual act.

Now he [Bloom] is himself paternal and these about him might be his sons. Who can say? The wise father knows his own child. He thinks of a drizzling night in Hatch street, hard by the bonded stores there, the first. Together . . . they hear the heavy tread of the watch as two raincaped shadows pass the new royal university. Bridie! Bridie Kelly! He will never forget the name, ever remember the night, first night, the bride-night. They are entwined in nethermost darkness, the willer with the willed, and in an instant (*fiat!*) light shall flood the world. (*U* 413)

Bloom prevents himself from becoming a father, however, on that occasion.

Did heart leap to heart? Nay, fair reader. In a breath 'twas done but—hold! Back! It must not be! In terror the poor girl flees away through the murk. She is the bride of darkness, a daughter of night. She dare not bear the sunnygolden babe of day. (*U* 413)

In this passage we find most of the elements of Joyce's theory of symbolic fatherhood: the incertitude of paternity, the sexual "wills," the darkness of sexuality, and finally the outburst of light signalling the arrival of paternity, the impulse generating the "sunnygolden babe of day," which Bloom represses.

When Stephen smashes at the lamp, light bursts out of the brothel chandelier, the old world-order ends, and the new one begins with the dawn of a new day. "Lucifer," as Stephen calls himself on *U* 558, is both destroyer and light-bearer, like King David. It is significant that both *Ulysses* and *Finnegans Wake* end with the sun rising: as Stephen walks up Eccles Street under "the double vibration of a jew's harp," Bloom feels "the incipient intimations of proximate dawn," and is tempted to stay out and watch the dawn which is about to appear (*U* 704–5). *Finnegans*

Wake ends with a magnificent sunrise and a universal cockcrow. When Stephen smashes the chandelier chimney of the brothel lamp, he is liberating the dawn of the new day, his day as King David, the destroyer of the old order and creator of the new.

With these interpretations in mind, it is possible to analyze in detail that portion of the Nighttown section that leads to Stephen's assault on the light and his affray with the soldiers.

The first two-thirds of the Circe episode (*U* 429–556) is almost entirely given up to Bloom and to his problems. Stephen appears briefly at *U* 431–33, where he expounds his "pornosophical" theory of gesture to Lynch, and "flourishes his ashplant shivering the lamp image, shattering light over the world," a foreshadowing of his action in the brothel. He also appears briefly at *U* 503–5, babbling self-consciously about creation and the creator. With the exceptions of those four pages Stephen does very little, while Bloom enjoys himself immensely.

At *U* 556, the action that leads to Stephen's violent gesture begins. Stephen recites his riddle, inviting the appearance of his mother's ghost, calls himself Lucifer (and Icarus) on *U* 558, and almost admits his guilt in his mother's death (*U* 559). *Götterdämmerung* is referred to on *U* 560, foreshadowing the downfall of the gods twenty-three pages later. On *U* 561 Lynch smacks Kitty and says "Pandy bat." This immediately evokes the memory of Father Dolan, the tyrannical father, and the paternal aggression of Clongowes. Father Dolan, however, is reassured by Father Conmee, who assures him that "Stephen is a very good little boy," that is, harmless to fathers. On *U* 563 Stephen finds numerical coincidences in the lives of Bloom and himself that suggest to him that history "moves to one great goal," and refers again to Father Dolan's aggression: "Hurt my hand somewhere." On *U* 569 Stephen mentions a helpless father Noah, whose son, Ham the "seeboy," saw his father when "his ark was open." [16] On *U* 571 Stephen recalls that he was offered a woman by the devil, and a melon (i.e., Molly) in a dream. He rejects these bribes on *U* 572 and shouts his defiance of the father:

STEPHEN
Break my spirit, will he? *O merde alors!* (*U* 572)

"He" shows up immediately; it is Stephen's father Simon Dedalus, in the forms of a buzzard and a huntsman, who starts a hunt for Stephen. Stephen as the guilty fox runs hunted across country, but as a dark horse wins his race (*U* 573). Privates Carr and Compton pass by in the street with Cissy Caffrey singing "My Girl's a Yorkshire Girl" and are identified as tools of God the father by Stephen: "Our friend, noise in the street" (*U* 574), echoing *U* 34. The soldiers bear the father's sign of blondness; in addition, they are called "necessary evils" by Stephen on *U* 595, an expression he had applied to fathers on *U* 207. They are God in the sense that they set off the crisis directly; by their singing they incite Zoe to start the pianola, which makes Stephen dance, which makes Stephen dizzy, which causes him to see his dead mother, which causes him to smash at the chandelier. The dance of the hours that takes place in the brothel (*U* 575–77) leads to the running-out of Time and the approach of apocalypse. Stephen's mother rises from the dead and the horrified Stephen begs her for "the word known to all men," the password of fatherhood (see *U* 49). The mother responds with prayers for Stephen's soul, and he bursts out with rage against God: "The ghoul! Hyena! . . . The corpsechewer! Raw head and bloody bones!" (*U* 581). Finally, shouting the name of his sword, Stephen raises his ashplant deliberately, "with both hands," and smashes the chandelier (*U* 583). Time's livid final flame leaps, space is ruined, and the new light is shattered over the world.

The first thing that Stephen does after the great apocalypse, after the downfall of the old order and his symbolic accession to maturity, is to rush out into the street in search of a feminine reality for him to fertilize. He runs up to Cissy Caffrey, the last in a series of representatives of his beloved that range from Eileen Vance through Mercedes and E. C. to the bird-girl on the beach, his "sister" Ireland, and woos her ecstatically. According to Cissy, he tried to get her "to go with him" (*U* 588), and at the height of his danger, regardless of the ravings of Private Carr and the bloody wars breaking out in his hallucination, Stephen woos Cissy.

STEPHEN
(*Ecstatically, to Cissy Caffrey.*)
    White thy fambles, red thy gan
    And thy quarrons dainty is. (*U* 598)

Stephen is quite aware of the fact that by wooing his beloved he is attacking the father; he notes again that his hand hurts him slightly, that old wound (*U* 589), he wishes to "sit down somewhere and discuss" something, possibly the death of kings (see *Richard II* 3.2.155–56). Stephen realizes that, in Blake's words

    The King & the Priest must be tied in a tether
    Before two virgins can meet together.[17]

All hell breaks loose, battle, black masses, civil wars, the King-father Edward VII eggs on his sons, and at the climax of the turmoil Private Carr rushes forward and knocks Stephen out (*U* 601). However, even while unconscious, Stephen woos his bird-girl; he stretches out his arms to her and sings "Who Goes with Fergus?" (*U* 608). He is yearning to practice his new paternal role and has no more brooding inhibitions about his powers, no more fears that he is "the eternal son and ever virgin." He sings constantly from this point on, although previously in *Ulysses* he had not been able to sing at all; this is a sign of his returning powers as a Davidic artist. He claims that Ireland belongs to him, which indeed it does, as the subject of his art. A man among men, he urinates side by side with Bloom (*U* 702–3). He rejects Bloom's offer of a place in the house, which would also involve a chance at Molly or Milly, because Bloom desperately needs a son and Stephen is no longer a son.[18] *Ulysses* is, in part, the story of a father's search for a son, but the easy parallel must not be drawn—the son is not in search of a father. The son is striving to *become* a father, to fulfill his Aristotelian drive toward completeness. In *Finnegans Wake* also, the only reason the sons seek the father is to destroy him.

Stephen must go into exile to begin his new life as a creator. Cissy Caffrey is an unworthy choice for Stephen; as an Irish girl walking out with British soldiers she is hardly the consort for the new "king" of Ireland. Nor are her friends any more worthy of the role; they all are involved with foreigners (*U* 431).[19] Molly and Milly are also unsatisfactory, since accepting either of them would also be accepting a role as Bloom's son, a little Harry Hughes enticed to his (spiritual) death by a Jew's daughter (*U* 690–92). Stephen, therefore, leaves the house of bondage and goes on his way under the chariot of David. As he goes, a Jew's harp sounds in Eccles Street for the beginning of his life as the new David, the mature creator, and the dawn prepares to rise.

appendix / notes / bibliography / index

epictetus and buckets in joyce

The sudden intrusion of Epictetus in the dean's conversation (*P* 187) has many interesting aspects apart from the one mentioned above, where the dean seems to identify himself as a lame slave by his naming of the lame slave Epictetus.

The intrusion is quite deliberate on Joyce's part. There is no hint of Epictetus in the corresponding section in *Stephen Hero* (*SH* 27–29, 42). Father Butt in that section does attempt to impress Stephen, but he does not drag in a first-century A.D. Greek stoic to do it. Atherton suggests that Joyce has the dean bring in Epictetus for purposes of irony: a Jesuit quotes a pagan in support of his argument while a rebel quotes Aquinas in support of his.[1] This seems to be a reasonable interpretation, but there might be other reasons for the mention of Epictetus.

It is perhaps an attempt at realism; the cold, enduring qualities preached by Epictetus might be those embraced by the dean. Another realistic association of Epictetus with the dean is Epictetus's relation to Christianity—Epictetus was the subject of an intense effort, in the nineteenth century, to make him a righteous heathen. There was even a suggestion that he had read parts of the New Testament and had met early Christians, and that he had derived his philosophy of serenity of soul and contempt of the world from them.[2]

Stephen's response to the dean's question, "You know Epictetus?" "An old gentleman . . . who said that the soul is very like a bucketful of water," contains more than a snub to the old dean. Epictetus's comparison of the soul to "a bucketful of water" occurs in book 3, section 3 of his *Discourses*.

What is weeping and lamenting? A matter of judgement. What
is misfortune? Judgement. What is faction, discord, criticism,
accusation, irreligion, foolishness? All these are judgements,
nothing else, and judgements passed on things beyond the will,
as though they were good and evil. Only let a man turn these
efforts to the sphere of the will and I guarantee that he will
enjoy peace of mind, whatever his circumstance may be.

    The soul is like a dish full of water, and the impressions
like the rays of light which strike the water. Now when the
water is disturbed the light seems to be disturbed too, but it is
not really disturbed. So when a man has a fit of dizziness, the
acts and virtues are not put to confusion, but only the spirit
in which they exist: when this is at rest, they come to rest too.
(*Trans. by P. E. Matheson [1916]*)

This characteristic bit of Stoic exhortation comes readily
to Stephen's mind; why only this one, and not any one of
dozens of similar passages in the *Discourses?* Perhaps
Stephen sneers "coarsely" at Epictetus's definition of the
soul to indicate to the poor old dean that whoever's soul
may be like water, his, the artist's, is like a rock. However,
another possibility is suggested by the context of the quotation. At the beginning of section 3 of book 3 comes the
assertion by Epictetus that

the very sight of good attracts one towards it, the sight of evil
repels. The soul will never reject a clear impression of good,
any more than we reject Caesar's currency. On this depends
every motion of men and of God. (*Matheson trans.*)

Just before the matter of Epictetus is brought up Stephen
has quoted Aquinas on the good: *Bonum est in quod tendit
appetitus* (P 186) . The phrase from Epictetus, "The very
sight of good attracts one towards it," is very close to
Stephen's doctrine, derived from this statement of Aquinas,
that perception of the good is kinetic while perception of
the true and the beautiful is static. He will base his whole
theory of art as recreation of static movements of truth
upon this Aquinan doctrine. Therefore, we may say that

the train of thought begun on *P* 186 continues on under
the desultory conversation until it surfaces at *P* 187 in
another form. But why should Stephen think of *this* section of Epictetus's *Discourses* in this context when the idea
that good attracts the mind can be found in many other
places, including Aristotle? I think a more satisfactory
answer lies elsewhere.

In this section of Epictetus occurs a rejection of unworthy fatherhood:

[Since the soul can never resist a clear impression of the good,
and since it is upon this property of the soul that "every notion
of man and of God depends"] therefore the good is preferred
to every tie of kinship.

I have no concern with my father, but with the good!

"Are you so hard-hearted?"

It is my nature; this is the currency which God has given
me. Therefore if the good is different from the noble and just,
then father and brother, country and all such things disappear.

I say, am I to neglect my good, that you may get it? Am I
to make way for you? Why should I?

"I am your father."

But not my good. (*Matheson trans.*)

What Stephen is doing, then, in quoting a portion of
Epictetus, is implicitly rejecting the dean's bid to be his
ghostly father, just as he rejects it explicitly on *P* 190.
(With the little "scenario" of age threatening youth with a
baculus (see above) we see a strong undercurrent of hostility to the father displayed in this section.) This technique of contextual allusion, most often associated with
Eliot and Pound, is characteristically Joycean, and we will
meet it again many times in *Ulysses* and *Finnegans Wake*.
In these works he evokes a large section of a source by
quoting a small section of it, or perhaps only one characteristic word or phrase of it. This technique permits clari-
fication of complex situations in an elegant and economical
manner.

Some other overtones of this quotation from Epictetus are interesting to explore. For example, from which source does Stephen get his phrase "bucket of water"? None of the translations of this section of Epictetus available to Joyce translate *lekane* as "bucket." Elisabeth Carter (1758) translates the word as "vessel"; George Long (1877) translates it as "dish." The Matheson translation, published in 1916, too late for *A Portrait*, translates it also as "dish." The word "bucket" was chosen deliberately by Joyce and has a specific symbolic meaning. Buckets appear in many contexts in *Ulysses* and *Finnegans Wake*. One of the most common contexts for the word is in the neighborhood of authoritarian violence, of "beastly death," of callous disregard of suffering, and of official deathdealings in the form of executions and wars. Bloom watches Larry O'Rourke's "curate" swab up the shop with mop and bucket (*U* 58); immediately afterward come references to the Russo-Japanese War and to Paddy Dignam's burial. On *U* 71 a listless boy holds a bucket of offal; a few lines below the mention of the boy Bloom remembers the burial again. There are many buckets in the Hades chapter itself; a server holds "a brass bucket with something in it" which proves to be holy water which Father Coffey shakes out over the grave (*U* 103–4). Later, Bloom, regarding Glasnevin, thinks, "Who passed away. Who departed this life. As if they did it of their own accord. Got the shove, all of them. Who kicked the bucket' (*U* 113). Bloom's cynical rewriting of the epitaphs of the unwilling dead establishes the phrase "kicked the bucket" as a reference to what Buck Mulligan called "beastly death." The bucket acquires the sinister significance of an instrument of the *dio boia* on *U* 164: "[A baby] born every second somewhere. Other dying every second. Since I fed the birds five minutes. Three hundred kicked the bucket." Bloom agrees with Stephen about the cruelty of the God of nature; Stephen's dissertation on the gluttony of God (*U*

420) repeats in expanded form Bloom's horror of the cold, cruel process of birth and death. Before another bucket reference Stephen uses a phrase "staggering bob" which was first used by Bloom on *U* 171: "Poor trembling calves. Meh. Staggering bob. Bubble and squeak. Butchers' buckets wobble lights. . . . Rawhead and bloody bones." Stephen throws "Raw head and bloody bones!" as a curse at God in the Nighttown chapter, and calls Him "The corpsechewer!" (*U* 581). The head of the executioner in the Cyclops chapter is enclosed in a "tengallon pot with two circular perforated apertures through which his eyes glowered furiously" (*U* 309). Buck Mulligan's callous dismissal of death as beastly and nothing more turns into a restatement of the bucket motif in the Nighttown section, as the spectre of Stephen's mother rises from the grave: "The mockery of it! Kinch killed her dogsbody bitchbody. She kicked the bucket" (*U* 580). Edward VII supervises and inflames the carnage in the Nighttown chapter with an "identification bucket" in his hand (*U* 590, 591). On *U* 594 the Croppy Boy is hanged and drawn; Edward VII, delighted with the horrors of the execution done in his name, "dances slowly, solemnly, rattling his bucket and [singing] with soft contentment." After Stephen has been struck down by Private Carr, inflamed with drink and hazy patriotism, Major Tweedy, as representative of the crown, declares the war over: "Carbine in bucket! Cease fire!" (*U* 601). Finally, there might be an echo of Rumbold's pot headgear in Bloom's asseveration that the police would gladly perjure themselves to secure a conviction: ". . . those policemen . . . were admittedly unscrupulous in the service of the Crown and . . . prepared to swear a hole through a ten gallon pot" (*U* 615).

This meaning of buckets as symbolizing the cruelty and violence of nature and of nature's God, as well as the savagery of equally authoritarian earthly figures like kings who foment wars and demand executions, is reinforced in

Finnegans Wake: "Nobucketnozzler" appears in the bloody company of "Homin" (perhaps Haman), "Broin Baroke," "Lonan" (perhaps Lenin), and "Guinnghis Khan" on *FW* 24.34–35; HCE, the cheap politician and cheat, has a "bucketshop store" (*FW* 46.3); the infuriated Cad threatens, among other things, that ". . . he would give him [HCE] his (or theumperom's or anybloody else's) thickerthanwater to drink and his bleday steppebrodhar's into the bucket" (*FW* 70.25–27). One of the suggested answers to Shem's riddle, "When is a man not a man?" is ". . . when the angel of death kicks the bucket of life" (*FW* 170.12–13), that is, when he is a corpse. Finally,[3] the enraged Jaun threatens extreme violence, both legal and extralegal, to anyone who makes advances to his sister: ". . . if I get the wind up what do you bet in the buckets of my wrath I mightn't even take it into my progromme, as sweet course, to do a rash act and pitch in and swing for your perfect stranger in the meadow of heppiness and then wipe up the street with the clonmellian, pending my bringing proceedings verses the joyboy before a bunch of magistrafes and twelve good and gleeful men" (*FW* 443.6–11). "The buckets of my wrath" is an echo of the seven vials of God's wrath to be poured out on the sinful earth, in Rev. 15:5–8, 16:1–21, the ultimate violence of the Most High on his suffering creation.

If "bucket" means in *A Portrait* what it means in *Ulysses* and *Finnegans Wake,* Stephen is deliberately mistranslating Epictetus to show that he is acquainted with the coercive power of the father, and does not care if he knows it. This, combined with the context of the Epictetus quotation that he chooses, reveals his attitude toward the father who tried many times to bully and terrorize him; he now despises the power of the father, and dismisses him from his thoughts. At this point in his career, at any rate, the artist sees a clear path ahead toward creation, toward fatherhood for himself.

1 The conflict of the generations

[1] In *The Wings of the Dove,* James originally intended to make Lionel Croy into a much more prominent figure than he turned out to be. "He but 'looks in,' poor, beautiful dazzling, damning apparition that he was to have been." (Preface to *The Wings of the Dove* [New York: Modern Library ed.], p. xviii.)

For a short note on fathers in modern literature, see Kevin Sullivan, *Joyce Among the Jesuits* (New York, 1958), pp. 53–54.

[2] See E. L. Epstein, "James Joyce and *The Way of All Flesh,*" *James Joyce Quarterly,* 7 (Fall 1969), 22–29.

[3] *Letters of James Joyce,* ed. Stuart Gilbert and Richard Ellmann, 3 vols (New York, 1957, 1966) 1, 312.

[4] Joyce felt his father's death keenly. In the same letter, he remarks that he has passed the weeks since his father's death "in prostration of mind," and that he was thinking of abandoning *Finnegans Wake:* "I could not collect my thoughts or do anything."

[5] Richard Ellmann, *James Joyce* (New York, 1959), pp. 181, 269–70, 285–86; Stanislaus Joyce, *My Brother's Keeper* (New York, 1958), pp. 57, 59, 60.

[6] Here Joyce actually suppresses material from his own life which he might have used in his portrait of Stephen—John Joyce occasionally *did* bluster at his eldest son. (See *The Dublin Diary of Stanislaus Joyce,* ed. B. H. Healey [Ithaca, N.Y., 1962], p. 46; Ellmann, *James Joyce,* p. 156.)

[7] I will not try here to resolve the difficult questions of Joyce's irony, and whether we are to take anything that Stephen says as Joyce's own opinion. However, I believe that Joyce always clearly signals irony whenever he intends it.

[8] Joyce later quotes a phrase from this sonnet, "unear'd womb," on *U* 202. See W. M. Schutte, *Joyce and Shakespeare* (New Haven, 1957), p. 182. For other references to offspring as images, projections, or portraits, see Sonnets 6, 9, 10, 11, 13, 16, 17.

[9] Ellmann, *James Joyce,* p. 212. See also Stanislaus Joyce, *My Brother's Keeper* (New York, 1958), p. 152.

[10] Ellmann, p. 212.

[11] *De Anima,* 2. 4. 415^{a}25–32, trans. J. A. Smith in *The Works of Aristotle,* ed. W. D. Ross (Oxford, 1931), vol. 3.

[12] The Latin translation of Aristotle used by Aquinas for his commentary on *De Anima* supports this interpretation; it has *quaecumque perfecta [sunt]* for *hosa teleia,* and Aquinas's commentary indicates that he interpreted *teleia* to mean "matured" rather than "phys-

ically capable." See *Aristotle's De Anima, in the version of William of Moerbeke and the commentary of St. Thomas Aquinas,* trans. Kenelm Foster and Silvester Humphries (New Haven, 1951) sec. 314, p. 214.

13 *Metaphysics,* 16. 1021ᵇ23–25; translation is from Aristotle *Metaphysics* books 1–9, trans. H. Tredennick (London, 1947), p. 267. This passage is actually the fourth description of "perfection" in this section. The other three either describe common meanings of the word or are related to the idea of the complete attainment of an end.

14 Gorman declares that Joyce read Aristotle in Victor Cousin's translation in Paris 1903; see Herbert Gorman, *James Joyce* (London, 1939), p. 94—hereafter cited as Gorman. This phrase has been variously translated. W. A. Hammond in his 1902 translation of *De Anima* renders it as "all animals which are perfect and not abnormal" (*Aristotle's Psychology,* trans. W. A. Hammond [London, 1902], p. 57). Philip Wheelwright translates it as "normally developed and not defective" (*Aristotle: Selections . . . ,* trans. Philip Wheelwright [New York, 1951], p. 130). The implication in Hammond's translation is that all that is necessary for reproduction is that the being in question be physically capable of it. The Wheelwright translation introduces the notion of development to maturity; Smith's translation makes this suggestion explicit with its use of the phrase *"reached its normal development."*

Ellmann echoes Gorman: "After a day reading Jonson [Joyce] would go on to Cousin's translation of Aristotle's *De Anima, Metaphysics,* and of course *Poetics"* (p. 124). However, Victor Cousin never translated *De Anima, Metaphysics* or *Poetics* or any work of Aristotle. A French translation of *De Anima* was made in 1846 by a disciple of Cousin—Barthélémy-Saint-Hilaire (*Traité de l'Ame* [Paris, 1846]). If Joyce read this translation, he would have seen that 415ᵃ 27–28 is rendered, "êtres vivants qui sont complets, et qui ne sont pas avortés, ni produits par génération spontanée." This translation clearly separates the "completed" beings *both* from the abortions *and* from the spontaneously generated beings; Joyce's "complete" is a literal translation of Barthélémy-Saint-Hilaire's "complets," and therefore the phrase in Joyce should probably be interpreted as signifying *completely developed* beings rather than *physically complete* creatures.

15 In *Finnegans Wake,* however, it almost seems as if the Eternal Creator Himself fears human creation as an assertion of paternity, and therefore an attempt to push Him from His Throne. His thun-

ders growl most when someone is writing a letter, a song, or a fable. See *FW* 23.5, 44.20, 113.9, 257.27, 314.8, 414.19, 424.20 (this last thunder-word is evoked by the word "invrention").

16 In *A Portrait* "race" seems to refer both to family lines and to nationality; by *Finnegans Wake* "race" seems to take in all of the human race; "The Irish Race and World" is the title of an important short episode in the *Wake* (*FW* 342.14–32).

17 Helmut Bonheim provides an interesting analysis of the father-son conflict in *Joyce's Benefictions,* but he sees it as basically the traditional romantic conflict between the Byronic rebel and the forces of authority and conformity. He declares that the suggestion of a father-son relationship between Bloom and Stephen is a "half-truth" (p. 40).

18 Joyce seems to have considered "Haveth Childers Everywhere" one of the more important expansions of HCE's initials; he chose this section to be published as one of the five booklets of sections from the *Wake* that appeared before the *Wake* as a whole did. It is the only one of the five which is directly about the father; the others describe the nature of the mother, the sons, and the daughter of the archetypal family. The five booklets are *Haveth Childers Everywhere* [*FW* 532–54] (Paris and New York, 1930; London, 1931), *Anna Livia Plurabelle* [*FW* 196–216] (New York, 1928; London, 1930), *Tales Told of Shem and Shaun* [*FW* 152–59, 282–304, 414–19] (Paris, 1929), later printed as *Two Tales of Shem and Shaun* [*FW* 152–59, 414–19] (London, 1932), *The Mime of Mick, Nick and the Maggies* [*FW* 219–59] (The Hague, 1933), *Storiella As She is Syung* [*FW* 260–75, 304–8] (London, 1937); see Walton Litz, *The Art of James Joyce* (London, 1961), pp. 147–48.

19 Perhaps there is also a reference to John of Gaunt's dying speech in *Richard II,* 2.1. 57–61.

20 For other references to *The Playboy* and other Synge works, see J. S. Atherton, *The Books at the Wake* (New York, 1960), p. 284.

21 *FW* 23.4.

22 "Pamjab!" and "Bumchub!" echo the "bombshoob" of the Willingdone episode (*FW* 10.9) that was sought so fiercely by the third soldier.

23 The most obvious complaints occur on *FW* 260.N1, 277.N2, and 293.N2. The subject is treated again in the "Peaches Browning" episode, *FW* 65.5–33.

24 See *FW* 279.N1: "The good fother with the twingling in his eye will always have cakes in his pocket to bethroat us with for our allmichael good."

FW 283.N3 is a particularly interesting example: "Slash-the-Pill lifts the pellet. Run, Phoenix, run!" This seems to be a re-wording of a stanza from an early poem by Robert Graves, "The Halls of Bedlam," which is about a father who runs mad and kills his children.

> Father in his shirt-sleeves
> Flourishing a hatchet—
> > Run, children, run!

Graves is mentioned in *FW* 283 three lines above the line to which note 3 refers: "bring alliving stone allaughing down to grave clothnails." ("Pellet" could contain the Greek *pelekus,* axe.)

Another prominent reference to a murderous father occurs on *FW* 115.28: "that undemonstrative relative . . . who settles our hashbill for us"; Joyce probably picked up the expression "settle your hash" from his American friends.

25 *FW* 373–80: The mob, singing the last of five stanzas of their warsong, "Water parted from the say," rush up the straining "gang-stairs," declaring that Hosty, their leader, will "speed the bogre's barque away." The "bogre" is branded (*FW* 374.32–33), kicked viciously (*FW* 375.3–4, 21–22), and hanged (*FW* 377.8–9, 17–18, 36), and dies slowly (*FW* 378.1–2, 17, 20–21, 24–26, 379.12 [they shoot him to speed up the process: see *U* 328], 13, 18).

26 Lincoln's assassin, Booth, is mentioned many times—the first time on *FW* 32.36 ("the viceregal booth"), where HCE, like Lincoln before his assassination, is in a theatre box watching a performance, and for the last time on *FW* 552.15, where John Wilkes Booth is merged with General William Booth of the Salvation Army; see also *FW* 26.10, 35.10 ("jackboots"), 72.20, 188.7, 257.19, 262.24, 314.21, 316.33, 332.35, 351.28, 368.24, and 480.30. The references to Succoth, the Hebrew Festival of Booths, may also conceal the personage of John Wilkes Booth—as a year-end festival of fertility it may also refer to the change of power from the old king to the new; see *FW* 13.28, 612.14, 15 (first "seecut," then "sukkot").

27 See Bonheim, *Benefictions,* pp. 58–72 passim, for a useful analysis of Mark's role in the book.

28 The manuscript of this sketch (Slocum-Cahoon E 3a) is now in the Lockwood Library collection of Joyce material at the University of Buffalo; see Peter Spielberg, *James Joyce's Manuscripts and Letters at the University of Buffalo* (Buffalo, 1962), p. 7. The typescript made by Stanislaus is at Cornell; see Robert E. Scholes, *The Cornell Joyce Collection* (Ithaca, N.Y., 1961), pp. 15–16. The

sketch was published in the *Yale Review,* 49 (Spring 1960), 360–69. See also Ellmann, pp. 149–52.

[29]   BM Add MSS 47473, p. 137; quoted in David Hayman, ed., *A First-Draft Version of Finnegans Wake* (Austin, Texas, 1963), p. 97, n. 28.

[30]   Smith trans. in Ross, *Works of Aristotle,* vol. 3.

[31]   Gorman, *James Joyce,* p. 95. Stephen repeats a version of this definition on *U* 432:

So that gesture . . . would be a universal language, the gift of tongues rendering visible not the lay sense but the first entelechy, the structural rhythm.

[32]   Smith trans., in Ross, *Works of Aristotle,* vol. 3.

[33]   I have deleted and added commas to this sentence, which appears in a confusing form in all editions of *Stephen Hero.*

[34]   See, for example, his Pola notebooks (quoted in Gorman, *James Joyce,* pp. 133–35); *SH* 213; *P* 212–13. For a rather hazy exposition of a related point, see *U* 633–34.

[35]   *De Anima* 3. 6. 430^b 6–16.

[36]   Ibid., 430^b 17–30.

[37]   Father Noon further suggests that "a modest tradition of Scotist aesthetics" instituted by Gerard Manley Hopkins while a professor at University College may have survived to Joyce's day. Further on (p. 72) Father Noon suggests that "possibly to heighten the irony in Stephen's predicament" Joyce assigned to him "a solicitude for the uniquely singular and individually ineffable thing."

[38]   S. L. Goldberg, *The Classical Temper: a Study of James Joyce's Ulysses* (London, 1961), p. 318.

[39]   Two places are also described; the Inn (or City), and the Universe (or mound of universal history).

[40]   For a development of this point, see Irene Hendry Chayes, "Joyce's Epiphanies," *Sewanee Review* (July 1946), 9.

2   a portrait of the artist

[1]   In *Finnegans Wake* one of the major traits of HCE is his stammer; *balbus* means *stammering* in Latin (see *FW* 287.19, 467.16, 518.34, 552.19, for other references to Balbus). Another trait of HCE's is his association with walls, in his roles as Humpty Dumpty, Tim Finnegan the hod-carrier, and Bygmester Solness, Ibsen's master-builder. The association of the Clongowes "square"

with fear and sexuality also helps to reinforce the references to the fearsome, creative father: "What did that mean about the smugging in the square? Why did the five fellows out of the higher line run away for that? . . . [Eileen] had said that pockets were funny things to have" (*P* 42–43).

² Joseph Campbell and Henry Morton Robinson, *A Skeleton Key to Finnegans Wake* (New York, 1944), p. 164. Robert S. Ryf, in *A New Approach to Joyce* (Berkeley and Los Angeles, California, 1962), p. 203, says that the father on the first page of *A Portrait* "is clearly a child's idea and surrogate of God." See also Hugh Kenner, *Dublin's Joyce* (Bloomington, Indiana, 1956), p. 114.

³ In *Finnegans Wake* versions of the phrase "There's hair," which is an abbreviation of the once fashionable meaningless phrase "There's hair like wire coming out of the Empire," seem to be associated with the father. The clearest connection between hair and paternal rule is found on *FW* 289.9–10, in "Derzherr, live wire" who thrust his "righthand son" out of his "Empyre," that is, the "Erzherr" blazing with lightning fired his sinful son out of His empyrean, very much as Zeus thrust his craftsman son Hephaestus out of Olympus. (See Kenner, *Dublin's Joyce*, p. 115.)

⁴ John V. Kelleher, "The Perceptions of James Joyce," *Atlantic Monthly*, 201 (March 1958), 85: "As the very first sentence [of *A Portrait*] informs us, he is not truly of the family into which he was born—there he is 'baby tuckoo,'" the cuckoo's fledgling in the cowbird's nest." See also Ronald Bates, "The Correspondence of Birds to Things of the Intellect," *James Joyce Quarterly*, 2 (Summer 1965), 287.

⁵ The "pigtail tarr" dances up to them; the rhythm of the passage suggests a hornpipe, perhaps the very hornpipe of *A Portrait*.

He's a pigtail tarr and if he hadn't got it toothick he'd a tell-tale tall of his pitcher on a wall with his photure in the papers for cutting moutonlegs and capers, letting on he'd jest be japers and his tail cooked up. (*FW* 232.36–233.3)

⁶ Matthew J. C. Hodgart and Mabel P. Worthington, *Song in the Works of James Joyce* (New York, 1959), p. 159.

⁷ This is the first appearance of the word "different," which later becomes the sign of the artist's apartness from his fellows; see sec. b.

⁸ Joyce was almost certainly acquainted with this verse. Prov. 30:1 of the Douay version identifies the source of the wise sayings in chapter 30 of Proverbs as "Gatherer the son of Vomiter." "Gatherer" and "Vomiter" ("Congregans" and "Vomens" in the Vulgate) are

literal translations of the Hebrew "Agur" and "Jakeh," in which form they appear in the King James version. (No one knows the significance, if any, of these names.) In *Ulysses*, Stephen mentions a "Maister Gatherer," who can only be the "Gatherer" of Prov. 30.

Gilbert [Shakespeare's brother] in his old age told some cavaliers he got a pass for nowt from Maister Gatherer one time. (*U* 209)

There is no Shakespearean figure called "Gatherer," either in Shakespeare's work, in the work of his contemporaries, or in his life or that of his family.

⁹ Note that the second of these biblical references is also about eyes. The true (i.e., symbolic) significance of eagles and eyes becomes clear hundreds of pages later; see sec. f. Hugh Kenner's suggestion (in *Dublin's Joyce*, p. 116) that the eagles are Roman eagles and symbols of the Church's threatening power, though certainly plausible, seems to me to explain less about the real situation of the book than the notion that they are biblical eagles.

¹⁰ Epiphany No. 6 in James Joyce, *Epiphanies*, ed. O. A. Silverman (Buffalo, 1956), p. 6.

¹¹ It is clear, however, that neither of the women is the primary cause of Stephen's fright. They are obviously defending him (jocularly, but really) against an angry third party. The situation, women defending weak males, occurs again on *U* 531–32 (the whores sheltering unmanned Leopold Bloom from Bello) and on *FW* 8.29–30: "This is the crimealine of the alps hooping to sheltershock the three lipoleums." ALP is trying to shield her sons from the dreadful Willingdone.

¹² Kevin Sullivan, *Joyce Among the Jesuits* (New York, 1958), pp. 14, 42–43, 51.

¹³ See J. S. Atherton's notes to his edition of *A Portrait* (Modern Novels Series [London, 1964]), pp. 239–40. See also Richard Ellmann, *James Joyce* (New York, 1959), p. 29.

¹⁴ In his Pola notebook Joyce made a note about the "cold flesh of priests." See Herbert Gorman, *James Joyce* (New York, 1939), p. 138.

¹⁵ For a short analysis of the light-dark opposition in the works of Joyce, see Kenner, *Dublin's Joyce*, pp. 116–17. See also Thomas F. Smith, "Color and Light in 'The Dead,'" *James Joyce Quarterly*, 2 (Summer 1965), 304–9.

¹⁶ This attempt at definition is repeated, in expanded form, in the Lessons episode of *Finnegans Wake*; see Campbell and Robinson, *Skeleton Key*, pp. 164–68.

[17] In *Finnegans Wake* Shaun never tires of mocking Shem's refusal to become engaged in battle; see, for example, *FW* 171.33–34, 174.5–21, 176.19–36, 177.1–7, 178.8–36, 179.1–8, 189.28–36, 190.1–9 (Shaun justifies conflict), 190.26–30, 423.7 ("polthronechair"), 15 ("that unbloody housewarmer").

[18] Gogarty reported that "Joyce knew no Greek" (in *As I Was Going Down Sackville Street* [London, 1936], p. 285). However, apart from Gogarty's doubtful status as a disinterested witness to the facts of Joyce's career, there is a good deal of evidence that Joyce picked up a number of classical and modern Greek phrases while he was writing *A Portrait, Ulysses,* and *Finnegans Wake* (see Ellmann, *James Joyce,* ill. facing p. 433; see also pp. 421, 526). One of the two books left on his desk in Zurich when he went off to the hospital for his last illness was a Greek lexicon (Ellmann, p. 755). His notebooks containing exercises in modern Greek dating from his sojourn in Zurich (1915–19) are in the Lockwood Memorial Library at the University of Buffalo; see Peter Spielberg, *James Joyce's Manuscripts and Letters at the University of Buffalo: a Catalogue* (Buffalo, 1962), pp. 161–67.

[19] In his notes to his edition of *A Portrait* (Modern Novels Series [London, 1964]), p. 242.

[20] In *Ulysses* Stephen shows that he feels he is in the house of an enemy in 7 Eccles Street, first by the unfriendly song he sings (*U* 690–91), and then by the intonation of Ps. 113, commemorating the exit of Israel from the house of bondage (*U* 698).

[21] The "few coloured tickets" on the seats of the tram turn up again in *Finnegans Wake,* on *FW* 194.31–32, as an attribute of ALP who, as the symbol of development and maturing through time, wears "tramtokens in her hair."

[22] See D. A. Chart, *The Story of Dublin* (London, 1907), p. 327. The name originated from the lots reclaimed from the marshlands around the Liffey.

[23] "Hophazards" seems to be a reference both to the random motions of molecular particles ("Brownian motion") and to the quantum theory of discrete energy discontinuities. Scientists have recognized the role that chance plays in the creation of order:

> The fact that local irregularities cannot account for the existence of river meanders does not rule out either random processes as a possible explanation. . . . It is a paradox of nature that . . . random processes can produce regular forms . . . L. B. Leopold and W. B. Langbein, "River Meanders," *Scientific American,* (June 1966), 60.

For further treatment of the topic of chance in Joyce, see E. L. Epstein, "Chance, Doubt, Coincidence and the Prankquean's Riddle," *A Wake Newslitter*, 6, No. 1 (February 1969), 3–7.

[24] Besides the mention of night, the prostitute's greeting is significant in another respect. The name "Will" in the works of Joyce is frequently a symbol of "will," both that of sexual drive and that of the artist in pursuing his vocation. See for example *P* 249 (five "Wills" mentioned), *U* 198, 201–2 (here associated with sex), 206, 209, 217; see also *FW* 31, on which appears a king who is the composite of William the Conqueror, William Rufus, William III, William IV, and William Ewart Gladstone. "Will" in Elizabethan poetry sometimes has the significance of sexual power; the OED entry on "will," def. 2, quotes *The Rape of Lucrece* in this connection:

> Thus, graceless, holds he [Tarquin] disputation
> 'Tween frozen conscience and hot-burning will . . .
>
> (246–47)

(See also *Measure for Measure*, 2.4.164.) Joyce knew of this meaning; he employs it in Stephen's villanelle: "And you have had your will of him" (*P* 218, 223).

[25] The use of darkness as a symbol of the young attacker of the old order may derive ultimately from Shelley. Demogorgon, the overthrower of Jupiter in *Prometheus Unbound,* is described as "a veiled form sitting on an ebon throne," and as a "mighty darkness/ Filling the seat of power, and rays of gloom,/Dart round . . ." (act 2, sc. 4). If the many references to Shelley did not make it obvious that Joyce had read *Prometheus Unbound,* the quotation on *U* 201 of the lyric "Life of Life!" from act 2 of *Prometheus Unbound* would prove it.

[26] The same emotional state occurs in *Ulysses,* on *U* 37–38, at another point where Stephen feels himself stalled in his development.

[27] See J. S. Atherton's notes to his edition of *A Portrait* (Modern Novels Series [London, 1964]), p. 244.

[28] Gogarty, who "rejoiced in [Burns's] bawdry," introduced Joyce to it; see Padraic and Mary Colum, *Our Friend James Joyce* (New York, 1958), p. 68.

The poem itself, however, is not attributed to Burns in the introduction to the "1827" edition but to an anonymous English poet. There was only one likely source of Burns's bawdry available to Gogarty in the early twentieth century—John Camden Hotten's predated edition of *The Merry Muses,* the so-called "1827" edition,

originally published in 1872. The collection of bawdy poems written by Burns (or collected by him) first appeared c. 1800, and there
were several editions afterwards—?1820, ?1825–30, 1843—but copies
of these editions were extremely rare by 1900. The "1827" edition,
on the other hand, had many reprints and was, until the Burns
Federation Edition of 1911, the only one generally available. Therefore, this edition, containing Hotten's introduction and the Tom-
and-Tim poems, would most likely be the edition from which
Gogarty quoted, and which Joyce may have seen. See J. W. Egerer,
A Bibliography of Robert Burns (Carbondale, Illinois, 1964), pp.
154–56; G. Legman, *The Horn Book: Studies in Erotic Folklore and
Bibliography* (New Hyde Park, N.Y., 1964), pp. 184, 200–204. Another poem from this introduction is alluded to in *Finnegans Wake:*

> Tom went out as a Mission-ary
> Unto the fields of Timbuctoo,
> There he met a Casso-wary,
> Who ate him, and his Hymn-book too.

See *FW* 288.22–23: "his perry humdrum dumb and numb nos-
trums that he larned in Hymbuktu . . ."

For further analysis of Tom and Tim, see E. L. Epstein, "Tom
and Tim," *James Joyce Quarterly*, 6, No. 2 (Winter 1968), 158–62.

[29] For an interpretation of Stephen's activity as that of a damned
soul, see Caroline Gordon, "Some Readings and Misreadings,"
Sewanee Review, 61 (Summer 1953), 388–93. Shem, the artist in
FW, is a devil in many places, especially in bk. 2, chap. 1.

[30] Elizabeth F. Boyd, in her article "Joyce's Hell-Fire Sermons,"
Modern Language Notes, 75 (November 1960), 570, traces this passage to a number of seventeenth and eighteenth-century Jesuits, or
possibly to Saint Alphonsus Liguori. The phrase "one of our own
fathers" does not, of course, occur in the original source, whatever
the original source may have been. (Sullivan, in *Joyce Among the
Jesuits*, pp. 134–41, identifies Joyce's immediate source as a sodality
manual used by him at Belvedere.)

[31] The equation of the beloved of the *Canticles*, the Virgin, and
the world is traditional. Stephen's immediate source in this passage
is the book he mentions by St. Alphonsus Liguori; Atherton suggests
it is the English translation of his *Visitations to the Blessed Sacrament*. It is a small step from the beloved as the World to the beloved as the souls of men. Stephen merges these four entities—the
beloved of the *Canticles*, the Virgin, the World, the soul—into one
feminine reality. See Atherton *Portrait*, p. 248.

[32] The continuation of the above quote "and he would be a priest

for ever according to the order of Melchisedec" combines a traditional reference to the order of priesthood with a covert, allusive
warning about the dangers of a false vocation. Melchisedec is juxtaposed with Daedalus by Dante in *Paradiso* 8.125–26; the context
treats of the diversity of vocations and the necessity, in an ordered
universe, for every man to follow his true vocation.

[33] This detail is autobiographical. Joyce was always interested in
women's clothes; in fact he once told Frank Budgen that he was no
longer interested in women's bodies, just in their clothes (Ellmann,
James Joyce, p. 644) .

[34] Stephen's doubt flying birdlike "hither and thither" before his
mind is echoed in chapter 4 when the bird-girl associated with his
vocational vision stirs the waters "hither and thither" with her foot
(*P* 171) . "A faint flame" trembles on her cheek also. "Hither and
thither" ends up in *FW* as one of the leitmotifs of *Anna Livia.* See
W. Y. Tindall, *The Literary Symbol* (New York, 1955) , p. 82, and
A Reader's Guide to James Joyce (New York, 1959) , pp. 89–90. See
also Ronald Bates, "The Correspondence of Birds to Things of the
Intellect," *James Joyce Quarterly,* 2 (Summer 1965) , 281–90.

[35] "Peter Parley" (Samuel Griswold Goodrich) describes his pub-
lications in the appendix to his autobiography *Recollections of a
Lifetime, or Men and Things I have seen,* 2 vols. (Miller, Orton and
Mulligan; New York, N.Y. and Auburn, N.Y., 1856) . He specifically
disclaims writing any work called *Peter Parley's Tales about Greece
and Rome,* and suggests that the book of that title was a pirated version of two of his ancient history texts. See Sullivan, *Joyce among
the Jesuits,* pp. 43–45.

[36] "In several of his works Joyce had made significant references
to hats. . . . these references tend to support the impression that
for Joyce a whole hat denotes maturity, adequacy, or identity." P. L.
Graham, P. B. Sullivan, and G. F. Richter, "Mind Your Hats Goan
In! Notes on the Museyroom Episode of *Finnegans Wake,*" *The
Analyst,* No. 21, p. 3. See also Tindall, *Reader's Guide,* pp. 254–55.

[37] In an earlier section of the Eumaeus chapter (*U* 620) Bloom's
reference to Simon Dedalus brings to Stephen's mind a family scene
very much like the one on *P* 162–63. Stephen blames the disorgani-
zation of the household as much on Simon's weak nature as on the
general nature of muddling humanity.

[38] Shaun, the glutton, refers later on to "a ribroast and jack-
knife" as a "sporten dish" (*FW* 455.30–31) . There is more than a
hint here of a knife in the ribs for someone from Shaun, who besides being a glutton and womanizer is also a politician.

[39] He had been striding "from the door of Byron's publichouse to the gate of Clontarf Chapel." These are significant termini, of course—Byron, a favorite of Joyce, the symbol of romantic revolt, and Clontarf, a symbol of Irish history. See Tindall, *Reader's Guide*, p. 76.

[40] *Critical Writings*, p. 70.

[41] This is an anticipation of the hero of *Finnegans Wake* who bears a Danish name (Earwicker, from *Eirikr*), a Norman name (Persse O'Reilly), and an English name (Mr. Porter), and who is still the Irishman Finnegan, all under the influence of Finn Mac-Cool. Blake, of course, anticipated Joyce's mystic nationalism by his creation of the giant Albion, who is the embodiment of England. See Northrop Frye, "Quest and Cycle in *Finnegans Wake*," *James Joyce Review*, 1 (2 Feb., 1957), 39–47.

[42] *Critical Writings*, p. 166.

[43] *Letters*, 1:146. Joyce has Stephen refer to the Jews as a race on *U* 205.

[44] See Herbert Howarth, *The Irish Writers* (London, 1958), passim.

[45] Cf. "The O'Donoghue of the Glens" (*U* 599); Joyce's friends assumed that "The Nolan" of "The Day of the Rabblement" was an "Irish chieftain like the MacDermott or the O'Rahilly" (Joyce's statement in the Gorman papers, quoted in Ellmann, *James Joyce*, p. 93).

[46] See Tindall, *Reader's Guide*, p. 75. The phrases that they shout, "Bous Stephanoumenos! Bous Stephaneforos!" mean no more than *crowned* (or *wreathed*) *ox* (see Atherton *Portrait*, p. 250), but I have not been able to discover their source. They are not to be found in the Greek New Testament, Homer, Aeschylus, Sophocles, Euripides, or Aristophanes. The words *stephanoumenos* and *stephaneforos* are common in Greek literature, however, mostly in references to kings and archons. A suggestive use of *stephanoumenos* occurs in Achilles Tatius's tale of *Leuxippe and Cleitophon*, 1:5; Apollo is *stephanoumenos*, having crowned himself with laurel from the tree into which Daphne has turned fleeing from him. Hence *stephanoumenos* could be considered the Greek equivalent, in this case, of the Latin *laureata*.

[47] See also *U* 207, 734.

[48] Joyce's sources for this symbol are not difficult to find. Obvious sources are Dante's image of the universe turning to God like a rose (his rose was white, however) and Yeats's "red-rose bordered hem" of his vision of beauty and his Rosicrucian roses upon the

rood of time (see *U* 391). Other sources with which Joyce may have been acquainted may be found in the poetry of Poliziano, Tasso, Ronsard, and Du Bellay. Another possible source is James Clarence Mangan. "Mangan as Orientalist . . . rioted in roses." (R. M. Hewitt, "Harmonious Jones," in *Essays and Studies by Members of the English Association* [Oxford, 1943], p. 54, quoted in Marzieh Gail, *Persia and the Victorians* [London, 1951], p. 16.) Mangan's interest in Persian poetry, which is filled from end to end with real and mystical roses, influenced the creation by him of such poems as "The Hundred-Leaved Rose," in which every line in all twenty-seven quatrains ends with "rose." See also W. Y. Tindall, *The Literary Symbol* (New York, 1955), pp. 79–82, and "Dante and Mrs. Bloom," *Accent*, 11 (Spring 1951), 85–92, and Barbara Seward, "The Artist and the Rose," *University of Toronto Quarterly*, (January 1957), 180–90.

[49] Joyce returns to this theme on *FW* 549; he lists the twelve months ("tolvmaans") of the Ku Klux Klan year but leaves out the eighth month, perhaps deliberately, so that again we have a chronometrical unit of twelve aimed at and only eleven achieved. See E. L. Epstein "Interpreting *Finnegans Wake*: a Halfway House," *James Joyce Quarterly*, 3 (Summer 1966), 255, 271; and C. G. Anderson, "The Sacrificial Butter," *Accent*, (Winter 1952), 10. See also *U* 558–59.

[50] Stephen's companions are also described in animal terms in the third section of chapter 5. See *P* 227, 235, 236, 237, 242.

[51] Shaun as Justius in *FW* "points the deathbone and the quick are still." (*FW* 193.29) Shaun is like Cranly in that he also preaches what sounds like conventional morality as a cloak for his baser purposes.

[52] "Epistola S. Ignatii de virtute obedientia," in *Thesaurus Spiritualis S. J.*, p. 397, quoted in Kevin Sullivan, *Joyce among the Jesuits* (New York, 1958), p. 122; Mr. Sullivan's translation.

[53] On p. 251 of the Scribbledehobble notebook, a page devoted to notes on *A Portrait* for inclusion in *Finnegans Wake*, Joyce has written: "George Clancy 'his equal' c'est egal: every journey from Ireland is a flight into Egypt . . ."; George Clancy is the original for Davin. (*James Joyce's Scribbledehobble: the Ur-workbook for Finnegans Wake*, ed. T. E. Connolly [Evanston, Illinois, 1961], p. 74.)

[54] This is Ignatius's definition of the ideal mental attitude of the Jesuit, from "Epistola S. Ignatii de virtute obedientiae," in *Thesaurus Spiritualis S. J.*, p. 397.

[55] *Exiles,* ed. and with an intro. by Padraic Colum (New York, 1951), p. 118.

[56] Stephen repeats this description of Ireland on *U* 595; in *Finnegans Wake* the symbol reappears as the sow of Irish history: "Cliopatrick (the sow)" (*FW* 91.6). The ultimate source for this metaphor is *Macbeth,* 4. 1. 64–65:

> Pour in sow's blood, that hath eaten
> Her nine farrow.

(Stephen adds the adjective "old" to the sow for symbolic reasons —the old versus the young.) However, in *Don Juan* there occurs a characteristically Byronic reflection on heroism which may have provided the bridge between the magical requirements of the witches in *Macbeth* and the destructive tendencies of Irish history:

> I want a hero . . .
>
> Vernon, the butcher Cumberland, Wolfe, Hawke,
>> Prince Ferdinand, Granby, Burgoyne, Keppel, Howe,
> Evil and good, have had their tithe of talk,
>> And fill'd their sign-posts then, like Wellesley now;
> Each in their turn like Banquo's monarchs stalk,
>> Followers of fame, "nine farrow" of that sow . . .
>>> (Canto the First, Verses 1, 2)

Wellesley (Wellington), the follower of fame, will be the central figure in the Museyroom episode in *Finnegans Wake* (*FW* 8–10) in which he will wage bloody war on his sons and lust after his daughters.

[57] See Gorman, *James Joyce,* pp. 96–97.

[58] Hugo Steger, *David rex et propheta* (Nürnberg, 1961), pp. 1–6, 116.

[59] Ibid., pp. 110, 129, 132.

[60] Ibid., pp. 138–46.

[61] Ibid., pp. 59–60.

[62] *City of God* 18. 14, in *Basic Writings of Saint Augustine,* ed. W. J. Oates, 2 (New York, 1948), p. 392. David is called "rex et propheta spiritus rector harmoniae mundi" by medieval writers; see Steger, pp. 118–21. For music as a medieval symbol of universal order, see Steger, pp. 65–75.

[63] Steger, p. 120.

[64] Ibid., pp. 118–19.

[65] Ibid., p. 119.

[66] Ibid., pp. 133, 135, 138.

[67]   Ibid., pp. 136, 137.

[68]   There was fierce debate in the early Christian era about the authenticity of the words "from wood"; Justin Martyr, in his *Dialogue with Tryphon,* sec. 73, declares that the Jews deliberately omitted the words from some manuscripts of the Psalms. Modern biblical scholarship has veered to the opinion that the words were interpolated by overzealous early Christians; see *The Ante-Nicene Fathers,* ed. A. Roberts and J. Donaldson (Edinburgh, 1885), 1, 235.

[69]   *Purgatorio* 10. 66, Laurence Binyon translation.

[70]   *Libri duo de poenitentia,* 2: 6.

[71]   Steger, *David rex,* pp. 75–98.

[72]   Ibid., pp. 25, 85–94.

[73]   Another example of clearsightedness is provided by Stephen's namesake, Stephen the Protomartyr; he is the first man to see "the Son of Man standing on the right hand of God"; see Acts 7:55, 56; *Purgatorio* 15. 109–14.

[74]   Another possible Augustinian echo is to be found on *U* 424, with the reference to the Roman goddess of coition, Pertunda; Augustine mentions her in *City of God* 6. 9. See *The Analyst,* No. 9, 3.

[75]   Weldon Thornton, *Allusions in Ulysses* (Chapel Hill, 1968), p. 65. However, Father Noon, who is Thornton's source, suggests that Joyce may have come across this phrase in some choir or sodality manual. I believe that there are too many references to medieval writers, many of them heretics, for sodality manuals to be Joyce's only sources.

        Joyce must have admired this phrase from Ambrose, *diebus ac noctibus iniurias patiens ingemiscit,* because a part of it appears first in his description of Cranly in *A Portrait:* "The gross name had passed over [Cranly's face] like foul water poured over an old stone image, patient of injuries" (*P* 232). However, he may have found "patient of injuries" in *Tristram Shandy,* 2, 12.

[76]   Joyce originally became interested in Joachim because of a reference in Yeats's "The Tables of the Law." He followed up his interest in a secondary source, Dollinger's *Fables and Prophecies of the Middle Ages* (1863; trans. 1872). He read some of Joachim in Marsh's library. See R. M. Adams, *Surface and Symbol* (New York, 1962), pp. 125–26, 180.

[77]   He is combined with Stevenson's sedulous ape: "He's so sedulous to singe always." Sedulius is treated in Joyce's 1907 lecture, "Ireland, Island of Saints and Sages." See *Critical Writings,* pp. 157, 159.

[78] See Atherton, *Books at the Wake*, pp. 13, 140–43; Tindall, *James Joyce*, pp. 11, 60; J. M. Morse, "Augustine, Ayenbite, and Ulysses," PMLA, 22 (December 1955),1143–59.

[79] *Critical Writings*, p. 221.

[80] Atherton believes that few of the Patristic writers besides Jerome, Aquinas, and Augustine provide phrases for the *Wake* (*Books at the Wake*, pp. 137–38, 145).

[81] Atherton, however, finds clear references to Jerome in several places in the *Wake;* see Atherton, *Books at the Wake*, pp. 143–44, 222.

[82] *Critical Writings*, p. 160. See also Thornton, *Allusions*, p. 30.

[83] Frances A. Yates, *Giordano Bruno and the Hermetic Tradition* (London, Chicago, 1964), p. 104, quoting Pico, *Opera omnia* (Bale, 1572), p. 106.

[84] Translation by Frances A. Yates, in *Giordano*, pp. 236–37. Three years after the publication of *La cena de le ceneri* (1584), the mage flying through the universe in search of knowledge turns up in the Faustbook of 1587, the source of the Faustus legend; the braggart Faustus claims to be able to fly through the universe on eagle's wings. Rimbaud, the "poète voyant," is another likely source for the artist as seer.

[85] See Maurice Beebe, "James Joyce and Giordano Bruno: a Possible Source for 'Dedalus,'" *James Joyce Review*, 1 (Dec. 15, 1957), 41–44.

[86] Archer Taylor, *The Literary History of Meistergesang* (New York, 1937), pp. 18–19.

[87] Georges Borach, "Conversations with Joyce," *College English*, 15 (March 1954), 325–27, quoted in Ellmann, *James Joyce*, p. 473. However, Joyce sometimes felt that *Meistersinger* was "pretentious stuff." (Ellmann, p. 278) For a short summary of Wagner' influence on Joyce, see William Blissett, "James Joyce in the Smithy of his Soul," in *James Joyce Today*, ed. T. Staley (Bloomington, Indiana, 1966), pp. 96–134.

[88] I am omitting the Renaissance and post-Renaissance stream of epics in which David's career is treated in a Virgilian way and which Joyce seems to have ignored: Malveggi's *Davide perseguitato* (1634), Cowley's *Davideis* (1657), Lesforgues' *David* (1660), Albano's *Davide re* (1691), and the *Davideis* of Thomas Ellwood (1712). Nor is there any evidence that Joyce was acquainted with Christopher Smart's *A Song to David* (1763).

[89] Delany, pp. 19, 24.

[90] Ibid., p. 121.

[91] Ibid., p. 122.

[92] Ibid., p. 295.

[93] Ibid., pp. 127, 319–24.

[94] Ibid., pp. 332, 339.

[95] Livy, *History*, 1:20. Joyce was well acquainted with Livy; his name appears many times in *Finnegans Wake*, sometimes as one of the components of Anna Livia's name and therefore the incarnation of history, but sometimes on his own (see *FW* 260.09, 260.13, 452.19).

[96] Livy, 38:17.

[97] Livy, 21:42.

[98] Sullivan, *Joyce among the Jesuits*, p. 159.

[99] "Tripudium" is also a technical term of augury in Cicero *De Divinatione* 1. 28, 77; 2. 73. Although Joyce read Cicero (see Sullivan, *Joyce among the Jesuits*, p. 159; Atherton, *Books at the Wake*, p. 242; see also *U* 124, 394, 622), there is no evidence that he read *De Divinatione*.

[100] The title is in French in the original.

[101] *Schumann and the Romantic Age*, trans. Geoffrey Sainsbury (New York, London, 1956), pp. 160–61. See also Frederick Niecks, *Robert Schumann* (London, 1925), pp. 132 ff., 177.

[102] See Tindall, *James Joyce*, p. 119; *Reader's Guide*, p. 51.

[103] Goethe always insisted that *Wilhelm Meisters Lehrjahre* was very carefully planned and that he intended it from the beginning as a symbolic totality; see his letters to his mother of September 20, 1780 and November 9, 1785; to Schiller of June 18, 1795, March 7, 1796, and November 19, 1796; to Knebel of March 29, 1801 and March 26, 1814; see also the diary of Goethe's friend Friedrich von Müller, entry for January 22, 1821. Schiller agreed that the work formed an artistic whole and that the symbolism was "tight"; see his letters to Goethe of December 23, 1794 and October 20, 1797.

[104] Goethe's autobiography *Dichtung und Wahrheit* described the same process, the poet growing like a plant from a seed to his majestic blossoming and "fathering-forth"; see R. Friedenthal, *Goethe: his life and times* (London, 1963), p. 418.

[105] Goethe's teleological vitalism was very close to that of Aristotle (and Joyce). See Friedenthal, pp. 491–92 passim, and Sir Charles Sherrington, *Goethe on Nature and Science* (2nd ed., Cambridge, 1949).

[106] Goethe had played with a puppet theatre in his youth, and had also staged episodes from the life of David. The technique of the puppet theatre influenced the writing of *Faust;* see Friedenthal, *Goethe: his life and times*, p. 28.

¹⁰⁷ Joyce was acquainted with Goethe, and also with *Wilhelm Meisters Lehrjahre* (if only by name). Goethe's name appears three times in *Stephen Hero* (*SH* 41, 43, 201), once in *A Portrait* (*P* 211), several times in *Finnegans Wake* (*FW* 71.26, 344.5, and 539.6). (Despite Atherton, *Books at the Wake,* p. 81, who declares that the name of Goethe appears only on *FW* 344.5 and 539.6, and "nowhere else," Goethe's name appears at *FW* 91.35, 256.16, 372.13, 394.27, and 501.9, as well as in many other places where it is "occluded" by "God," "goat," and so on). The works of Goethe are referred to several times in the works of Joyce: *Faust* is quoted or parodied in *Ulysses* (*U* 204, 422), and referred to in *Finnegans Wake* (*FW* 74.9, 83.29, 252.2, 288.9, 292.22, 356.1). The *Walpurgisnacht* influenced sections of the Circe episode. The *Conversations with Eckermann* are mentioned on *FW* 71.8, *Werther* (perhaps) on *FW* 344.5, *Götz von Berlichingen* on *FW* 301.2, *Hermann und Dorothea* on *FW* 283.28, and *Reineke Fuchs* on *FW* 480.23 (Atherton, *Books at the Wake,* pp. 81, 82, 83, 251). *Wilhelm Meister* is mentioned on *U* 184, where it forms the first contribution to the Shakespeare discussion in the library; Mignon, the enigmatic little girl whom Wilhelm befriends, is mentioned on *FW* 157.33, and her famous song "Kennst du das Land" is echoed on *FW* 479.29, "Weissduwasland." (Atherton, *Books at the Wake,* p. 83.) There is, in addition, a reference to *Wilhelm Meister* in one of Joyce's letters to Frank Budgen (October 9, 1932):

The enclosed is a little silly but rather graceful—I mean the picture of myself and daughter and Wilhelm Meister. There is something Mignonesque about her and, if it comes to that, I do not mind being called a "harmonieux vieillard" when there are so many unharmonious striplings about. (*Letters,* 3:261)

("Wilhelm Meister" is probably one of Lucia's young men, perhaps one of those young Swiss architects that Frau Giedion-Welcker kept throwing at Lucia; see Ellmann, *James Joyce,* p. 675. The "harmonieux vieillard" is Joyce himself as Mignon's father, the weird old harper Lothario in *Wilhelm Meister* who is subject to fits and who attempts to murder children—a Joycean father. I am not sure why Joyce refers to Lothario in French; the phrase does not occur in the most famous French adaptation of *Wilhelm Meister,* Ambroise Thomas's popular opera *Mignon.*)

¹⁰⁸ Through his life Joyce seems to have been simultaneously denigrating Goethe and reading him avidly; see *Critical Writings,* pp. 82, 99, 136, and Ellmann, *James Joyce,* pp. 406, 655, and 743.

[109] For this interpretation of the David-symbol in *Wilhelm Meister*, see H. H. Boyesen, *Goethe and Schiller* (New York, 1879), p. 103.

[110] For an analysis of this passage, see E. L. Epstein, "King David and Benedetto Marcello in the Works of James Joyce," *James Joyce Quarterly*, 6 (Fall 1968), 83–86.

[111] See Joseph Klausner, *The Messianic Idea in Israel* (New York, 1955), pp. 19–21, 28–32, 42–44; Gershom E. Scholem, *On the Kabbalah and its Symbolism* (New York, 1965), p. 145.

See Ellmann, *James Joyce*, p. 527, for a note on Joyce's knowledge of *Hatikvah*.

The Hebrew word for exile, *galut,* appears disguised during the Hades chapter as a description of the man in the mackintosh: Bloom thinks, "Now who is that lankylooking galoot over there in the macintosh [*sic*]?" (*U* 109). The man in the mackintosh is an exile—he is later called "Dusty Rhodes," a wandering tramp, and "walking Mackintosh of lonely canyon" (*U* 427).

The theme of the return of the exile—Ulysses, the Hebrew people, the man in the mackintosh—ties up with the ship-symbolism in the Circe chapter. (The ship coming is, primarily, the *Rosevean* with bricks [*U* 51, 249, 625], but it symbolizes the return of all exiles.) Bloom, testifying to his innocence to the Dublin court, declares that he "was mentioned in dispatches. I did all a white man could. (*With quiet feeling.*) Jim Bludso. Hold her nozzle again the bank" (*U* 458). "Jim Bludso" is a poem by John Hay, the American poet-statesman. In it, Jim Bludso, the skipper of a riverboat threatened with an explosion, fiercely shouts that he will hold "her nozzle again the bank / Till the last galoot's ashore." Bloom is the *galut* Ulysses, as well as the exiled Jew, who is waiting for his Messiah to bring the *galut* to his native shore—Ithaca, or Palestine, or a transfigured Ireland.

[112] It is possible that Joyce found this matter treated in some secondary source, perhaps two of the many books of A. E. Waite upon the mystical traditions of the Jews: *The Doctrine and Literature of the Kabalah,* London, 1902, and *The Secret Doctrine in Israel,* London, 1913. Waite, whose treatment of esoterica influenced Yeats (see the essay by W. Y. Tindall in *The Permanence of Yeats,* ed. J. Hall and M. Steinmann [New York, 1950], p. 270, and Giorgio Melchiori, *The Whole Mystery of Art* [London, 1960], pp. 47–48, 172), and who spent his long life explicating Rosicrucianism and Cabalism, sums up the two previous books on Hebrew mysticism in *The Holy Kabbalah,* London, 1929 (repr. New Hyde Park, N.Y.,

1960). On the other hand, Joyce could have found a full account of Hebrew speculation on the twin Messiahs in the article "Messiah" in *The New Schaff-Herzog Encyclopedia of Religious Knowledge*, New York, London, 1910, vol. 7. There is some evidence that Joyce had read this entry. In it, it is stated that the Messiah ben Joseph is to expiate "Jeroboam's sin"; HCE is called Jeroboam on *FW* 558.15. The name of the author of the entry in the encyclopedia, Conrad von Orelli, Professor of Old Testament Studies at the University of Basel, appears on *FW* 243.34 as "Sant Pursy Orelli."

113 A. E. Waite, *The Holy Kabbalah*, pp. 319–24. For the influence of the Cabalah on Joyce, see Tindall, *James Joyce*, p. 79, *Reader's Guide*, pp. 282–83; Campbell and Robinson, *Skeleton Key*, pp. 164–66, 193–96; Atherton, *Books at the Wake*, pp. 44–45, 87, 134. Atherton believes that Joyce read the article on "Kabballah" in the eleventh edition of the *Encyclopedia Britannica;* Atherton, p. 87.

114 Even in the Talmud the traditions are not consistently expounded. In one place it is affirmed that the Messiah ben Joseph will suffer a violent death, as in Isa. 53; in other places it declares that evil has no hold on him. The Zohar in one place suggests that the Messiah will die and rise again, but in another place asserts that the Messiah ben Joseph will die and that the Messiah ben David will not. See Waite, pp. 319–24. For Bloom as Messiah, see Stanley Sultan, *The Argument of Ulysses* (Columbus, Ohio, 1964), pp. 249–62.

115 See Waite, *Holy Kabbalah*, p. 320.

116 Ibid., pp. 322–23.

117 Presumably her sexual consolation; "ring" bears a ribald meaning in *Merchant of Venice* 5. 1, ("Nerissa's ring") and in Rabelais's tale of Hans Carvel (*Gargantua and Pantagruel*, 3. 27). It could also mean "marriage ring."

118 "The Candle of the Welsh"; Dave is also Welsh, probably St. David, patron saint of Wales, as well as "the barmaid's flame." The writing of *Ulysses* was begun on St. David's Day, March 1 (Ellmann, *James Joyce*, p. 538; *Letters*, 3:52).

119 "Be introduced to yez" as well as Molly's sexual "yes."

120 "Will" bore an intensely *sexual* significance in the Elizabethan period; see above, n. 24.

121 "Echo, read ending!" equals *Ecco ridente (in cielo)*, Count Almaviva's first aria in Rossini's *Barber of Seville*, in which the count sings of the dawn and the sun laughing in the sky; the phrase in Joyce incorporates suggestions of ending and beginning. "Siparioramoci" combines *sipario*, theatre curtain (Ital.) with *separiamoci*, let us separate (Ital.). (I am indebted to Mr. Charles Parish for this last suggestion.)

[122] This is a reworking by Joyce of a dozen lines in *The Holy Office:*

> And for each maiden, shy and nervous,
> I do a similar kind service.
> For I detect without surprise
> That shadowy beauty in her eyes,
> The "dare not" of sweet maidenhood
> That answers my corruptive "would."
> Whenever publicly we meet
> She never seems to think of it;
> At night when close in bed she lies
> And feels my hand between her thighs
> My little love in light attire
> Knows the soft flame that is desire.
>
> *(The Holy Office, 61–72)*

It is the artist in *The Holy Office* who sees himself as an incubus; in *Finnegans Wake* the contact of brother and sister causes the ending of one cycle and the beginning of another.

For a source for *FW* 486.36–467.1–2, see E. L. Epstein, "Popular Poetry in *Finnegans Wake,*" *A Wake Newslitter,* 6, No. 1 (February 1969) , 14–15.

[123] See Tindall, *James Joyce,* pp. 63–64, 100; *Reader's Guide,* p. 243. That Dave the Dancekerl is King David is indicated both by the "dance" in his name and by his singing and harping:

Lumtum lumtum! Now! The froubadour! I fremble! . . . Could you wheedle a staveling encore out of your imitationer's jubalharp? . . . He's so sedulous to singe always if prumpted . . . Sweet fellow ovocal, he stones out of stune. But he could be near a colonel with a voice like that. . . . A full octavium below me! *(FW* 462.25–26; 466.17–18, 21–22, 35–36; 467.8)

"Lumtum lumtum" imitates the harp that sounds in *Il Trovatore* as the fraternal troubadour enters.

[124] See Tindall, *James Joyce,* p. 109. A number of connections between Dave the Dancekerl and the davy of the Willingdone Museyroom can be found. The davy is Welsh, a Welch Fusilier (or St. David) ; when Dave the Dancekerl enters, Juan says "I knew I smelt the garlic leek!" *(FW* 462.29–30), the leek as the symbol of Wales, and the Gaelic League, and refers to him as "Canwyll y Cymry." The phrase, " 'Twas the quadra sent him [Dave] . . ." *(FW* 467.30), also provides a link from Dave the Dancekerl through Hosty (otherwise the Roman voyeur Hostius Quadra) to Davy the seeboy and to Davy Stephens from *Ulysses;* see E. L. Epstein, "Hostius Quadra,"

A Wake Newslitter, 6, No. 2 (April 1969), 19–20. The murderous davy and Buckley are linked at *FW* 464.3, as Juan calls Dave the Dancekerl "David R. Crozier"; Butt as Buckley shoots the Russian general with a "crozzier." (*FW* 353.20) The davy "stooping" is also Buckley; *bücken* means "to stoop" in German. Another reason for the Celtic appurtenances of Davy may be that Matthew Arnold, in his essay *On the Study of Celtic Literature*, considered that the Celt stands for the Romantic revolt against Philistinism.

125 "Hiena hinnessy" represent a Napoleonic victory (Jena) and blondness (*fionn*, Irish) laughing like a "hiena"; "lipsyg dooley" represents defeat (Leipzig) and blackness (*dubh*, Irish), sighing; in a few places in the worksheets for *Finnegans Wake* the third soldier, Shimar Shin as he is here named, is represented by a symbol which combines Shaun's ∧ and Shem's ⌐ : ⌐ See BM Add. MSS. 47482.A.2. and 47482A. facing p. 92; both of these manuscript sources are reproduced in *A First-Draft Version of Finnegans Wake*, ed. David Hayman (Austin, Texas, 1963), pp. 30, 50.

126 See Stanislaus Joyce, *My Brother's Keeper*, p. 41.

127 See J. S. Atherton, "Sport and Games in *Finnegans Wake*," in *Twelve and a Tilly*, ed. J. P. Dalton and C. Hart (London, 1966), pp. 55–58.

128 Earwicker is haunted in his sleep by the mysterious activities of three soldiers and two girls in the woods. If the three soldiers represent the three components of male genitalia, the two girls similarly represent the physical configuration of female genitalia, and their combined activity is a symbolization of the sex act. Earwicker fears his sons' sexual ability because it means that they are capable of becoming fathers. ALP supports this interpretation of three-and-two as sexual activity on *FW* 584, at the height of her sexual ecstasy.

Tipatonging him on in her pigeony linguish, with a flick at the bails for lubrication, to scorch her faster, faster. . . . Three for two will do for me. (FW 584.3–5, 10)

(She sings it to the tune of "Tea for Two.") For a recent analysis of this motif, see Margaret Solomon, *Eternal Geomater* (Carbondale, Illinois 1969).

129 *Zohar*, Mantua ed., 1, fol. 72a, 127.

130 A. D. Hope, "The Esthetic Theory of James Joyce," *Australasian Journal of Psychology and Philosophy*, 21 (December 1943), 94, 95, 96; repr. in *Joyce's Portrait: Criticisms and Critiques*, ed. Thomas E. Connolly (New York, 1962), pp. 183–203.

131 For Ham as seeboy, see Gen. 9:20–27, and Glasheen, *Second*

Census, pp. 104–6. See also William Troy, "Notes on *Finnegans Wake,*" in *James Joyce: Two Decades of Criticism,* ed. S. Givens (New York, 1948), p. 314.

[132] The fable resembles a Hindu version of chess called "The Maharajah and the Sepoys," in which one powerful piece is beset by a number of weaker ones. See E. Falkner, *Games Ancient and Oriental and How to Play Them* (London, 1899), p. 217 ff.

[133] Later on the description of the excited seeboy "Upjump and pumpim" (*FW* 10.16) becomes "Upanishadem!" (*FW* 303.13) Both are based, of course, upon Wellington's apocryphal order at Waterloo, "Up, boys, and at 'em!" Cf. *FW* 93.22–23: "Artha kama dharma moksa. Ask Kavya for the kay." See also Atherton, *Books at the Wake,* pp. 228, 248, 287; C. Hart, *Structure and Motif in Finnegans Wake* (Evanston, Illinois, 1962), pp. 96–104; and B. P. Misra's note in *A Wake Newslitter,* n.s. 3, No. 1 (February 1966), 14.

[134] The last chapter of *A Portrait* was not written until the first months of 1915; see Ellmann, *James Joyce,* p. 365.

[135] It should also be noted, as clear evidence of Joyce's ironic view of Stephen, that although "the radiant image of the eucharist" (*P* 221) brings with it a gust of returning inspiration and allows Stephen to finish his poem, he really neither believes nor disbelieves in the power of the eucharist, as he later admits to Cranly (*P* 239).

3 stephen's dance

[1] One of John Joyce's expressions, especially when drunk; see Stanislaus Joyce, *My Brother's Keeper* (New York, 1958), p. 77.

[2] As usual, Joyce is less than accurate in a technical matter like heraldry. The Joyce arms are "Argent an eagle with two heads displayed gules, over all a fess ermine. *Crest:* A demi-wolf argent ducally gorged or." E. MacLysaght, *Irish Families, their Names, Arms and Origins* (Dublin, 1957), entry "Joyce."

[3] See W. Schutte, *Joyce and Shakespeare* (New Haven, 1957), p. 21.

[4] It is actually derived from *tripedio,* which is itself derived from the Greek *tripodizo;* see A. Walde, *Lateinisches Etymologisches Wörterbuch,* 3rd ed. (Heidelberg, 1951), entry *"tripudium."* Cicero, in *De Divinatione* 1. 28, 77, and 2. 73, and in *Ep. ad fam.* 6. 6, 7, uses the term in a different sense, as a term in augury, and derives *tripudium* from *"terra"* and *"pavium,"* a striking of the earth. *"Pavium,"* however, itself derives from the root for "foot."

[5] See E. L. Epstein, note in *James Joyce Review,* 1, No. 3 (15 Sept., 1957), 37–38; see also *Letters,* 1:151.

[6] See *Letters* 2:285, 390n, 456, 457n; Ellmann, pp. 427, 566; J. S. Atherton, *Books at the Wake* (London, 1959), pp. 118, 123, 282.

[7] See William York Tindall, *Reader's Guide to James Joyce* (New York, 1959), p. 144. Darkness shining in light is related to the doctrine of the *caligine Domini,* the "divine obscurity," the "dark ocean" of God, first defined by Dionysius the pseudo-Areopagite, and mentioned by Joyce in his second lecture (1912) on Blake; see *Critical Writings,* p. 222. For another possible source for darkness shining in light, see *Paradise Lost* 3. 372–82.

[8] Bloom also uses the word "saltwhite" to describe the color of a corpse on *U* 114.

[9] See Tindall, *Reader's Guide,* p. 143.

[10] *Critical Writings,* p. 81. My interpretation of this passage is partly based upon Tindall's *Reader's Guide,* p. 141, and Stanley Sultan, *The Argument of Ulysses,* (Columbus, Ohio, 1964), pp. 46–47.

[11] *Critical Writings,* p. 81n; see also Weldon Thornton, *Allusions in Ulysses* (Chapel Hill, 1968), pp. 27–28.

[12] *The Complete Writings of William Blake,* ed. Geoffrey Keynes (London, 1966), p. 604. For other statements on the daughters of Memory, see Blake's *Descriptive Catalogue* of 1809 (Keynes, pp. 565–66), and his Annotations to Reynolds's *Discourses* (Keynes, p. 452). (In this last, Blake's source for the phrase is Milton.)

[13] Mangan has a similar image for the end of time in his poem "To My Native Land":

> And till all earthly power shall wane,
> And Time's grey pillar, groaning, fall;
> Thus shall it be, and still in vain
> Thou shalt essay to burst the thrall . . .

[14] For references to the *Ring* in *A Portrait,* see chap. 2, sec. f. For an account of the influence of Germanic apocalyptic writings on Joyce, see Atherton, *Books at the Wake,* pp. 218–23.

[15] The passage is so translated in the Ronald Knox version of the Bible (London, New York, 1944).

[16] "Arks" is a prostitute's mispronunciation of "arse" to Bloom; see *U* 370. The seeboy in the Willingdone Museyroom sees the "harse" of his father.

[17] Keynes, *William Blake,* p. 177.

[18] I do not intend to analyze Bloom's paternal needs here. However, it is perfectly obvious that he sees Stephen as the substitute for his lost son Rudy. See *U* 609.

[19] The Daughters of Erin (*Inghinidhe na hEireann*) who mourn over Bloom on *U* 498–99, were founded by Maud Gonne expressly to stamp out fraternization between Irish girls and British soldiers, By showing Edy Boardman, Bertha Supple, and Cissy Caffrey as avidly pursuing British soldiers Joyce seems to be denying the possibility of a national renaissance of character in Ireland.

appendix

[1] J. S. Atherton's notes to his edition of *A Portrait* (Modern Novels Series [London, 1964]), p. 251.

[2] The most popular source for this relationship is probably F. W. Farrar, *Seekers after God* (London, 1863, and often reprinted). See the introduction and bibliography to the Loeb Classical Library edition of the works of Epictetus (London, 1926), edited by (of all names!) W. A. Oldfather.

[3] I do not mean to suggest that these are the only meanings for "bucket." The word appears in a number of other contexts in *Finnegan*.

bibliography

WORKS BY JAMES JOYCE

Anna Livia Plurabelle. New York, 1928; London, 1930.

Chamber Music. Ed. W. Y. Tindall. New York, 1954.

The Critical Writings of James Joyce. Ed. Ellsworth Mason and Richard Ellmann. New York, 1959.

Epiphanies. Ed. O. A. Silverman. Buffalo, 1956.

Finnegans Wake. (Text from Viking Press edition, New York. American 8th printing [1958] with corrections inserted. Further corrected from Introduction to *A Concordance to Finnegans Wake,* ed. Clive Hart Minneapolis, Minnesota, 1963, pp. xiii–xiv.)

Haveth Childers Everywhere. Paris, New York, 1930; London, 1931.

James Joyce's Scribbledehobble: the Ur-workbook for Finnegans Wake. Ed. T. E. Connolly. Evanston, Illinois, 1961.

Letters of James Joyce. Ed. Stuart Gilbert and Richard Ellmann. 3 vols. New York, 1957, 1966.

The Mime of Mick, Nick and the Maggies. The Hague, 1933.

A Portrait of the Artist as a Young Man. (Text from revised text, ed. Chester Anderson, New York, 1964.)

Stephen Hero. New Directions ed. Norfolk, Connecticut, 1963.

Storiella As She is Syung. London, 1937.

Tales Told of Shem and Shaun. Paris, 1929. (Later printed as *Two Tales of Shem and Shaun.* London, 1932.)

Ulysses. (Text from Modern Library edition, New York. Newly reset, 1961.)

OTHER WORKS

Adams, Robert Martin. *Surface and Symbol.* New York, 1962.

Ambrose. *Libri duo de poenitentia,* in Roberts and Donaldson (q.v.) .

Anderson, C. G. "The Sacrificial Butter," *Accent,* 12 (Winter 1952) , 3–13.

Aristotle. *Aristotle's De Anima, in the version of William of Moerbeke; and The commentary of St. Thomas Aquinas,* trans. Kenelm Foster and Silvester Humphries. New Haven, 1951.

———. *Aristotle's Psychology,* trans. W. A. Hammond. London, 1902.

———. *Metaphysics,* trans. H. Tredennick. London, 1947.

————. *Selections* . . . , trans. Philip Wheelwright. New York, 1951.

————. *The Works of Aristotle,* ed. W. D. Ross. 12 vols. Oxford, 1908–52. (Vol. 3, *De Anima,* trans. J. A. Smith, 1931.)

Atherton, J. S. *The Books at the Wake.* London, 1959.

————. "Sport and Games in *Finnegans Wake,*" in *Twelve and a Tilly.* Ed. J. P. Dalton and Clive Hart. London, 1966.

Augustine. *Basic Writings of Saint Augustine,* ed. W. J. Oates. 2 vols. New York, 1948.

Bates, Ronald. "The Correspondence of Birds to Things of the Intellect," *James Joyce Quarterly,* 2 (Summer 1965), 281–90.

Beebe, Maurice. "James Joyce and Giordano Bruno: A Possible Source for 'Dedalus,'" *James Joyce Review,* 15 December 1957, pp. 41–44.

————. "Joyce and Aquinas: The Theory of Aesthetics," *Philological Quarterly,* 36 (January 1957), 20–35.

Blake, William. *The Complete Writings of William Blake.* Ed. Geoffrey Keynes. London, 1966.

Blissett, William. "James Joyce in the Smithy of his Soul," in *James Joyce Today.* Ed. T. Staley. Bloomington, Indiana, 1966.

Bonheim, Helmut. *Joyce's Benefictions.* Berkeley, California, and Los Angeles, 1964.

Borach, Georges. "Conversations with Joyce," *College English,* 15 (March 1954), 325–27.

Boyd, Elizabeth F. "Joyce's Hell-Fire Sermons," *Modern Language Notes,* 75 (November 1960), 561–71.

Boyesen, H. H. *Goethe and Schiller.* New York, 1879.

Brion, Marcel. *Schumann et l'ame romantique.* Paris, 1954. Trans. Geoffrey Sainsbury as *Schumann and the Romantic Age.* New York, London, 1956.

Butler, Samuel. *Life and Habit.* Vol. 4 of Shrewsbury edition, ed. Henry Festing Jones and A. T. Bartholomew. London, 1923–26.

————. *The Way of All Flesh.* London: Everyman ed., 1933.

————. *The Way of All Flesh,* ed. William York Tindall. New York: Harper's Modern Classics Series, 1950.

Campbell, Joseph, and Henry Morton Robinson. *A Skeleton Key to Finnegans Wake.* New York, 1944.

Chart, D. A. *The Story of Dublin.* London, 1907.

Chayes, Irene Hendry. "Joyce's Epiphanies," *Sewanee Review* (July 1946), pp. 2–19.

Cicero. *De Divinatione.*

Colum, Padraic and Mary. *Our Friend James Joyce.* New York, 1958.

Connolly, Thomas E. *The Personal Library of James Joyce: A De-scriptive Bibliography*. Buffalo, 1955.

Dante. *Divine Comedy*. Trans. Laurence Binyon. London, 1938.

Delany, Patrick. *An Historical Account of the Life, and Reign of David, King of Israel* . . . 2 vols. Dublin, 1740, 1743.

Egerer, J. W. *A Bibliography of Robert Burns*. Carbondale, Illinois, 1964.

Ellmann, Richard. *James Joyce*. New York, 1959.

Epictetus. *Works*. Ed. and trans. W. A. Oldfather. London, 1926.

Epstein, E. L. Note in *James Joyce Review*, 15 September 1957, pp. 37–38.

———. "King David and Benedetto Marcello in the Works of James Joyce," *James Joyce Quarterly*, 6 (Fall 1968), 83–86.

———. "Tom and Tim." *James Joyce Quarterly*, 6 (Winter 1968), 158–62.

———. "Chance, Doubt, Coincidence and the Prankquean's Riddle," *A Wake Newslitter*, 6, No. 1 (February 1969), 3–7.

———. "Popular Poetry in *Finnegans Wake*," *A Wake Newslitter*, 6, No. 1 (February 1969), 14–15.

———. "Hostius Quadra," *A Wake Newslitter*, 6, No. 2 (April 1969), 19–20.

———. "James Joyce and *The Way of All Flesh*," *James Joyce Quarterly*, 7 (Fall 1969), 22–29.

Falkner, E. *Games Ancient and Oriental and How to Play Them*. London, 1899.

Farrar, F. W. *Seekers after God*. London, 1863.

Friedenthal, Richard. *Goethe: His Life and Times*. London, 1963.

Frye, Northrop. "Quest and Cycle in *Finnegans Wake*," *James Joyce Review*, 2 February 1957, pp. 39–47.

Glasheen, Adaline. *A Second Census of Finnegans Wake*. Evanston, Illinois, 1963.

Gogarty, Oliver St. John. *As I Was Going Down Sackville Street*. London, 1936.

Gordon, Caroline. "Some Readings and Misreadings," *Sewanee Review*, 61 (Summer 1953), 388–93.

Gorman, Herbert. *James Joyce*. New York, 1939.

Graham, P. L., P. B. Sullivan, and G. F. Richter. "Mind Your Hats Goan In! Notes on the Museyroom Episode of *Finnegans Wake*," *The Analyst*, No. 21.

Hall, J., and M. Steinmann, eds. *The Permanence of Yeats*. New York, 1950.

Hart, Clive. *Structure and Motif in Finnegans Wake.* Evanston, Illinois, 1962.

Hayman, David. *A First-Draft Version of Finnegans Wake.* Austin, Texas, 1963.

Hewitt, R. M. "Harmonious Jones," in *Essays and Studies by Members of the English Association.* Oxford, 1943; quoted in Marzieh Gail, *Persia and the Victorians.* London, 1951.

Hodgart, Matthew, and Worthington, Mabel. *Song in the Works of James Joyce.* New York, 1959.

Hope, A. D. "The Esthetic Theory of James Joyce," *Australasian Journal of Psychology and Philosophy,* 21 (December 1943), 93–114; repr. in *Joyce's Portrait: Criticisms and Critiques.* Ed. Thomas E. Connolly. New York, 1962.

Howarth, Herbert. *The Irish Writers, 1880–1940: Literature under Parnell's Star.* London, 1958.

James, Henry. *The Wings of the Dove.* New York: Modern Library edition; text is that of New York edition with author's preface, New York, 1909.

Joyce, Stanislaus. *The Dublin Diary of Stanislaus Joyce,* ed. G. H. Healey. Ithaca, N.Y., 1962.

———. *My Brother's Keeper.* New York, 1958.

Kelleher, John V. "The Perceptions of James Joyce," *Atlantic Monthly,* 201 (March 1958).

Kenner, Hugh. *Dublin's Joyce.* Bloomington, Indiana, 1956.

Klausner, Joseph. *The Messianic Idea in Israel.* New York, 1955.

Legman, G. *The Horn Book: Studies in Erotic Folklore and Bibliography.* New Hyde Park, N.Y., 1964.

Leopold, L. B., and W. B. Langbein. "River Meanders," *Scientific American,* 214 (June 1966), 58–68.

Litz, Walton. *The Art of James Joyce; Method and Design in Ulysses and Finnegans Wake.* London, 1961.

Livy. *Livy, with an English translation by B. O. Foster et al.* 14 vols. London, New York, 1919–59.

MacLysaght, E. *Irish Families: Their Names, Arms, and Origins.* Dublin, 1957.

Misra, B. P. Note in *Wake Newslitter,* n.s. 3, No. 1 (February 1966), 14.

Morse, J. Mitchell. "Augustine, Ayenbite, and Ulysses," *PMLA,* 22 (December 1955), 1143–59.

Niecks, Frederick. *Robert Schumann.* London, 1925.

Noon, W. T., S.J. *Joyce and Aquinas.* New Haven, 1957.

Orelli, Conrad von. "Messiah," *The New Schaff-Herzog Encyclopedia*

of Religious Knowledge . . . 12 vols. New York, London, 1910.
"Peter Parley" (Samuel Griswold Goodrich) . *Recollections of a Lifetime, or Men and Things I Have Seen.* New York, N.Y., Auburn, N.Y., 1856.
Roberts, A., and J. Donaldson, eds. *The Ante-Nicene Fathers.* 10 vols. Grand Rapids, Michigan, 1950–56.
Ryf, Robert S. *A New Approach to Joyce; the Portrait of the Artist as a Guidebook.* Berkeley, California, and Los Angeles, 1962.
Scholem, Gershom E. *On the Kabbalah and Its Symbolism.* Trans. Ralph Manheim. New York, 1965.
Scholes, Robert E. *The Cornell Joyce Collection; A Catalogue.* Ithaca, N.Y., 1961.
Schutte, W. M. *Joyce and Shakespeare; A Study in the Meaning of Ulysses.* New Haven, 1957.
Seward, Barbara. "The Artist and the Rose," *University of Toronto Quarterly,* (January 1957) , 180–90.
Sherrington, Sir Charles. *Goethe on Nature and Science.* 2nd ed. Cambridge, 1949.
Slocum, John J., and Herbert Cahoon. *A Bibliography of James Joyce, 1882–1941.* New Haven, 1953.
Smith, Thomas F. "Color and Light in 'The Dead,'" *James Joyce Quarterly,* 2 (Summer 1965) , 304–9.
Solomon, Margaret. *Eternal Geomater.* Carbondale, Illinois, 1969.
Spielberg, Peter. *James Joyce's Manuscripts and Letters at the University of Buffalo.* Buffalo, 1962.
Steger, Hugo. *David rex et propheta.* . . . Nürnberg, 1961.
Sullivan, Kevin. *Joyce among the Jesuits.* New York, 1958.
Sultan, Stanley. *The Argument of Ulysses.* Columbus, Ohio, 1964.
Taylor, Archer. *The Literary History of Meistergesang.* New York, 1937.
Thornton, Weldon. *Allusions in Ulysses: An Annotated List.* Chapel Hill, 1968.
Tindall, William York. "Dante and Mrs. Bloom," *Accent,* 11 (Spring 1951) , 85–92.
―――. *James Joyce: His Way of Interpreting the Modern World.* New York, 1950.
―――. *The Literary Symbol.* New York, 1955.
―――. *A Reader's Guide to James Joyce.* New York, 1959.
Troy, William. "Notes on *Finnegans Wake,*" in *James Joyce: Two Decades of Criticism.* Ed. S. Givens. New York, 1948.
Waite, A. E. *The Doctrine and Literature of the Kabalah.* London, 1902.

———. *The Holy Kabbalah.* . . . London, 1929. Repr. New Hyde Park, N.Y., 1960.

———. *The Secret Doctrine in Israel.* London, 1913.

Walde, A. *Lateinisches Etymologisches Wörterbuch.* 3rd ed. Heidelberg, 1951.

Yates, Frances A. *Giordano Bruno and the Hermetic Tradition.* London, Chicago, 1964.